Re-Orienting the Renaissance

Also by Gerald MacLean

THE COUNTRY AND THE CITY REVISITED: England the Politics of Culture, c.1550–1850 (*co-editor with Donna Landry and Joseph Ward*)

CULTURE AND SOCIETY IN THE STUART RESTORATION: Literature, Drama, History (*editor*)

MATERIALIST FEMINISMS (*with Donna Landry*)

THE RETURN OF THE KING: An Anthology of English Poems, Commemorating the Stuart Restoration, 1660 (*editor*)

THE RISE OF ORIENTAL TRAVEL 1580–1720

THE SPIVAK READER (*co-editor with Donna Landry*)

TIMES WITNESS: HISTORICAL REPRESENTATION IN ENGLISH POETRY 1603–1660

THE WOMAN AS GOOD AS THE MAN by Poulain de la Barre (*editor*)

Re-Orienting the Renaissance

Cultural Exchanges with the East

Edited by

Gerald MacLean

Foreword by

William Dalrymple

First published in 2005 by
PALGRAVE MACMILLAN
Houndmills, Basingstoke, Hampshire RG21 6XS and
175 Fifth Avenue, New York, N.Y. 10010
Companies and representatives throughout the world.

PALGRAVE MACMILLAN is the global academic imprint of the Palgrave
Macmillan division of St. Martin's Press, LLC and of Palgrave Macmillan Ltd.
Macmillan® is a registered trademark in the United States, United Kingdom
and other countries. Palgrave is a registered trademark in the European
Union and other countries.

ISBN-13: 978-1-4039-9233-8 hardback
ISBN-10: 1-4039-9233-9 hardback

This book is printed on paper suitable for recycling and made from fully
managed and sustained forest sources.

A catalogue record for this book is available from the British Library.

Library of Congress Cataloging-in-Publication Data

    Re-orienting the Renaissance : cultural exchanges with the East /edited
by Gerald MacLean; with a foreword by William Dalrymple.
        p. cm.
    Includes bibliographical references and index.
    Contents: Introduction / George MacLean – The status of the Oriental
traveller in Renaissance Venice / Deborah Howard – St George between
East and West / Jerry Brotton – Mummy is become merchandise / Philip
Schwyzer – A double perspective and a lost rivalry / Barnaby Rogerson –
The French Renaissance in search of the Ottoman empire / Philip
Mansel – Petrarch and 'that mad dog Averroes' / Robert Irwin – Arab
views of Europeans, 1578–1727 / Nabil Matar – The treacherous
cleverness of hindsight / Caroline Finkel.
    ISBN 1-4039-9233-9
    1. Renaissance. 2. East and West. I. MacLean, Gerald M., 1952–

CB361.R48 2005
303.48'2405'09024—dc22   2005048767

10 9 8 7 6 5 4 3 2 1
14 13 12 11 10 09 08 07 06 05

Printed and bound in Great Britain by
Antony Rowe Ltd, Chippenham and Eastbourne

Contents

Note on Transcription

In transcribing words and names from Arabic and Turkish, I have followed the style preferred by the contributors. Quotations follow the sources cited in the notes.

Notes on Contributors

Jerry Brotton is Senior Lecturer in Renaissance Studies at Queen Mary, University of London. He is the author of *Trading Territories: Mapping the Early Modern World* (1997), *Global Interests: Renaissance Art between East and West*, with Lisa Jardine (2000), and *The Renaissance Bazaar: From the Silk Road to Michelangelo* (2002). He is currently writing a history of King Charles I's art collection.

William Dalrymple's *White Mughals* won the Wolfson Prize for History 2003 and the Scottish Book of the Year Prize, and was shortlisted for the PEN History Award, the Kiryama Prize and the James Tait Black Memorial Prize. A stage version by Christopher Hampton has just been co-commissioned by the National Theatre and the Tamasha Theatre Company. He is married to the artist Olivia Fraser, and they have three children. They now divide their time between London and Delhi. William is always keen to hear what readers think of his work (www.williamdalrymple.uk.com).

Caroline Finkel is the author of *The Administration of Warfare: the Ottoman Military Campaigns in Hungary, 1593–1606* (1988), *The Seismicity of Turkey and Adjacent Area: A Historical Review, 1500–1800* (1995) (co-authored), and most recently *Osman's Dream: The Story of the Ottoman Empire, 1300–1923* (2005) (www.osmansdream.com). She lives in Istanbul.

Deborah Howard is Professor of Architectural History in the University of Cambridge, and a Fellow of St John's College, Cambridge. Her books include *Jacopo Sansovino: Architecture and Patronage in Renaissance Venice* (1975, 1987); *The Architectural History of Venice* (1980, 1987, revised enlarged edition 2002); and *Venice and the East: The Impact of the Islamic World on Venetian Architecture 1100–1500* (2000).

Robert Irwin is a writer and Research Associate of the History Department of the School of Oriental and African Studies, and a Fellow of the Royal Society of Literature. He has published six novels. His non-fiction includes *The Arabian Nights: A Companion* (2003) and *The Alhambra* (2004). *For Lust of Knowing: The Orientalists and Their Enemies* will be published in 2006.

Gerald MacLean is Professor of English at Wayne State University in Detroit and has held visiting appointments at Bosphorus University, Istanbul and the Institute for Arab and Islamic Studies, University of Exeter. His most recent book is *The Rise of Oriental Travel: English Visitors to the Ottoman Empire 1580–1720* (2004).

Philip Mansel received his doctorate for a thesis on the Court of France from London University in 1978. Specialising in the history of France and the Middle East, he is the author of, among other works, lives of Louis XVIII and the Prince de Ligne, histories of Constantinople and Paris, and *Dressed to Rule* (2005), a study of court costume from Louis XIV to Elizabeth II. He is currently working on a history of the Levant. He is a Fellow of the Royal Historical Society and editor of *The Court Historian*, newsletter of the Society for Court Studies.

Nabil Matar is Professor of English and Head of the Department of Humanities and Communication at Florida Institute of Technology. His book, *Britain and Barbary, 1589–1689*, the last in his trilogy on Britain and the Islamic Mediterranean, is forthcoming in 2005. His next project is on 'Early Modern Europe through Arabic Eyes'.

Barnaby Rogerson helps run the specialist publisher, Eland, with a distinguished list of 60 of the great classics of travel literature, www.travelbooks.co.uk. He is the author of *Heirs of the Prophet* (2005), *A Biography of the Prophet Muhammad* (2003), *Marrakech the Red City* (editor, with Stephen Lavington, 2003), *A Traveller's History of North Africa* (2001), and half a dozen guide books, most notably *Morocco*, *Tunisia* and *Cyprus* for Cadogan.

Philip Schwyzer is Lecturer in English at the University of Exeter. He is the author of *Literature, Nationalism and Memory in Early Modern England* (1994), and is currently working on a study of early modern literature and archaeology.

Foreword: The Porous Frontiers of Islam and Christendom: A Clash or Fusion of Civilisations?

William Dalrymple

Sometime in the early 1140s a scholar from north Italy made an arduous crossing of the Alps and the Pyrenees and eventually arrived in the newly reconquered Spanish town of Toledo. There, Gerard of Cremona was given the position of canon at the cathedral, formerly the Jama Masjid or Friday Mosque, which had recently been seized from the town's Muslims.

Before the rise of Islam, Toledo had been the capital city of Visigothic Spain, and its capture by Alfonso VI of Castile was an important moment in the Christian *reconquista* of the land known to Islam as al-Andalus. Many of the Muslims of the city had, however, chosen to stay on under Castilian rule, and among them was a scholar named Ghalib 'the Mozarab'. It is not known how Gerard and Ghalib met and became friends, but soon after Gerard's arrival the two began to cooperate on a series of translations from Toledo's Arabic library, which had survived the looting of the conquering Christians.

Gerard and Ghalib's mode of translation was not one that would be regarded as ideal by modern scholars. Ghalib rendered the classical Arabic of the texts into Castilian Spanish, which Gerard then translated into Latin. As many of the texts were Greek classics which had themselves arrived in Arabic via Syriac there was much room for error. But the system seems to have worked. In the course of the next half-century, Ghalib and Gerard translated no fewer than 88 Arabic works of astronomy, mathematics, medicine, philosophy and logic, the very branches of learning which underpinned the great revival of scholarship in Europe referred to as the twelfth-century Renaissance.

Gerard and Ghalib's translations were not alone. Other translations from the Arabic at this period filled European libraries with a richness of learning impossible even to imagine a century earlier: editions of Aristotle, Euclid, Plato and Ptolemy, commentaries by Avicenna (Ibn Sina) and astrological texts by al-Khwarizmi, encyclopaedias of astronomy, illustrated accounts of chess and guides to precious stones and their medicinal qualities.

It was a crucial but sometimes forgotten moment in the development of western civilisation: the revival of medieval European learning by a wholesale transfusion of scholarship from the Islamic world. It was probably through Islamic Spain that such basic facets of western civilisation as paper, ideas of courtly love, algebra and the abacus passed into Europe, while the pointed arch and Greco-Arab (or Unani, from the Arabic word for Greek/Ionian) medicine arrived via Salerno and Sicily, where the Norman king Roger II (known as the 'Baptised Sultan') was commissioning the Tunisian scholar al-Idrisi to produce an encyclopaedic work of geography.

Some scholars go further: Professor George Makdisi has argued convincingly for a major Islamic contribution towards the emergence of the first universities in the medieval West, showing how terms such as having 'fellows' holding a 'chair' or students 'reading' a subject and obtaining 'degrees', as well as practices such as inaugural lectures and academic robes, can all be traced back to Islamic concepts and practices. Indeed, the idea of a university in the modern sense – a place of learning where students congregate to study a wide variety of subjects under a number of teachers – is generally regarded as an Arab innovation first developed at the al-Azhar university in Cairo. As Makdisi has demonstrated, it was in cities bordering the Islamic world – Salerno, Naples, Bologna, Montpellier and Paris – that first developed universities in Christendom, the idea spreading northwards from there.[1] As the contributions to this volume show, the Islamic influence on the European Renaissance of the fourteenth, fifteenth and sixteenth centuries was no less fundamental.

The tortuous and complex relationship of western Christendom and the world of Islam has provoked a variety of responses from historians. Some, such as the great medievalist Sir Steven Runciman, take the view (as he wrote at the end of his magisterial, three-volume history of the Crusades) that 'our civilisation has grown ... out of the long sequence of interaction and fusion between Orient and Occident'.[2] Runciman believed that the Crusades should be understood less as an attempt to reconquer the Christian heartlands lost to Islam so much as the last of the Barbarian invasions. The real heirs of Roman civilisation were not the chain-mailed knights of the rural West, but the sophisticated Byzantines of Constantinople and the cultivated Arab caliphate of Damascus, both of whom had preserved the Hellenised urban civilisation of the Antique Mediterranean long after it was destroyed in Europe. For a later period, Fernand Braudel's magnificent *The Mediterranean World* (1949) has also shown the degree to which both sides of the Mediterranean, Christian and Muslim, shared a single economic world.

Others, however, have seen relations between Islam and Christianity as being basically adversarial, a long drawn-out conflict between the two rival civilisations of East and West: as Gibbon famously observed of the Frankish victory at the Battle of Tours in AD 732 which halted the Arab advance into Europe:

> A victorious line of march had been prolonged from the Rock of Gibraltar to the banks of the Loire; the repetition of an equal space would have carried the Saracens to the confines of Poland and the Highlands of Scotland; the Rhine is not more impassable than the Nile or the Euphrates, and the Arabian flee might have sailed into the mouth of the Thames. Perhaps the interpretation of the Koran would now be taught in the schools of Oxford, and her pulpits might demonstrate to a circumcised people the sanctity and truth of the Revelation of Mahomet.[3]

Today, in the aftermath of 9/11, the relationship of Christianity and Islam has become one of the central questions of our time, and our understanding of its history is now more important than ever. The contributors to this volume all unanimously take the Runciman or Braudel side in the debate, and show in their essays quite how closely interconnected Christendom and Islam were in the Renaissance; some even go as far as believing the Renaissance would simply have been impossible without the input of the Islamic world.

In this view they stand at odds with what has become one of the dominant narrative of our times, certainly in the US, where the relationship of Islam and Christianity is almost always seen in confrontational terms. The two cheerleaders for this tendency are Samuel Huntingdon and his mentor, Bernard Lewis.

Underlying most of Lewis's work is the assumption that there are two fixed and opposed forces at work in the history of the Mediterranean world: on the one hand, western civilisation which he envisages as a Judeo-Christian bloc; and on the other, and quite distinct, a hostile Islamic world hell-bent on the conquest and conversion of the West. As he wrote in one influential essay, 'The Roots of Muslim Rage': 'The struggle between these rival systems has now lasted some fourteen centuries. It began with the advent of Islam, in the seventh century, and has continued virtually to the present day. It has consisted of a long series of attacks and counterattacks, jihads and crusades, conquests and reconquests.'[4] It was this essay that contained the phrase 'the clash of civilisations', later borrowed by Samuel Huntingdon for his controversial *Foreign Affairs* article and book.[5]

Lewis's trenchant views have certainly made him a number of enemies, notably the late Edward Said, who wrote in *Orientalism* (1978) that Lewis's work 'purports to be liberal objective scholarship but is in reality very close to being propaganda *against* his subject material'.[6] In the aftermath of the Islamist attacks on America, Lewis's reputation has, however, undergone something of a revival. Not only have two of his books – *What Went Wrong?* and *The Crisis of Islam* – been major US bestsellers, Lewis's ideas have formed the intellectual foundations for the neo-con view of the Muslim world. Lewis has addressed the White House, and Dick Cheney and Richard Perle have both been named as disciples.[7]

A series of prominent polemical pieces in the *Washington Post* and *Wall Street Journal*, reprinted in his recent volume of collected essays, *From Babel to Dragomans: Interpreting the Middle East* (2004), gives an idea of the sort of advice Lewis would have offered his fans in the White House, and illustrates how influential an interpretation of history can be on contemporary policy. For Lewis used the attack on the World Trade Center to encourage the US to attack Saddam Hussein, implicitly making a link between the al-Qa'eda operation and the secular Iraqi Ba'athist regime, while assuring the administration that they would be feted by the populace who 'look to us for help and liberation', and thanked by other Muslim governments whose secret 'dearest wish'[8] was an American invasion to remove Saddam. It is here that Said's charge of Lewis acting as a propagandist against his subject rings most true.

In several places Lewis argues that Islamic hostility to America has less to do with American foreign policy in the Muslim world, notably American support for Israel, than a generalised Islamic 'envy' and 'rage' directed against its ancient cultural rival. This, he claims, derives from 'a feeling of humiliation – a growing awareness, among the heirs of an old, proud and long-dormant civilisation, of having been overtaken, overborne and overwhelmed by those whom they regarded as their inferiors'.[9]

Lewis has had such a profound influence that, according to *The Wall Street Journal*, 'the Lewis doctrine, in effect, had become US policy'.[10] If that policy has now been shown to be fundamentally flawed and based on a set of wholly erroneous assumptions, it follows that for all his scholarship, Lewis's understanding of the subtleties of the contemporary Islamic world is, in some respects at least, dangerously defective.

It also shows the urgency of showing the jobs facing historians who study the relationship of Christianity and Islam, and underlines the extreme importance of their work in overturning a misreading of history that has impacted in a very fundamental and visible way on contemporary politics.

* * *

The Prophet Muhammad, it is clear, did not think he was 'founding a new religion' so much as bringing the fullness of divine revelation, partially granted to earlier prophets such as Abraham, Moses or Jesus, to the Arabs of the Arabian Peninsula. After all, Islam accepts much of the Old and New Testaments and obeys the Mosaic laws about circumcision and ablutions, while the Qur'an calls Christians the 'nearest in love' to Muslims, whom it instructs in Surah 29 to 'dispute not with the People of the Book [that is, Jews and Christians] save in the most courteous manner ... and say, "We believe in what has been sent down to us and what has been sent down to you; our God and your God is one, and to him we have surrendered." '

It is important to remember the degree to which the Muslim armies were welcomed as liberators by the Syriac and Coptic Christians who had suffered discrimination under the strictly Orthodox Byzantines: as Richard Fletcher put it in his excellent study *The Cross and the Crescent: Christianity and Islam from Muhammad to the Reformation*: 'To the persecuted Monophysite Christians of Syria and Egypt, Muslims could be presented as deliverers. The same could be said of the persecuted Jews ... Released from the bondage of Constantinopolitan persecution they flourished as never before, generating in the process a rich spiritual literature in hymns and devotional work.'[11]

Recent excavations by the Jerusalem-based archaeologist Michele Piccirillo have dramatically underlined this point. They have shown that the conquest of Byzantine Palestine by the Arabs resulted in an almost unparalleled burst of church-building and the construction of some remarkable Hellenistic mosaics, implying that under the rule of the Ummayad Caliphs of Damascus, religious practice was freer and the economy flourishing.[12]

Early Byzantine writers, including the most subtle theologian of the Early Church, St John Damascene, assumed that Islam was merely a heterodox form of Christianity. This perception is particularly fascinating as St John had grown up in the Ummayad court of Damascus – the hub of the young Islamic world – where his father was chancellor, and he was an intimate friend of the future Caliph al-Yazid. In his old age, John took the habit at the desert monastery of Mar Saba where he began work on his great masterpiece, a refutation of heresies entitled *The Fount of*

Knowledge. The book contains a precise critique of Islam, the first written by a Christian, which John regarded as closely related to the heterodox Christian doctrine of Nestorianism. This was a kinship that both the Muslims and the Nestorians were aware of. In 649 a Nestorian bishop wrote: 'These Arabs fight not against our Christian religion; nay, rather they defend our faith, they revere our priests and saints, and they make gifts to our churches.'[13]

Throughout the medieval period, Christians and Muslims continued to meet as much in the context of trade and scholarship as they did on the battlefield. The tolerant and pluralistic civilisation of Muslim al-Andalus allowed a particularly fruitful interaction. A revealing moment, highlighted by Fletcher, was when, in 949, a Byzantine embassy presented the court of Cordoba with the works of the Greek physician Dioscorides:

> There were no scholars in Spain who knew Greek, so an appeal was sent back to Constantinople in answer to which a learned Greek monk named Nicholas was sent to Spain in 951. A Muslim scholar from Sicily with a knowledge of Greek was also found. Together these two expounded the text to a group of Spanish scholars. This group was a most interesting one. It included native Andalusian Islamic scholars such as Ibn Juljul, who later composed a commentary on Dioscorides; a distinguished Jewish physician and courtier, Hasday ibn Shaprut; and a Mozarabic bishop Recemund of Elvira (he who was sent on an embassy to Germany) who was the author of the *Calendar of Córdoba*, a work containing much agronomical and botanical information. It was a truly international and interdenominational gathering of scholars.[14]

Throughout the Crusades, the Venetians and other Italian trading cities kept up a profitable trade with their Muslim counterparts, resulting in a great many Arabic words surviving in Venetian dialect and a profound Islamic influence on Venetian architecture.[15] Even Christian clerics who cohabited with Muslims in the Crusader kingdoms came to realise that as much bound them together as separated them. As William of Tripoli reported from Acre in 1272: 'Though their beliefs are decorated with fictions, yet it now manifestly appears that they are near to the Christian faith and not far from the path of salvation.' At the same time the Muslim traveller Ibn Jubayr noted that despite the military struggles for control of Palestine, 'yet Muslims and Christian travellers will come and go between them without interference'.

There were of course no shortage of travellers on both sides who could see no good in the infidels amongst whom they were obliged to mingle, and tensions often existed between Muslim rulers and the diverse religious communities living under their capricious thumb: by modern standards Muslims and Jews under Muslim rule – the *dhimmi* – were treated as second-class citizens. But there was at least a kind of pluralist equilibrium (what Spanish historians have called *convivencia*, or 'living together') which had no parallel in Christendom and which in Spain was lost soon after the completion of the Christian *reconquista*: on taking Grenada, the Catholic kings expelled the Moors and Jews, and let loose the Inquisition on those – the New Christians – who had converted. There was a similar pattern in Sicily. After a fruitful period of tolerant coexistence under the Norman kings, the Muslims were later given a blunt choice of transportation or conversion.

As the writers in this volume show, the course of the Renaissance was moulded in a very fundamental way by these close linkages, connections and mutual commercial, intellectual and cultural influences that had developed in the medieval period between Islam and Christendom, and the degree of traffic between the two: by the importation of silks, textiles and other luxury eastern goods; by the mutual influence of design and aesthetic practices; by the trans-Mediterranean movement of wealth and trade; by the European taste for eastern spices, currants and coffee, and by the Ottoman need for Cornish tin and bell metal; by Sultan Mehmed II's taste for Quattrocento Italian medals and classical Greek histories, and Süleyman's for Florentine Renaissance sculpture; by the exchange of ideas of medicine, mapping, navigation and philosophy; and most striking of all, by the human presence of leading Renaissance figures such as Gentile Bellini and Constanzo da Ferrara – as well as huge numbers of Venetian and other Italian merchants scattered from Budapest to Cairo[16] – living for extended periods of time in the Ottoman East. At all levels, the Ottoman world impinged directly on Renaissance life, and the intellectual awakening that the Renaissance represented owed almost as much to the interplay of East and West as it did to any process of self-regeneration drawing from Greek and Roman roots.

* * *

Against this compelling picture of inspirational and catalytic interconnectivity, Bernard Lewis posits a very different picture: of two hostile blocs clashing incessantly for 1,500 years. In particular, the idea that the Islamic world has been humiliated by a West it once despised and ignored, and that it has never come to terms with this reversal, is a thesis that links Lewis's historical work and his journalism, and has come to form his central theme.

For a thousand years, argues Lewis, Islam was technologically superior to Christendom and dominated its Christian neighbours; but since the failure of the Ottoman siege of Vienna in 1683, the Muslim world has been in retreat. Militarily, economically and scientifically it was soon eclipsed by its Christian rivals. Failure led first to a profound humiliation, then to an aggressive hatred of the West: 'This is no less than a clash of civilisations – the perhaps irrational but surely historic reaction of an ancient rival against our Judeo-Christian heritage, our secular present, and the worldwide expansion of both.'[17]

It is a thesis which Lewis first formed in his *The Muslim Discovery of Europe* (1980) and developed with a more contemporary spin in *What Went Wrong?* (2002) and *The Crisis of Islam* (2003). The idea reappears in various guises in no fewer than five essays in *From Babel to Dragomans*.[18]

During the period immediately following the European Renaissance – the sixteenth and seventeenth centuries – Lewis believes that there was an especially crucial and fatal failure of curiosity about development in Europe. In the conclusion to *The Muslim Discovery of Europe*, Lewis contrasts the situation in Britain and Ottoman Turkey at this period:

> The first chair of Arabic in England was founded by Sir Thomas Adams at Cambridge university in 1633. There, and in similar centres in other west European countries, a great effort of creative scholarship was devoted to the languages, literatures, and cultures of the region ... All this is in striking contrast to the almost total lack of interest displayed by Middle Easterners in the languages, cultures and religions of Europe ... The record shows that, until the latter part of the eighteenth century the information [compiled by the Ottoman state about Europe] was usually superficial, often inaccurate, and almost always out of date.[19]

There were some changes in the eighteenth century, such as the adoption of European-style diplomacy and military techniques, but it was only in the early nineteenth century that there was any substantial change in Muslim attitudes. In an essay entitled 'On Occidentalism and Orientalism' Lewis writes:

> By the beginning of the nineteenth century, Muslims first in Turkey and then elsewhere, were becoming aware of the changing balance,

not only of power but also of knowledge, between Christendom and Islam, and for the first time they thought it worth the effort to learn European languages ... It was not until well into the nineteenth century that we find any attempt in any of the languages of the Middle East to produce grammars or dictionaries which would enable speakers of those languages to learn a Western language. And when it did happen, it was due largely to the initiative of those two detested intruders, the imperialist and the missionary. This is surely a striking contrast [to the situation in Europe] and it has prompted many to ask the question: why were the Muslims so uninterested?[20]

By then it was too late: during the course of the nineteenth and twentieth centuries the colonial West imposed itself by force on Muslim countries from the Middle East to Indonesia, 'a new era in which the Muslim discovery of Europe was forced, massive, and for the most part, painful'.[21]

Lewis emphasises that until the nineteenth century there was little question of Muslims going to study in Europe. As he writes in the essay 'Europe and Islam': 'The question of travel for study did not arise, since clearly there was nothing to be learned from the benighted infidels of the outer wilderness.' Again and again, Lewis returns to his idea that Muslim awareness 'of belonging to the most advanced and enlightened civilisation in the world' led to the lack of a spirit of enquiry that might otherwise have propelled individuals to explore the non-Muslim world:

> Few Muslims travelled voluntarily to the land of the infidels. Even the involuntary travellers, the many captives taken in the endless wars, had nothing to say after their ransom and return, and perhaps no one to listen ... a few notes and fragments ... constitute almost the whole of Muslim travel literature of Europe.[22]

Such a view was tenable when there was only vague awareness of what Islamic libraries actually contained, but discoveries over the last 30 years have shown that this apparent lacuna was more the result of lack of archival research on the part of Lewis than any failing by Muslim writers. Lewis's findings, while always well argued, now appear somewhat dated. It is true that the Muslim world fell behind the West, and (as Fletcher nicely puts it) the 'cultural suppleness [and] adaptability' shown by the early Muslim states who absorbed the learning of Byzantium and ancient Persia 'seemed to run out in later epochs', but it is not true that the reason for this was a lofty disdain for or hatred of the

West, nor that Muslims failed to take an intense and often enthusiastic interest in developments there.[23]

* * *

Perhaps the best counterblast to this central strand of Lewis's thought are three remarkable books by Nabil Matar, the great Christian Palestinian scholar who has spent the last three decades delving in archives across the Islamic world, and whose most recent groundbreaking essay, 'Arab Views of Europeans, 1578–1727', is included in this collection.

Matar's first two books, *Islam in Britian, 1558–1685* (1998) and *Turk, Moors and Englishmen in the Age of Discovery* (2000), show the degree to which individuals from the Islamic and Christian world mixed and intermingled during the sixteenth and seventeenth centuries, while the most recent, *In The Land of the Christians: Arabic Travel Writing in the Seventeenth Century* (2003), directly counters Lewis's idea that Muslim interest in the West only really began in earnest in the nineteenth century.[24] Here a succession of previously unknown seventeenth-century travel narratives unfold in English translation, with Arab writer after writer describing their intense interest in and excitement with western science, literature, politics and even opera. As Matar emphasises in his introduction:

> The writings in this volume reveal [that] travellers, envoys, ambassadors, traders and clerics were eager to ask questions about *bilad al-nasara* (the lands of the Christians) and to record their answers – and then turn their impressions into documents. They all wrote with precision and perspicacity, producing the most detailed and empirically based information about the way in which non-Europeans view Europeans in the early modern period. No other non-Christian people – neither the American Indians nor the sub-Saharan Africans nor the Asiatics – left behind as extensive a description of the Europeans and of the *bilad al-nasara*, both in the European as well as the American continents, as did Arabic writers.[25]

Recent research in Indian Muslim and Iranian archives has revealed a similar fascination with the developments in the West in the early modern period.[26]

Matar's work is full of surprises for anyone who believes that Christian–Muslim relations have always been exclusively confrontational. In *Turks, Moors and Englishmen*, we learn, for example, that in

1603, Ahmad al-Mansur, King of Morocco, was making a proposal to his English ally, Queen Elizabeth I. The idea was a simple one: that England was to help the Moors colonise America. The King proposed that Moroccan and English troops, using English ships, should together attack the Spanish colonies in America, expel their hated Spanish enemies, and then 'possesse' the land and keep it 'under our [joint] dominion for ever'. There was a catch, however. Might it not be more sensible, suggested the King, that most of the future colonists should be Moroccan rather than English: 'those of your countrie doe not fynde themselfes fitt to endure the extremetie of heat there, where our men endure it very well by reason that heat hurtes them not.' After due consideration, the Moroccan offer was not taken up by Her Majesty.[27]

Such a proposal might seem extraordinary today, but at the time it clearly raised few eyebrows. After all, as Matar points out, the English were close allies of both the Moroccans and their overlords, the Ottomans – indeed, the Pope regarded Elizabeth as 'a confederate with the Turks'. The English might have their reservations about Islam, but these were nothing compared to their hatred and fear of 'Popery'.[28] As well as treaties of trade and friendship, this alliance led to several joint expeditions, such as an Anglo-Moroccan attack on Cadiz in 1596. It also led to a great movement of people between the two worlds. Elizabethan London had a burgeoning Muslim community which encompassed a large party of Turkish ex-prisoners, some Moorish craftsmen, a number of wealthy Turkish merchants and a 'Moorish solicitor', as well as 'Albion Blackamore, the Turkish Rope-daunser'.[29]

If there was a small but confident Muslim community in London, then much larger numbers of Englishmen could be found living across the Ottoman Empire as Matar shows in *Islam in Britain*. British travellers regularly brought back tales of their compatriots who had 'crossed over' and were now prospering in Ottoman service: one of the most powerful Ottoman eunuchs during the sixteenth century, Hasan Aga, was the former Samson Rowlie from Great Yarmouth, while in Algeria the 'Moorish King's Executioner' turned out to be a former butcher from Exeter called 'Absalom' (Abd-es-Salaam).[30] When Charles II sent Captain Hamilton to ransom some Englishmen enslaved on the Barbary Coast his mission was unsuccessful as they all refused to return: the men had all converted to Islam and were now 'partaking of the prosperous Successe of the Turks', living in a style to which they could not possibly have aspired back home. The frustrated Hamilton was forced to return empty-handed: 'They are tempted to forsake their God for the love of Turkish women', he wrote in his report. 'Such ladies are', he added, 'generally very beautiful'.[31]

There is a serious point underlying such anecdotes, for they show that throughout history, Muslims and Christians have traded, studied, negotiated and loved across the porous frontiers of religious differences. Probe relations between the two civilisations at any period of history, and you find that the neat civilisational blocks imagined by Lewis or Huntingdon soon dissolve.

What is most interesting in many of the cases described by Matar is that Islam overwhelmed as often by its power of attraction as by the sword. Indeed, as the English ambassador Sir Thomas Shirley pointed out, the more time Englishmen spent in the East, the closer they moved to adopting the manners of the Muslims: 'conuersation with infidelles doeth mutch corrupte', he wrote, 'many wylde youthes of all nationes ... in euerye 3 yeere that they staye in Turkye they loose one article of theyre faythe'.[32] In 1606 even the British consul in Egypt, Benjamin Bishop, converted and promptly disappeared from records. It was a similar situation in India where up until the mid-nineteenth century substantial numbers of Britons were taking on aspects of Mughal culture, marrying Mughal women and converting to Islam.[33]

In one matter, however, Matar demonstrates something that will surprise no one: that English cooking, then as now, left much to be desired. For while English society was thrilled to taste Turkish cooking, when the Ottoman Governor of Algiers presided over a feast '*alla Turchescha*' at his residence, the Magribian guests proved rather less impressed by English fayre. This emerges from the story of one unfortunate English captive who was captured in a sea-battle and 'Taken Prisoner by the Turks of Argiers', who put him to work as a cook. This proved a mistake for everyone involved. Unused to the exotic ingredients of the region, the Englishman found himself producing such 'mad sauces, and such strange *Ragoux* that every one took me for a Cook of the *Antipodes*'. Worse yet was the reaction of his Master to a sauce specially prepared from fish liver that 'hath the most loathsom taste'; he ordered that the cook should be given 'ten Bastonadoes' and advised that he should be returned to the slave market. As far as the 'Turks of Argiers' were concerned, the English, it seems, made better galley slaves than gourmets.[34]

Notes

1. George Makdisi, The *Rise of Colleges: Institutions of Learning in Islam and the West* (Edinburgh: Edinburgh University Press, 1981), and *The Rise of Humanism in Classical Islam and the Christian West* (Edinburgh: Edinburgh University Press, 1990). See also Hugh Goddard, *A History of Christian–Muslim Relations* (Edinburgh: Edinburgh University Press, 2000).

2. Sir Steven Runciman, *A History of the Crusades. Volume 3: The Kingdom of Acre* (Harmondsworth: Penguin, 1965), p. 480.

3. Edward Gibbon, *The History of the Decline and Fall of the Roman Empire*, ed. J. B. Bury, 7 vols (London: Methuen, 1909–14), 6: ch. 52:16.

4. Collected in Bernard Lewis, *From Babel to Dragomans: Interpreting the Middle East* (London: Weidenfeld and Nicolson, 2004), for this passage see p. 320.

5. Lewis in fact first coined the phrase in an article about Suez published in 1957, and has used it intermittently ever since.

6. Edward Said, *Orientalism* (Harmondsworth: Penguin, 1978), p. 316. The adjacent pages played host to a celebrated exchange between Lewis and Said in 1982.

7. Bernard Lewis, *What Went Wrong? The Clash between Islam and Modernity in the Middle East* (London: Weidenfeld and Nicolson, 2002), and *The Crisis of Islam: Holy War and Unholy Terror* (New York: Modern Library, 2003).

8. Lewis, *From Babel*, pp. 379, 370.

9. Lewis, *From Babel*, pp. 375, 328.

10. See Peter Waldman, 'A Historian's Take on Islam Steers US in Terrorism Fight', *Wall Street Journal*, 4 February 2004.

11. Richard Fletcher, *The Cross and the Crescent: Christianity and Islam from Muhammad to the Reformation* (2003; rpt. London: Penguin, 2005).

12. See Michele Piccirillo, *The Mosaics of Jordan*, ed. Patricia Bikai and Thomas Dailey (Amman, Jordan: American Center of Oriental Research, 1992), which illustrates some of the remarkable 'Byzantine' floor mosaics excavated by Piccirillo. Those constructed during the Ummayyad period show, surprisingly, such Hellenistic subjects as satyrs with flutes leading Christianised Bacchic processions, while angelic cupids swoop above orange trees. Similar tendencies can be found in the mosaics of the Ummayad winter palace in Jericho built by Caliph Hisham el Malik. There is an interview with Piccirillo in my book, *From the Holy Mountain: A Journey among the Christians of the Middle East* (London: HarperCollins, 1997).

13. Margaret Smith, *Studies in Early Mysticism in the Near and Middle East* (1931; rpt. Oxford: Oneworld, 1995), p. 120.

14. Fletcher, *Cross and Crescent*, p. 59.

15. The Islamic influence on Venice has recently received magnificent treatment from Deborah Howard in her book *Venice and the East: The Impact of the Islamic World on Venetian Architecture 1100–1500* (New Haven, CT: Yale University Press, 2000). As well as showing the profound Islamic influence on buildings such as the Doge's palace and the Palazzo Ducale, she also charts Arab influence on Venetian painting, town planning, domestic architecture, jewellery and speech. Her essay in this volume, 'The Status of the Oriental Traveller in Renaissance Venice', supplements this work.

16. Howard, in this volume, finds that as many as 68 Venetians were in Damascus during the three-year period 1455–57.

17. Lewis, *From Babel*, p. 330.

18. Some notable examples from Lewis's writings include: 'While European travellers to the East had already produced a considerable literature, there was nothing comparable on the Muslim side', *Islam and the West* (New York: Oxford University Press, 1993), p. 210; and the following from the essays reprinted in *From Babel*: 'Ottoman awareness of Christian Europe was ... still very limited ... Of the intellectual life of Europe virtually nothing was

known ... The failure to take Vienna in 1683 ... marked a major turning point' ('Europe and Islam', p. 125); 'a feeling of humiliation – a growing awareness of having been overtaken' ('The Roots of Muslim Rage', p. 328); 'For many centuries Islam was the greatest civilisation on earth ... And then everything changed' ('Targeted by a History of Hatred', p. 373); 'Muslims were becoming aware of the changed balance, not only of power but of knowledge ... Why were the Muslims so uninterested?' ('On Occidentalism and Orientalism', pp. 433–4). And see Bernard Lewis, *The Muslim Discovery of Europe* (London: Weidenfeld and Nicolson, 1982).

19. Lewis, *Muslim Discovery*, pp. 296–7.
20. Lewis, *From Babel*, p. 434.
21. Lewis, *Muslim Discovery*, p. 12.
22. Lewis, *From Babel*, pp. 132, 433, 210.
23. Fletcher, *Cross and Crescent*, p. 161.
24. See Nabil Matar, *Islam in Britain, 1558–1685* (Cambridge: Cambridge University Press, 1999), and *Turks, Moors, and Englishmen in the Age of Discovery* (New York: Columbia University Press, 1999). In 'Europe and Islam', Lewis dates 'the first influential Arab account of a European country' to the years following 1831; see *From Babel*, p. 128.
25. Nabil Matar, ed., *In the Lands of the Christians: Arabic Travel Writing in the Seventeenth Century* (New York and London: Routledge, 2003), p. xxii.
26. For early Indian Muslim interest in and knowledge of the West, see Sanjay Subrahmanyam's fascinating 'Connected Histories: Notes toward a Reconfiguration of Early Modern Eurasia', *Modern Asian Studies*, 31:3 (July 1997), special issue: *The Eurasian Context of the Early Modern History of Mainland South East Asia, 1400–1800*, pp. 735–62; also good is Gulfishan Khan, *Indian Muslim Perceptions of the West during the Eighteenth Century* (Oxford: Oxford University Press, 1988). Michael Fisher has edited an edition of Dean Mahomet's eighteenth-century account of his journey from India to Europe which, remarkably, he wrote in English. Fisher is currently working on publishing for the first time the voluminous corpus of Mughal travel accounts. For Iran, see Mohamad Tavakoli-Targhi, 'Modernity Heterotopia and Homeless Texts', *Comparative Studies of South Asia, Africa, and the Middle East* 18:2 (1998), and his *Refashioning Iran: Orientalism, Occidentalism, and Historiography* (New York: Palgrave, 2001). For recent work on intimate Ottoman relations with Europe, see Daniel Goffman, *Britons in the Ottoman Empire 1642–1660* (Seattle: University of Washington Press, 1998), and Philip Mansel, *Constantinople: City of the World's Desire, 1453–1924* (London: Murray, 1995).
27. See Matar, *Turks, Moors*, p. 9.
28. Inter-Christian rivalry was always a powerful factor leading to alliances and arrangements between Muslims and Christian states. Just before the fall of Constantinople to the Ottoman Turks in 1453, the Orthodox monks famously refused to agree to submit to the Papacy in return for military aid against the Ottomans. As the Byzantine dignitary Lucas Notaras famously observed: 'It is better to see in the city the power of the Turkish turban than that of the Latin tiara.'
29. See Matar, *Turks, Moors*, p. 22.

30. See Matar, *Islam in Britain*, pp. 53, 39. For more on English captives in North Africa, see also Linda Colley, *Captives: Britain, Empire and the World 1600–1850* (London: Cape, 2002), and Robert C. Davis, *Christian Slaves, Muslim Masters: White Slavery in the Mediterranean, the Barbary Coast, and Italy, 1500–1800* (Basingstoke: Palgrave Macmillan, 2003).
31. Quoted in Matar, *Islam in Britain*, p. 37.
32. Quoted in Matar, *Turks, Moors*, p. 28.
33. This is explored in detail in my *White Mughals: Love and Betrayal in Eighteenth-Century India* (London: HarperCollins, 2002). In the wills of the late eighteenth century, one in three British men in India were leaving their goods either to an Indian wife or an Anglo-Indian child.
34. *The Adventures of (Mr. T. S.) An English Merchant, Taken Prisoner by the Turks of Argiers* (London: Moses Pitt, 1670), pp. 31, 32; discussed by Matar, *Turks, Moors*, pp. 78–9. In the event, 'T. S.' writes, 'I was forced to suffer the punishment with Patience', but – Providence intervening – was only removed 'to another employment, which I heartily longed for. I was made by a wonderful change of Fortune Keeper of the King's Baths' (pp. 32, 33–4) and from here, his further 'Adventures' take a notably picaresque turn as he finds himself a sex-slave. For a detailed study of *The Adventures* that curiously passes over these comic interludes in the kitchens, see 'T. S. in Captivity: North African Slavery, 1648–70', Part IV of Gerald MacLean, *The Rise of Oriental Travel: English Visitors to the Ottoman Empire, 1580–1720* (Basingstoke: Palgrave, 2004), pp. 177–220.

Introduction: Re-Orienting the Renaissance

Gerald MacLean

Re-Orienting the Renaissance seeks to shift the angles from which we regard those unprecedented developments in learning and the arts that it is generally agreed occurred throughout western Europe between the late thirteenth and seventeenth centuries. From differing perspectives and from different kinds of evidence, the authors of this book show how a nineteenth-century term, 'Renaissance', has often encouraged us to forget just how many of the artistic, social, religious, philosophical, scientific, technical and cultural developments that distinguished the period depended upon the movement and exchange of ideas, skills and goods between what have come to be thought of as separate spheres: East and West. Had it not been for the importation of eastern goods and skills, many of the achievements most commonly associated with the European Renaissance would not have occurred; had it not been for continuing cultural rivalry among Christian and Muslim princes and aristocrats to display their wealth and magnificence in ways that others would understand and perhaps even emulate or envy, many of the artistic achievements of the period might not have taken the forms they did. In chapters ranging from Ottoman history to Venetian publishing, from portraits of St George to Arab philosophy, from cannibalism to diplomacy, the authors interrogate what all too often seem to be settled certainties, such as the clear border demarcating East from West, the inevitability of conflict between Islam and Christianity, and the regeneration of European civilisation nourished entirely by taproots in classical Greece and imperial Rome.

The contributors to this book draw attention to some of the misunderstood, misrecognised and ignored historical evidence of powerful connections and mutual influences that linked East with West before the creation of borders that today we take for granted. Conflicts,

1

misunderstandings and theological differences there were, but the story told here is of a time when Christianity and Islam were not invariably locked in battle or mutual disregard, and it insists that we think again whenever we hear the term 'Renaissance' being used casually to describe an exclusively European movement involving the recovery of exclusively European ideas, values and attitudes from Antiquity. The authors invite us to recognise how, whatever else it might have been, the 'confluence of artistic, literary, scientific, and cultural developments that made the Renaissance' – in the words of *The Encyclopedia of the Renaissance* – can be fully understood only in the light of Christian Europe's relations with eastern and Islamic cultures and in the light of mutual recognitions and exchanges between Christian and Muslim. In the sphere of portraiture, a well-known example of such dialogue is that between the portrait attributed to the fifteenth-century Persian artist Bihzâd, of an artist painting a portrait and the 'Seated Scribe' that has been attributed to both Costanzo da Ferrara and Gentile Bellini.[1]

The Renaissance: scholarly contexts

The Renaissance was a time of widespread movements of wealth and power, and of people and goods. It witnessed, we might say, a displacement from familiar, settled patterns of local life, and the appearance of ideas, objects and opportunities that came from elsewhere. Traditional accounts focus on those artistic and cultural movements that, starting with the Italian city-states, spread westward and northward, gradually transforming social attitudes and material values throughout western Europe.[2] In these familiar senses, the Renaissance was a great leap forward in artistic practices, in scientific, religious and philosophical ideas, and in new and improved styles and standards of living. During these years, it has often been argued, the self-knowing and self-actualising individual emerged to dominate the scene.[3] This Renaissance individual was most often, but not always, gendered male. Humanists thought about him, while artists painted him, sculptors under the influence of antique models displayed his perfect form, and dramatists and poets gave voice to the inner conflicts and newly awakened ambitions that made him distinct from his medieval ancestors. In this new world where mankind was at the centre of things, talented men and women could overcome circumstances of birth and achieve greatness. They wrote important works of history, philosophy and literature not only in Latin but also in vernacular languages, with the result that national literatures rapidly developed to rival those of Antiquity. Renaissance men and women amassed huge fortunes and built splendid palaces and churches for which they employed the services of great architects and innovative decorators. They filled them with magnificent statuary, sumptuous tapestries and costly paintings by important and talented living artists. They courted powerful rulers and influenced policy. In all their achievements, the traditional view has it, men and women of the Renaissance were deliberately seeking to imitate and exceed the glories of classical European civilisations. They were also inventors. The printing press was doubtless their greatest technical innovation, but they also mapped and navigated more of the globe than previous generations, and they built new and better ships which carried more people and more goods between more places. New World gold and silver helped finance everything.[4] Life, for many, improved.

This is a view of the Renaissance that leads us to understand the massive upheavals that took place over three centuries solely in Eurocentric terms, and deriving largely from the appearance of men and women of great and original genius at a time of mobile wealth. The notion of Europe rebirthing itself from itself, however, is not entirely a nineteenth-century idea since works such as Giorgio Vasari's *Lives of the Painters* (1550) described the times as a re-flourishing of forgotten artistic skills and talents formerly perfected in the Hellenic and Roman eras. But the Renaissance involved far more of the world than the confines of Christian Europe and its Hellenistic past.

In *Re-Orienting the Renaissance*, the authors look beyond Europe and demonstrate how the Renaissance would have been entirely different, if not impossible, had it not been for direct and regular contact with the eastern, largely Muslim, world, and the constant exchange of goods and ideas. It must be said that this argument is not without precedent. As long ago as 1968, in *The Ottoman Impact on Europe*, Paul Coles argued that 'the development of Europe cannot be fully understood without a knowledge of the era of Turkish power', and noted that 'while the Ottoman empire suffered from growing administrative problems, the states of western and central Europe gradually increased their commercial and military resources'.[5] Yet *Re-Orienting the Renaissance* challenges and displaces the progress-and-decline model of historical development implicit in Coles' thesis, with its foundational underpinning of a direct causal link between the two, by demonstrating the need to recognise more complex forms of differential development and cross-cultural interactivity at work. In doing so, this book aims to advance understanding of the period between the fourteenth and seventeenth centuries as a period in world history when trade, dialogue and cultural interaction were as characteristic of Christian relations with Islam as the more sensationalistic moments of armed conflict. The Renaissance was no simple shift of power and civilisation from a declining East to an ascending West.[6]

Art, humanism and Renaissance man

The case for the traditional view has never been better made than in Paul Johnson's compelling *The Renaissance: A Short Introduction* (2000). Effortlessly, Johnson's book exemplifies the values of the rhetorical tradition of the Renaissance humanists that it describes: the ability to present a convincing case persuasively, combined with an astonishing breadth of detailed knowledge. To these, Johnson adds a sharp critical understanding of potential counter-arguments such as those that might be made, for example, by scholars trained in the traditions of Marxist historiography and materialist criticism. After describing the historical contexts and economic developments that gave meaning to the Renaissance and enabled it, Johnson delivers an emphatic 'But' and insists that material circumstances do not control human activity. 'But it must be grasped', Johnson writes, 'that the Renaissance was primarily a human event, propelled forward by a number of individuals of out-standing talent, which in some cases amount to genius'.[7] And that is what Johnson's short introduction provides, a masterful survey of the great Renaissance themes and the great Renaissance men who inhabited and exemplified them. A 'short introduction' to something as complex as the Renaissance obviously needs focus, and Johnson elegantly sketches in the 'background' before dismissing it with that 'But' and turning away from questions of how, not only economic factors, but also culture itself can influence historical events. He turns instead to the answer proposed by the Renaissance humanists themselves that history is made by great men of exceptional ambition and ability. Despite the acknowledgement of historical forces as 'background', Johnson offers a nineteenth-century view of the Renaissance, a history made by remark-able men. It is a view that would have made sense to Machiavelli.

In Anglophone scholarship of the last 25 years, debates in Renaissance studies have been at the forefront of New Historicism and have been central to the development of Cultural Studies. Both these critical move-ments have grown from ways of viewing history as a more complicated process than simply the activity of great individuals and the importance of their backgrounds. Stephen Greenblatt's enormously influential *Renaissance Self-Fashioning* of 1980 made Renaissance studies the very heart of lively revisionist attempts to rewrite the cultural history of the early modern period. Perhaps what has given Greenblatt's book its lasting status as the foundational work of New Historicism was the urgency with which Greenblatt made the case that knowing about self-fashioning in the Renaissance really was crucially important for people living today. What mattered was not just that we needed to understand what was going on then, but that we needed to admit to the ways our personal and political interests continued to shape what we would look for and find in the Renaissance. Paul Johnson writes that 'the Renaissance was the work of individuals, and in a sense was about individualism'.[8] What Greenblatt did, we might say, was to put himself into the picture and invite us along for the ride.

Some historians continue to object that New Historicism is about producing a history with much of the past left out because it relies too heavily upon thick description – examining a single past work to show how its conventions and features illuminate its more general historical moment. The settled waters of academic historiography have also been troubled by interdisciplinary and multidisciplinary approaches to the past. As with Greenblatt's own work since *Renaissance Self-Fashioning*, the New Historical approach has taken a globalising turn in recent years and, as with Cultural Studies more widely, has long since been transformed by empire-, nation- and race-sensitive feminist scholarship. In 1996, Lisa Jardine's *Worldly Goods: A New History of the Renaissance* appeared, treating Ottoman Istanbul as an exemplary Renaissance city and putting trade between Europe and the Muslim world firmly at the heart of the Renaissance. Two years later, Nabil Matar's *Islam in Britain, 1558–1685* was published, describing the powerful reach and influential purchase of Muslim thought and culture within Renaissance Britain. By emphasising the dependence of Renaissance artists on materials and aesthetic practices from the East and by unveiling the allure that Islam held for many Christians at the time, Jardine and Matar not only dislodged the traditional Eurocentric perspective but also rendered it untenable. By the late 1990s, re-orienting the Renaissance was already underway.[9]

Orientalising the Renaissance

In certain respects, the effect upon Europe of encounters with the Islamic East has never really been in doubt. Gunpowder famously came from the East. So did paper and woodblock printing, making possible the printing revolution that transformed intellectual life in western Europe, just as gunpowder transformed warfare. The earliest universities in Europe were inspired by the famous Arab centres of learning such as al-Azhar University in Cairo, while translations from Arabic works of astrology, mathematics, medicine, philosophy and logic fuelled the European scholarly revival sometimes known as the Twelfth-Century Renaissance.[10] Later, without so-called Arabic numerals and the decimal system, accurate book-keeping would not have developed to assist the great banking families who paid for the paintings and the armies, the palaces and the explorers, the libraries and the scholars, without which and without whom the Renaissance would not have occurred.[11] Historians specialising in medieval and Renaissance trade, medicine, mathematics, philosophy, sculpture, architecture, decorative arts, textiles and poetry have long recognised how the influence of Arab, Ottoman and Islamic cultures became ever more intertwined with developments in Christian Europe after the fall of Constantinople to the Ottomans in 1453 and after the fall of Granada to Catholic Spain in 1492. These events helped to set in motion the revival of classical learning inspired by the flow of Greek and Arabic manuscripts throughout Europe. Gold and silver from the New World both fuelled and accelerated the rates of cultural exchange. The question is not whether, despite differences and disagreements, there was commercial and cross-cultural exchange between Muslim and Christian, or whether Renaissance artists and intellectuals engaged with eastern aesthetics and Islamic ideas. The question is rather how to describe and assess those widespread cultural exchanges that were taking place.

In *The Influence of Islam on Medieval Europe*, W. Montgomery Watt points to the way that trade and 'political presence in Spain and Sicily' had made the 'superior culture of the Arabs gradually known' throughout western European by the thirteenth and fourteenth centuries, and offers three helpful points:

> first, the contributions of the Arabs to western Europe were chiefly in respect of matters which tended to the refinement and the improvement of its material basis; second, most Europeans had little awareness of the Arab and Islamic character of what they were adopting; third, the 'gracious living' of the Arabs and the literature that accompanied it stimulated the imaginations of Europe and not least the poetic genius of the Romance peoples.[12]

Watt's conclusion, that 'the influence of Islam on western Christendom is greater than is usually realized',[13] is slowly but happily proving less true than it once was. In the field of art history, Julian Raby's *Venice,*

Dürer and the Oriental Mode (1982) and Deborah Howard's studies of Jacopo Sansovino (1975) and, more recently, her *Venice and the East* (2000) have established the crucial influences of eastern design and aesthetics upon the art and architecture of western Europe during the fourteenth and fifteenth centuries.[14] In numerous studies since the 1980s, Michael Rogers has examined how Süleyman's court drew upon and creatively competed with the artistic production of the courts of Christian Europe.[15] Building in part on their insights, Jerry Brotton's *The Renaissance Bazaar* has emphasised the mutually transforming cultural exchanges going on in this movement of people, ideas, wealth, learning and art that we call the Renaissance. Unlike Paul Johnson, Brotton aims to describe 'the historical period starting in the early fifteenth century when eastern and western societies vigorously traded art, ideas, and luxury goods in a competitive but amicable exchange that shaped what we now call the European Renaissance'.[16] What is perhaps most striking about Brotton's achievement, in his short introduction, is that he synthesises what specialist scholars working in disparate fields already knew, to present an entirely convincing case regarding how it is no longer possible to think of the Renaissance entirely or exclusively in Eurocentric terms.[17]

This re-orienting of Renaissance scholarship has also already begun responding to the challenges posed by Edward Said's *Orientalism* (1978). Scholars are generally agreed that we need a better way of thinking about East–West relations before the Napoleonic invasion of Egypt, the event that initiates the period of most interest to Said. The earlier pre-colonial period receives very little attention in Said's book, while the Ottoman Empire receives none at all. Important recent studies of the influence of Islam on medieval Europe by L. P. Harvey, Hugh Kennedy and Hugh Goddard, and in collections edited by Dionisius Agius and Richard Hitchcock and by David Blanks, have shown Said's psycho-ethnographic model of cultural 'othering' to be largely unsuitable for understanding the period immediately preceding the Renaissance.[18] Said's neglect of the Ottoman Empire has not gone unnoticed in recent studies of English Renaissance drama, such as those by Ania Loomba, Daniel Vitkus and Richmond Barbour, which have further complicated Said's claim that western understanding of the East during the Renaissance was dominated by 'Christian supernaturalism'.[19] Nabil Matar's study of *Turks, Moors, and Englishmen in the Age of Discovery* (1999) details how intricately English life and thought were being changed by increasing contact and commerce with the Muslim world.[20] Meanwhile, scholars of Ottoman history have expanded and transformed our understanding of Ottoman culture during the early modern period. Research into Ottoman archival sources has challenged directly the persistent and misleading view that the Ottoman Empire went into decline following the reign of Kanuni Sultan Süleyman I (r. 1520–66), known to the West as 'the Magnificent' and to the Ottomans as 'the Lawgiver'.[21] If the nineteenth century needed to historicise the artistic achievements of fourteenth- and fifteenth-century Italy by declaring them to signal a rebirth of European magnificence and civilisation, it also needed to ignore the great civilising achievements of the Ottomans by viewing that empire as if it were a latter-day version of Rome, doomed to decay and fall.

Contact and cultural exchange

It was Nicola Pisano (c. 1220–84), according to Paul Johnson, who sculpted the first characteristically Renaissance figures, rendering 'men and women as living, breathing, individual creatures'. Pisano was trained in one of the southern Italian workshops established by the Holy Roman Emperor Frederick II, the self-styled 'wonder of the world' (*stupor mundi*) who had himself crowned King of Jerusalem in 1229. Frederick's early but recognisably Renaissance vision of himself as a wealthy and powerful patron of the arts led him to build palaces throughout southern Italy that 'imported ideas and technologies from the eastern Mediterranean and the Orient', and to train builders and artists to revive and to imitate classical forms.[22] As early as the thirteenth century, then, the European Renaissance can be found stimulating itself by appropriating styles and techniques from the East – though as Philip Mansel reminds us in his essay here, artistic tastes can often clash with political views.

   Renaissance emperors competed with one another in their public and private buildings and in lavish exhibitions of courtly pageantry. To an already divided Christian world, the capture of Constantinople by Mehmed II in 1453 ended an historical era marked by the gradual loss of sacred lands to Islam, and finally severed Christendom into western and eastern communities. But it also brought the Ottoman Empire directly into the frame of western Europe. Mehmed 'the Conqueror', like Frederick, was an emperor who understood the importance of magnificence and the need to patronise learning and the arts. Within a few years of capturing Constantinople, Mehmed set about making conspicuous his own imperial majesty with a massive building programme which included mosques and no fewer than two palaces in the former Byzantine capital. Mehmed ordered that plans for the layout of the second of these, the Topkapı palace, should not just follow but improve upon Italian designs, and he employed decorators and master builders from all over Italy to achieve that ideal. While the Topkapı was under construction, artistic links between Florence and Pera were especially close. Francesco Berlinghieri dedicated his *Geographia* (c. 1481) to Mehmed, the sultan to whom Niccolò Ardinghelli presented a copy of Leonardo Aretino's commentary on Polybius. Gentile Bellini was living in Istanbul, busily painting his famous portrait of Mehmed and a series of lost erotica. Francesco Rosselli's engraved 'View of Istanbul' probably dates from the early 1480s, and it is most likely that the fifteenth-century Italian engravings, now in the Topkapı palace library, were gathered at the time of Mehmed.[23]

From the time of Fatih Mehmed, the Ottoman court in Istanbul was joined with the great courts of Europe in a competitive cultural dialogue that intimately linked artistic patronage and display with trading agreements and political manoeuvrings. Renowned throughout Europe, Süleyman I earned himself the title of 'the Magnificent' in the West for the sheer opulence of his court and the enormous concentration of wealth and military power it represented. Such were the ties between East and West in the mid-sixteenth century that the Valois king, François I, who is often said to have brought the Renaissance to France, sent his ring in supplication to Süleyman before going into battle against Emperor Charles V, at Pavia in 1525.[24] Defeated, François nevertheless persisted in plotting against the Holy Roman Empire and in seeking friendship with Süleyman. In 1533 he received an embassy from Süleyman's great admiral, Hayreddin Barbarossa, and began negotiating an astonishing alliance with the Ottomans against Charles V. In 1535 he dispatched Jean de La Forest to Istanbul to begin discussing campaign strategies, and the next year sent Guillaume Postel as his official interpreter with a commission to travel through Syria and Egypt to collect books and manuscripts.[25] The French king's approaches to the Ottoman court earned him the scorn of Pietro di Arezzo, known as Aretine, whom Ariosto called the 'flagello dei Principi', the 'scourge of princes'. 'How', quizzed Aretine, 'can a man be called either King or free ... if he goes and begs aid from barbarians, foes of his race, and turns against his creed?'[26] As if to counter the scorn of the Italian, the French satirist Rabelais wrote praising François for his patronage of the arts and learning, in particular 'the learned languages ... Greek, Hebrew, Arabic, Chaldean and Latin'.[27] In 1536 François and Süleyman signed military and trading agreements – the 'capitulations' (*ahid-name*) – that 'altered the entire balance of power in the Mediterranean' by allowing France direct trade with Ottoman ports.[28] Meanwhile, Postel returned with rare and valuable manuscripts in Greek and Arabic for the King's library, from which the Bibliothèque Nationale would emerge, and François renovated his château at Fontainebleau, decorating the tables with Turkish and Persian carpets.[29] François' taste for eastern culture may have started in his early years: a manuscript illumination by Robinet Testard shows the young François, aged about ten, sitting with his sister playing the Persian board game known in English as chess.[30]

Commerce

In the technical and intellectual fields, the European Renaissance relied upon skills and ideas originating even further east than Istanbul. In mapping, navigation and seamanship, like philosophy, medicine, sculpture and architecture, exchanges between Muslim and Christian were crucial; each learned from the other. There would, however, have been no Renaissance without gunpowder, paper and the mathematics that made accounting possible. In these key respects alone, skills and inventions imported from Asia may be said to serve as preconditions for the European Renaissance. Moreover, once we consider the variety of consumer goods that were being exchanged between Christian and Muslim peoples during this period, it becomes clear how many aspects of everyday life in Europe involved direct and immediate contact with the products and aesthetics of the Muslim world. In the 1580s, Elizabeth signed trading agreements allowing English merchants to trade directly in Ottoman ports alongside the Venetians and French. A document of the time lists major imports to England:

> The commodities they bringe from those partes are all sortes of Spices, Rawe Silke, Appoticarie drugs, India blewe, and Cotton Woll, as also yarne and cloaths made thereof, Galles, Currants, Sweete Oyle, Sope, Quiltes, Carpete and divers other commodities.[31]

Among wealthy and powerful families, Jardine and Brotton have shown, costly paintings, valuable tapestries and purebred horses regularly circulated in all directions across religious and state borders. But we clearly need to broaden and extend their argument by noticing how, in England at least, luxury goods from the East not only infiltrated the everyday life of the growing numbers of largely urban, middling sorts of people with disposable incomes, but also provided new opportunities for employment among the artisanal and labouring classes. In England, as throughout western Europe, those spices and drugs, blue dyes and cheap cottons, those currants, oils and carpets were becoming increasingly familiar parts of everyday life; nor were the great London merchants alone in making a living from buying and selling imported goods.

Textiles were central to the way trade from the East changed life in Renaissance England. At the court of Henry VIII, masquerading in Ottoman costume may have been a privileged entertainment restricted to the court's elite.[32] But by the end of Elizabeth's reign, imported eastern carpets and clothing made from Persian silks bought directly by expatriate agents could be found decorating properties and persons throughout the land. The importation, finishing and retailing of raw silk and silk cloth not only made English merchants and shopkeepers rich, but also employed an increasing domestic labour force, mostly of women. One contemporary commentator reckoned that between 1590 and 1630 the number of people working in the city and suburbs of London alone who were employed in the 'winding and twisting only of forraign raw silk' rose from 300 to 'over fourteen thousand souls'.[33] These labouring women may not have been able to afford the fabrics they were making, but they would have become accustomed to sweetening their food with sugar, which since the fourteenth century had been imported from Morocco. In 1565 over 5,400 hundredweight of sugar valued at over 18,000 pounds was imported into England from Morocco.[34]

Textiles and sugar were not the only items imported to Renaissance England. By the second half of the sixteenth century, eastern porcelain and glassware had begun replacing native pewter, a process that had begun much earlier in Italy and France. When Thomas Dallam went shopping in London in 1599 to pack for his sea voyage to Istanbul, he bought several essential items that he would be re-exporting back to the East – oil, sun dried raisins, cloves, mace, pepper and sugar.[35] Sugar was no longer the only imported sweetener commonly found influencing the national diet of the English. The fashionable taste for Zante currants had become so widespread throughout the middling and lower classes that the acerbic Scots traveller, William Lithgow, complained of those 'Liquorous lips ... here in England ... who forsooth can hardly digest Bread, Pasties, Broth ... without these curraunts'.[36] Among the first generation of professional travel writers, Lithgow was not alone in complaining about the orientalisation of the English diet and manners. Dramatists satirised and puritan preachers railed against the newfangled fashions of those who were becoming rich from the eastern trade and the consequent alterations in attitudes, expectations and styles of life. Commercial and cultural interests during this period were seldom identical with theological or political goals, but seldom were they entirely separate. In March 1642, currants became politics. The House of Commons banned the import of Zante currants by an Act of Parliament that was immediately vetoed by King Charles I. This was one of the very last pieces of legislation to be disputed between Parliament and Crown before the outbreak of the English civil war.[37]

For western Europe generally, the trade in consumer goods crossed class and gender lines and helped former luxuries become necessities. From eastern and Mediterranean shores came gold, silver, silk, porcelain, sugar, tea, coffee, currants, oil, wine, honey, pepper, leather, carpets, horses, opium. By the Restoration of Charles II in 1660, the process of cultural assimilation was so well established that it could be taken for granted. On the London stage in 1700, Mirabell, the hero of William Congreve's *The Way of the World*, declared tea and coffee to be 'native drinks' with only the mildest irony. Goods that regularly left English shores for the Ottoman Empire included finished woollen cloth and rabbit skins from the West Country that would warm the legs of the wealthier citizens of Istanbul and Izmir. But there was also a darker side to Renaissance trade. Other English exports tended to the business of war. For the silks of the East the English sent back bell-metal and Cornish tin to be manufactured into cannons and bullets at the great foundries of Istanbul;[38] for North African sugar and gold, oak timbers crossed from England to re-mast Algerian corsairs liable to sail against English ships.[39] Darker yet was the trade in human lives. In 1675, the Iraqi traveller Ilyas Hana al-Mawsuli set sail for the New World and reported, without comment or surprise, 'halfway we met an English ship loaded with a cargo of black slaves'.[40]

Renaissance women between East and West

For over two decades, the question of whether the Renaissance is a useful concept for women's history has been on the agenda of feminist scholars. The more specific question of whether the Renaissance has any meaning in relation to women living in the Muslim world at the time is certainly beyond my present scope, though recent scholarship on Ottoman women does provide some leads.[41] Since 1977, when Joan Kelly asked 'Did Women have a Renaissance?', scholars have retrieved from the archives, in both East and West, the astonishing lives and achievements of women who lived during the period and sculpted, painted, wrote poetry, contributed to knowledge, patronised artists and engaged in trade.[42] We know that women living in rural areas of the Ottoman Empire, even those in provincial towns, were largely kept ignorant of world events, and that most of what we know about them depends on the scant evidence pertaining to women from the upper reaches of court society. Some women were literally exchanged between Christian and Muslim countries as servants and slaves, though it is worth recalling that women from the *harem* could rise through the ranks to positions of considerable influence, and evidence suggests that many felt no sense of shame because of their humble origins.[43] Ümm Gülsüm, wet-nurse (*daye kadın*) to Fatih Mehmed, built two mosques in Istanbul and one in Edirne.[44] Women of European origins were among the most famous and powerful individuals of the Ottoman Empire: Hurrem Sultan, known as Roxelana, was probably Ukrainian; Nurbanu (d.1583), who rose to power as Murad III's mother and negotiated directly with Catherine de Medici, began life christened Ceclia Venier-Baffo;[45] Esther Handali (d.1590), Nurbanu's Kira – her commercial and diplomatic agent – was probably a Sephardic Jew of Spanish origin.[46] In addition to records concerning powerful women in the Ottoman court, there is also substantial archival evidence of Ottoman women who were taken captive into the service of European families, but their story has yet to be told.[47]

If our knowledge of how Ottoman women participated in and found their lives being affected by the Renaissance remains partial, obscure and often speculative, this generalisation largely holds true for women in western Europe also. Most women of the time were barred from taking leading roles in the male-dominated concerns of art and literature, architecture and philosophy, commerce and diplomacy, discovery and exploration, and so seldom appear in the records. Those women we do know about tend to be exceptions; and although we know more of these exceptions in western Europe than in the Ottoman Empire, there were nevertheless women of extraordinary talent and means throughout the Islamic world as well as Christian Europe. We now know, for example, that women throughout western Europe and the Ottoman Empire were far more likely to be able to read than we might once have expected. Ottoman women may not have directly benefited from the revolution in printing until the 1820s, but the names of several earlier Ottoman women poets and copies of their works do survive, and this preservation attests to their importance. On the other hand, despite the flood of reading material that the presses sent spinning throughout western Europe, access to production remained a great struggle, if not impossibility, for most women. As Suraiya Faroqhi observes in her study of women's culture in the Ottoman Empire, 'all patriarchal cultures, not excluding our own, tend in one way or another to exclude female achievements from the general consciousness'.[48] Wherever one looks, the surviving records for the period of the Renaissance were largely written by, for and about men.

Nevertheless, we now know more about the self-fashioning of the women who wielded great political power – such as Catherine de Medici, Queen Isabella of Castile and Queen Elizabeth I – than we did two decades ago, and to their names we can add those of Hurrem Sultan (Roxelana), Nurbanu and Safiye, the mother of Sultan Mehmed III, and later women such as Kösem, mother of Murad IV and Ibrahim, who held sway within the Ottoman Empire by manipulating their husbands and sons. Meanwhile, scholars have also widened our understanding of Renaissance women poets, writers, artists and musicians. Alongside European women who exemplify key aspects of Renaissance learning and arts, Faroqhi introduces several Ottoman women who were respected poets, scholars and patrons of the arts at the time. The poetry of Mihri Hatun (c.1470–after 1515) was widely known beyond her hometown of Amasya and was eventually honoured by Sultan Beyazid II (r.1481–1512) who sent her gifts. Like other Renaissance poets, Mihri Hatun challenged poetic conventions, disputed with other poets and wrote of unrequited love. Against powerful cultural expectations, her father encouraged her education and supported her decision not to marry. Her writing expressed ideas and ideals that would have found fit audience among women throughout Europe, where the pioneering work of Christine de Pisan earlier that century had initiated widespread debates over the status of women.[49] Addressing directly one of the main topics of this European *querelle des femmes*, Mihri Hatun wrote:

> You say women have little understanding, and that you do not listen to them for that reason. Yet Mihri, who prays for you [and wishes you well], explains – and clever and mature people confirm it: a talented woman is better than a thousand untalented men, a woman of understanding is better than a thousand stupid men.[50]

Her direct and disputatious manner drew a response from the poet Necati, who wrote defending talented women. Other notable examples of learned women in Ottoman society include Piri Hanim, who studied alongside learned men, and the mystic Ayişe, or Hubbi, Hatun, who took formal instruction in the Halvetiye order of Sufi mysticism by exchanging letters with eminent sheikhs.[51] During the sixteenth century, when notable women poets such as Tullia d'Aragona, Louise Labé, Catherine des Roches and Gaspara Stampa were writing in Italian and French, in Istanbul Nisayi and Hubbi Hatun were composing elegant Ottoman poetry, with its complex roots in Persian and Arabic vocabulary, employing the devices of allusion, and innuendo.[52] Hubbi Hatun, Faroqhi assures us, 'is less famous than Fitnat, whose "real" name was Zübeyde (died 1780). Fitnat lived in Istanbul',[53] so she may have been born when Lady Mary Wortley Montagu was writing her celebrated letters from the English embassy in Pera. Istanbul monuments built through the patronage of women that Lady Mary might have seen include the magnificent mosque complex of Hurrem built by the celebrated architect Sinan in 1538, the double bath-house he designed and built for her in 1556, and the striking 'New Mosque' on the Golden Horn initially commissioned in 1597 by Safiye, mother of Sultan Mehmed III, but not built until the 1660s. Already by the middle of the sixteenth century in Istanbul, '37 per cent of all officially recorded' pious foundations had been established by women.[54] For women who were fortunate, clever, artistically talented, wealthy, well-born and well-educated, the Renaissance was a time of great possibility in both East and West.

Women and textiles between East and West

Commercial exchange may not have brought Muslim and Christian women into personal contact with each other in the same ways it could for men, but textile production and East–West trade did affect increasing numbers of women's lives directly. The westward movement of silk, as already noted, served an increasing demand from affluent urban women, while also employing larger numbers of middling and lower-class women at all stages of production and marketing. Within the Ottoman Empire, as in most of Europe, men and women's attention to clothing and their relation to the textile industries involved social displays of wealth that regularly disregarded sumptuary laws aimed at preserving distinctions of rank and status. An Ottoman decree of 1564 ordering non-Muslim women to wear only skirts of angora wool or a silk and cotton blend, 'probably manufactured in Bursa', may well have been passed to help the women who were employed making these garments by boosting and assuring demand.[55] Opportunities for Ottoman women to support themselves outside the family were certainly limited, but producing and dealing in textiles provided an outlet for some who had to support themselves. As throughout Europe, there were tradeswomen who became wealthy from dealing in costly embroidered and printed fabrics. Other Ottoman women lived by selling their own needlework or by spinning mohair from home.[56] Women who travelled between villages selling shawls, called, *bohçacı kadın*, carried their wares wrapped about their hips under a suitably fashioned overcoat which made them instantly recognisable.

During the Renaissance, costume and the textile trades also brought European and Ottoman women into various forms of indirect contact and mutual recognition. At the top end of the import/export business, diplomatic gifts regularly contained valuable examples of a nation's best products. In the early 1590s, Queen Elizabeth I and Safiye, mother of Mehmed, heir to the sultanate and at that time the most powerful woman in the Ottoman Empire, exchanged gifts of richly worked costumes and pieces of finely died fabrics. Although the two women never met, we may nevertheless imagine them achieving a strange intimacy by handling materials that would clothe the other woman's body. An inventory dated February 1592 lists Elizabeth's gifts to 'the Grand Signor' and to 'the Sultana', and details the contents of no fewer than 23 great chests of the finest in English-produced textiles.[57] In October 1593, Elizabeth sent a further ten 'garments of cloth of gold' and two 'pieces of fine holland' to the Ottoman court. By August the next year, a letter from Safiye promising to intercede with the reigning sultan, Murad III, on behalf of English mercantile interests, had arrived, together with a return gift. A translation of Safiye's letter was read aloud and the magnificent garments sent as gifts were ceremonially presented to Elizabeth at Greenwich. There remains something of a mystery concerning the exact contents of Safiye's gift, but garments intended for the Queen's body were certainly included. One account describes 'an upper gowne of cloth of gold very rich, an under gowne of cloth of silver, and a girdle of Turkie worke, rich and faire', while another mentions 'two garmentes of cloth of silver', 'one girdle of cloth of silver' and 'two handekerchers wrought with massy gould'.[58] What are we to make of the particular intimacy of girdles as a ceremonial gift between powerful women? It may be that some items of Safiye's gift to Elizabeth never left Istanbul; a jewelled tiara seems to have been delayed, and the finger may point at the Kira, Esperanza Malchi, whose job was to keep discipline among the women inside the *harem* and to serve as Safiye's contact with the outside world. Some years later, after Safiye's son had become Mehmed III and Safiye herself had become the all-powerful Valide Sultan, the Kira Esperanza felt her own position elevated and wrote directly to Queen Elizabeth herself, announcing that she was forwarding 'a robe and a girdle and two handkerchiefs worked with gold and three worked with silk according to the custom of this kingdom and a necklace of pearls and rubies' as well as 'a crown of diamond gems' on behalf of her mistress. This may be the delayed tiara. For her own part,

Esperanza Malchi included a personal request: 'As there are to be found in your kingdom', she wrote, 'rare distilled waters of every kind for the face and odiferous oils for the hands, Your Majesty would favour me by sending some of them by my hand for this most serene Queen [i.e. Safiye]'.[59] At least one of the great ladies at the Ottoman court, for whom personal appearance counted as a professional skill, had heard rumours about Englishwomen and their skin-care products and wanted some.

For wealthy European and Ottoman women of the fifteenth and sixteenth centuries, each other's clothing and costume focused mutual recognition and attraction. In courts throughout Renaissance Europe, ladies dressed themselves in eastern costume to perform in masques. In Istanbul, the wives of early ambassadors being presented at the Topkapı palace regularly found their clothing was certain to attract attention to their persons. In 1607, Anne, Lady Glover was obliged to remove her gloves when visiting the court of the rather pious Sultan Ahmed I. The wife of Sir Peter Wych, ambassador to Murad IV from 1628 to 1639, assured the ladies of the *harem* that she was not shaped like the high-hooped skirt she was wearing by removing it.[60] While visiting the Ottoman Empire, European travellers made or purchased locally produced costume books containing hand-coloured illustrations of national dress and its many regional variants.

The engraved portraits of men, but more frequently women, dressed in local costumes, which Nicolas de Nicolay produced for his *Navigations* (1568),[61] circulated widely throughout Europe and provided an early ethnography based on the wide variety of local costumes to be found throughout the Ottoman Mediterranean. Nicolay's plates were often based on carefully staged on-site sittings for which the Frenchman hired local prostitutes to model regional costume.[62] Nicolay's plates were often reprinted for translations and inspired regular imitation. A magnificent folio compilation of 67 multiple-image engravings made by Julius Goltzius from portraits by J. J. Bouissard, titled *Habitus Variarum Orbis Gentis*, appeared in 1581. Each plate features multiple costume portraits of women from Europe, Asia and Africa and includes – among many others – portraits of women representing Venice, Salonica, Pera, Mitilene, Metz, Augsburg, Pisa, Rome, Naples, Milan, Rome, Beyruth, Swabia, the Levant, Arabia, Caramania, Istanbul, Aleppo, Damascus, Ethiopia, 'Africa', Tripoli, Beirut, Macedonia, Alexandria, Ragusa, and, conspicuously placeless, some 'Gypsy women'.[63]

More modest in scope but more widely available, the plates featuring the national costumes of European women that appear in Wenceslas Hollar's later *Theatrum Muliebrum* (1633) show the influence of eastern fabrics and designs. The costume portraits of Ottoman women in George de la Chappelle's more sumptuous *Receuil de divers Portraits des Principales Dames de la Porte du Grand Turc, Tireé au natural sur les lieux* (Paris, 1648),[64] include a 'Turkish' princess, a Greek woman, Greek maiden and a Jewish woman, all with panoramas of Istanbul in the background, as if the models were posing in their finest costumes on the heights of Pera. De la Chappelle's volume also portrays the 'Queen of Athens', a 'Turkish dancing girl', a 'Turkish' woman riding on horseback, as well as Armenian, Persian and Tartar women, all in splendid array, and remind us how swiftly the printing press had begun to produce and to circulate national stereotypes.

Without resorting to printing and for the benefit of more restricted audiences, Ottoman artists were developing their own conventions for representing persons, costumes and national differences. Magnificent, handcrafted costume books were produced in Istanbul for sale to European collectors and for presentation as gifts on state occasions. These are often works of imperial grandeur that celebrate and boast of the breadth and extent of Ottoman control, and at the same time they cannot but have helped to stimulate desire for eastern textiles. One collection from the 1620s contains finely differentiated and fully coloured portraits of, among many others: a Greek Orthodox nun, a Circassian woman, a Janissary in service to the English ambassador, a 'Christian virgin in the Street', a 'Christian virgin in the House', a married Christian woman, a Grecian woman, a Christian widow, an Armenian woman, a Jewish woman at home, a 'Turkish virgin in the Street', a 'Turkish woman married in the Street' and a 'Turkish whore in the Street', all of them in suitably distinct and brilliantly coloured costumes. The collection also includes a portrait of a 'Woman that sells Cloaths', one of those tradeswomen called *bohçacı kadın*, 'the woman with the wrappers'.[65]

These costume books circulated powerful images of eastern textiles at a time when garments made from such materials were in demand throughout western Europe. Renowned for their great skills at embroidery with gold thread, the Ottoman craftswomen who made the finest pieces came to be in such great demand that, in 'the Habsburg parts of Hungary and at Christian courts in south-eastern Europe ... some members of the nobility attempted to obtain such women as slaves for their own residences'.[66] So there was a darker side to the Renaissance for women too.

The more we know about the lives and achievements of a growing number of remarkable Renaissance women, and the more we struggle to find out about women whose lives were not exceptional enough to be a matter of record, the less we may be inclined to believe that the Renaissance was entirely restricted to events involving western European male individuals after all. More research will be required before we can fully understand how interaction between East and West influenced the lives of women during the Renaissance, or understand fully just how influential women might have been in the great movements of the period.

Re-Orienting the Renaissance

This book is organised thematically from papers that were invited on the theme of 'Re-telling the Renaissance' and first presented, courtesy of the Institute for Arab and Islamic Studies, at the University of Exeter. The aim of that event was to bring together a number of scholars and writers from a number of different disciplines and fields whose work directly challenges many of the ways we are still invited to think of the Renaissance as an exclusively European event. The first three chapters pursue commercial and cultural interactions between Christian and Muslim, between East and West; the fourth and fifth chapters explore various methods by which Europeans represented the Ottomans and their purposes in doing so; the final three chapters complicate matters further by examining views from the Muslim world by taking into account Arabic and Ottoman sources.

Chapters by Deborah Howard, Jerry Brotton and Philip Schwyzer set the frame for the book by showing how trade between East and West not only rendered borders rather porous but also brought with it crucial forms of cultural exchange without which the widespread artistic and intellectual movement that came to be called the Renaissance could not have taken place. Howard's essay establishes how, by the fifteenth century, Venetians took it for granted that their material and cultural life was inextricably bound up with the East. The story begins, in other words, at a moment when there was no simple East–West divide but rather an accepted and normative flow of mutually sustaining values, goods and attitudes. Brotton's chapter develops and moves this interchange across western Europe and shows how, during the fifteenth and sixteenth centuries, the iconography of a 'Turkish' (Anatolian-born) Christian martyr – St George – was shared among Italian, German, Dutch and English artists and exploited for a variety of national and political purposes. Schwyzer's chapter, focusing on the late sixteenth and early seventeenth centuries in England, argues that the trade in medicinal *mumia* from Egypt figured at the centre of a widespread and hitherto ignored anxiety about what constituted, quite literally, the body politic of the Protestant English. From conditions of commercial, artistic and cultural exchange to actual, physical incorporation, these first chapters cover the period under consideration and show how conditions of relatively untroubled commercial interaction only started to come unstuck with the rise of competing western European nationalisms.

Chapters by Barnaby Rogerson and Philip Mansel reinforce and extend a central argument of this book that, despite major differences, there was no necessary or inevitable conflict between the Christian West and Islamic East. They do so by investigating western visitors to the East during the sixteenth and seventeenth centuries, a phenomenon that was almost entirely a one-way development at this time. Rogerson's comparative examination of a Flemish diplomat and writer and a Danish engraver living together in sixteenth-century Istanbul shows how, despite the different forms in which they represented what they saw, both long-term expatriates shared a remarkable capacity for sympathetic understanding of a society and a culture that were quite different from their own. In surveying reports by French travellers to the Ottoman Empire during the sixteenth century, Mansel's chapter argues that intellectual and scientific developments of the time intensified French interest in the people, culture, flora and fauna of the East. Together, these central chapters demonstrate how new forms of enquiry and methods of representation that were features of what we call the Renaissance – travel writing and pictorial imaging, humanistic ethnography and natural history – developed from and were dependent upon the skills and open-mindedness of western visitors living in Ottoman lands.[67]

Chapters by Robert Irwin, Nabil Matar and Caroline Finkel are based on comparative analyses that bring contemporary Arabic and Ottoman sources to bear upon the questions raised by the book as a whole and, in doing so, complicate and nuance what might otherwise seem to be a uniform set of eastern influences upon the West. While one general argument of the book is, indeed, that what has come to be understood as the European Renaissance could not and would not have taken place in the ways it did without such material, cultural and intellectual influences, these chapters turn our attention to the remaining problems with such a view and argue that without a detailed understanding of what was happening at the time among Muslim nations we are very likely to misunderstand the nature and scope of those influences and thus misunderstand those very real developments. Irwin's chapter tackles the thorny problems of language and translation, of intellectual influence and philosophical misunderstanding in the Petrarchan moment, and shows how misinformation continues to bedevil our views of how knowledge travelled between East and West. Matar uncovers a previously ignored Arabo-Islamic legal discourse that was developing in counterpoint to European humanism. In doing so, he shows that the Magharibi were aware of Europeans, were interacting with them, and saw them as part of a familiar Mediterranean world, conceived of in terms that were not very different from the cultural and historical space theorised by Fernand Braudel. Finkel's chapter challenges received models, academic and popular, that have been used to portray the history of the Ottoman Empire as one of decline in the face of European progress. After demolishing the notion of an uncontested claim to historical truth or value, Finkel outlines some Ottoman perspectives on things European. Features that once seemed integral to an intact 'Renaissance' or to the Ottoman 'classical' period, conceived as parallel but separate worlds, converge and dissolve in the historical figures Finkel describes of several Ottoman 'Renaissance' men whose achievements in arts and sciences suggest a differential flourishing of civility and culture rather than a rebirth of exclusively European origins.

In the move from Howard's reversal of normative aesthetic and representational categories and values when the West meets itself coming back from the East, to Finkel's displacement of the historiographical categories that give concepts such as 'the Renaissance' both form and meaning, the journey of this book formally enacts the reversal and displacement characteristic of a deconstructive reading. Instead of regarding the Renaissance in its own terms, this book challenges the authority of self-description by reversing the values implicit in the oppositional structures that give that description meaning, and then displaces them. This deconstruction does not, as is often claimed by those who wish it were so, leave us with nihilistic and ahistorical doubts, but rather with the very kinds of informed questions raised by this book that point us away from settled certainties about European 'progress' in the face of eastern 'stagnation' or 'decline' and towards new directions of enquiry. The authors of this book leave us asking: How can we ever again speak of 'the Renaissance'? At the same time, they demand that we also ask: How can we not speak about it when to do so might be to begin to unravel the seeming perdurability of conflict between the East and the West?

Acknowledgements

My thanks to Professor Tim Niblock and Dr Mohammad-Salah Omri of the Institute for Arab and Islamic Studies, University of Exeter, for appointing me

Visiting Professor in 2004, and to Mohammad-Salah especially for helping to organise the conference 'Re-Telling the Renaissance, East and West', held at IAIS in May at which this book had its origins. Special thanks are due to Professor Lisa Jardine for sponsoring our application to the British Academy for financial support, and to the Centre for Mediterranean Studies and the School of English at the University of Exeter for additional assistance. My special thanks to Christopher LeBrun, RA, who generously allowed us to use 'Venice IV' from his 2004 exhibition for the webpage to the Exeter event, and to the Marlborough Gallery which kindly arranged for the digital reproduction. I also want to extend special thanks to the audience and all the participants who contributed to that event – most notably Edmund Bosworth, John and Pat Boyd, William Dalrymple, Iman Hamam, Richard Hitchcock, Rosemary Hooley, Nick McDowell, Rhoads Murphey and Ann Williams. Luciana O'Flaherty and the anonymous readers at Palgrave Macmillan were quick off the mark; since then Dan Bunyard and Michael Strang have been exemplars of attentive efficiency and patience. Sarika Chandra, Colin Heywood, Elisabeth Sauer, Dana Seitler and Cannon Schmitt, all kindly commented on drafts of my Introduction to its improvement; to each my thanks. Suraiya Faroqhi generously sent me her Stories of *Ottoman Men and Women*, studies which deserve fuller attention than they receive in this Introduction. Without Caroline Finkel, in Istanbul and London, and without Philip Mansel and Jerry Brotton sometimes in London, none of this could have happened. I know I am not alone in thanking William Dalrymple for coming to Exeter and, more recently, for writing the Foreword. Once again, without Donna Landry willingly listening to incoherent chatter, reading early drafts, answering the phone and enduring my panic attacks, none of this would have happened.

Notes

1. 'European History: From the Stone Age to a New Millennium', advertising brochure for *The Encyclopedia of the Renaissance* (Farmington Hills, MI: Gale, 2003), p. 6. The 'Seated Scribe' is reproduced widely and discussed in relation to the portrait by Bihzād in Jerry Brotton, *The Renaissance Bazaar: From the Silk Road to Michaelangelo* (Oxford: Oxford University Press, 2002). See also Phillipa Scott, *Turkish Delights* (London: Thames and Hudson, 2001), who reproduces the 'Seated Scribe' and discusses its relation to a 'series' of such portraits by 'Persian, Mughal, and Turkish artists', pp. 16–17.
2. Recent studies of the Renaissance as a pan-European movement, but largely excluding the Ottoman Empire, include Keith Whitlock, ed., *The Renaissance in Europe: A Reader* (New Haven, CT: Yale University Press, 2000) and John Jeffries Martin, ed., *The Renaissance: Italy and Abroad* (London: Routledge, 2002).
3. For a recent reworking of the concept of Renaissance individualism based on English literary sources only, see Elizabeth Hanson, *Discovering the Subject in Renaissance England* (Cambridge: Cambridge University Press, 1998), and, for a lively and informed challenge to the notion, see John Jeffries Martin, *Myths of Renaissance Individualism* (Basingstoke: Palgrave Macmillan, 2004).
4. For a useful brief account of the relevant developments in economic history, see Robert Markley, 'Riches, Power, Trade and Religion: the Far East and the English Imagination, 1600–1720', in Daniel Carey, ed., *Asian Travel in the*

Renaissance (Oxford: Blackwell, 2004), 169–91, esp. pp. 176–8 on the question of financing Renaissance trade. See also Andre Gunder Frank, *ReOrient: Global Economy in the Asian Age* (Berkeley, CA: University of California, 1998), and Kenneth Pomerantz and Steven Topik, *The World that Trade Created: Society, Culture, and the World Economy, 1400 to the Present* (New York: Sharpe, 1999).

5. Paul Coles, *The Ottoman Impact on Europe* (London: Thames and Hudson, 1968), back cover.
6. On the problem of Ottoman decline, see Finkel in this volume, and Daniel Goffman, *The Ottoman Empire and Early Modern Europe* (Cambridge: Cambridge University Press, 2002), pp. 112–15 and passim.
7. Paul Johnson, *The Renaissance: A Short History* (London: Weidenfeld, 2000), p. 18.
8. Johnson, *Renaissance*, p. 21.
9. In relation to the critique of New Historicism, it may be noted how the recent surge of interest in Islam and the East among Renaissance scholars trained in literary and cultural studies has often developed in disregard of Ottoman historiography; see Dan Goffman, 'Afterword: Early Modern English Ambivalence toward the Ottomans', in Goran Stanivukovic, ed., *Mapping the Mediterranean in Early Modern English Writings* (forthcoming).
10. See George Makdisi, *The Rise of Colleges: Institutions of Learning in Islam and the West* (Edinburgh: Edinburgh University Press, 1981), and *The Rise of Humanism in Classical Islam and the Christian West* (Edinburgh: Edinburgh University Press, 1990).
11. On Fibonacci and the European debt to Arab mathematics, see Brotton, *Renaissance Bazaar*, pp. 44–8.
12. W. Montgomery Watt, *The Influence of Islam on Medieval Europe* (1972; rpt. Edinburgh: Edinburgh University Press, 1987), pp. 28, 29.
13. Watt, *Influence*, p. 84.
14. Julian Raby, *Venice, Dürer and the Oriental Mode* (London: Sothebys, 2002); Deborah Howard, *Jacopo Sansovino: Architecture and Patronage in Renaissance Venice* (New Haven, CT: Yale University Press, 1975), and *Venice and the East: The Impact of the Islamic World on Venetian Architecture 1100–1500* (New Haven, CT: Yale University Press, 2000).
15. See, in addition to indispensable works such as Michael Rogers, ed., *The Topkapı Saray Museum: The Albums and Illustrated Manuscripts* (Boston: Little, Brown, 1986), further references to Michael Rogers' extensive publications in J. M. Rogers and R. M. Ward, *Süleyman the Magnificent* (New York: Tabard, 1988), pp. 222–3, and Caroline Finkel's essay in this book.
16. Brotton, *Renaissance Bazaar*, p. 1; and see Rosamond E. Mack, *Bazaar to Piazza: Islamic Trade and Italian Art, 1300–1600* (Berkeley, CA: University of California Press, 2002).
17. In her recent *Creating East and West: Renaissance Humanists and the Ottoman Turks* (Philadelphia: University of Pennsylvania Press, 2004), Nancy Bisaha analyses fascination with the Ottomans among Italian humanist writers, both broadening and confirming her earlier argument that the humanist's secular assessment of the Ottoman Empire was enormously influential and rooted in both classicism and fear; see her ' "New Barbarian" or Worthy Adversary? Humanist Constructs of the Ottoman Turks in Fifteenth-Century Italy', in David Blanks and Michael Frassetto, eds., *Western Views of Islam in*

Medieval and Early Modern Europe: Perception of Other (New York: St. Martin's Press, 1999), pp. 185–205.

18. See L. P. Harvey, *Islamic Spain, 1250–1500* (Chicago: Chicago University Press, 1990), and *Muslims in Spain, 1500–1614* (Chicago: Chicago University Press, 2005); Richard Fletcher, *Moorish Spain* (Berkeley: University of California Press, 1993); Hugh Kennedy, *Muslim Spain and Portugal: A Political History of al-Andalus* (London: Longman, 1996); Hugh Goddard, *A History of Christian–Muslim Relations* (Edinburgh: Edinburgh University Press, 2000); Dionisius Agius and Richard Hitchcock, eds., *The Arab Influence in Medieval Europe: Folia Scholastica Mediterranea* (Reading: Ithaca, 1996); and David Blanks, ed., *Images of the Other: Europe and the Muslim World Before 1700* (Cairo: American University in Cairo Press, 1997).

19. Said, *Orientalism*, p. 122, and see Ania Loomba, *Gender, Race, Renaissance Drama* (Manchester: Manchester University Press, 1989); Daniel Vitkus, *Turning Turk: English Theater and the Multicultural Mediterranean, 1570–1630* (New York: Palgrave, 2003); Richmond Barbour, *Before Orientalism: London's Theatre of the East, 1576–1626* (Cambridge: Cambridge University Press, 2003). In *Mimesis and Empire: The New World, Islam, and European Identities* (Cambridge: Cambridge University Press, 2001), Barbara Fuchs turns to theatrical and literary texts for evidence of national identity-formation in early modern England and Spain. Theorising the pre-colonial moment of Orientalism has a healthy history of writings that take the form of critical engagements with Said's work, among which see Peter Burke's seasoned position in 'The Philosopher as Traveller: Bernier's Orient', in Jaf Elsner and Joan-Pau Rubiés, eds., *Voyages and Visions: Towards a Cultural History of Travel* (London: Reaktion, 2000), pp. 124–37.

20. Nabil Matar, *Turks, Moors, and Englishmen in the Age of Discovery* (New York: Columbia University Press, 1999).

21. Recent studies in English of early modern Ottoman history include: Palmira Brummet, *Ottoman Seapower and Levantine Diplomacy in the Age of Discovery* (Albany, NY: State University of New York Press, 1994); Suraiya Faroqhi, *Kultur und Alltag im osmanischen Reich* (Munich: Beck'sche, 1995), trans. Martin Bott, *Subjects of the Sultan: Culture and Daily Life in the Ottoman Empire* (London: Tauris, 2000), and *The Ottoman Empire and the World Around It* (London: Tauris, 2004); Caroline Finkel, *Osman's Dream: The Story of the Ottoman Empire* (London: Murray, 2005); Daniel Goffman, *Ottoman Empire*; Colin Imber, *The Ottoman Empire, 1300–1600* (Basingstoke: Palgrave Macmillan, 2002); Colin Imber, Keiko Kiyotaki and Rhoads Murphey, eds., *Frontiers of Ottoman Studies*, 2 vols (London: Tauris, 2004); Cemal Kafadar, *Between Two Worlds: The Construction of the Ottoman State* (Berkeley, CA: University of California Press, 1995); Leslie Peirce, *The Imperial Harem: Women and Sovereignty in the Ottoman Empire* (New York: Oxford University Press, 1993); Gabriel Piterberg, *An Ottoman Tragedy: History and Historiography at Play* (Cambridge: Cambridge University Press, 2003).

22. Johnson, *Renaissance*, p. 53.

23. On the construction of the Topkapı, see Gülru Necipoğlu, *Architecture, Ceremonial and Power: The Topkapı Palace in the Fifteenth and Sixteenth Centuries* (Cambridge, MA: MIT Press, 1991), pp. 4–15, and David Landau and Peter Parshall, *The Renaissance Print, 1470–1550* (New Haven, CT: Yale

University Press, 1994), pp. 91–4, for a summary – largely based on Julian Raby's archival scholarship – of the Florentine connections.

24. Desmond Seward, *Prince of the Renaissance: The Life of François I* (London: Cardinal, 1974), p. 188. See also R. J. Knecht, *Renaissance Warrior and Patron: The Reign of Francis I* (1994; rpt. Cambridge: Cambridge University Press, 1996).
25. Seward, *Prince of the Renaissance*, p. 166.
26. Cited in Seward, *Prince of the Renaissance*, p. 198.
27. Seward, *Prince of the Renaissance*, p. 170.
28. Seward, *Prince of the Renaissance*, p. 188. But on the effectiveness of the early capitulations, see Joseph Matuz, 'À propos de la validité des capitulations de 1536 entre l'Empire ottoman et la France', *Turcica* 24 (1992): 183–92.
29. Seward, *Prince of the Renaissance*, p. 163.
30. Reproduced in Seward, *Prince of the Renaissance*, p. 19.
31. British Library Ms Cotton Nero B viii, f.53b.
32. 'On Shrove Sunday the same yere, the kyng prepared a goodly banket, in the Parliament Chambre at Westminster, for all the ambassdours, whiche then wer here, out of diverse realms and countries ... his grace with the Erle of Essex, came in appareled after Turkey fashion, in long robes of Bawdkin, powdered with gold, hattes on their heddes of Crimosyn Velvet ... girded with two swords, called Cimiteries', [Edward Halle], *Hall's Chronicle; Containing The History of England* (London: Johnson et al., 1809), p. 513. The English were not, of course, alone in their admiration for Ottoman textiles; see, for example, Veronika Gervers, *The Influence of Ottoman Turkish Textiles and Costume in Eastern Europe with Particular Reference to Hungary* (Toronto: Royal Ontario Museum, 1982).
33. Cited in Alfred C. Wood, *A History of the Levant Company* (1935; rpt. London: Cass, 1964), p. 76.
34. British Library Ms Lansdowne 8, fol. 17.
35. Thomas Dallam, 'Diary', in Theodore J. Bent, ed., *Early Travels in the Levant* (London: Hakluyt, 1893), p. 2.
36. William Lithgow, *The Totall Discourse of The Rare Adventures and Painefull Peregrinations* (1632; rpt. Glasgow: MacLehose, 1906), p. 58.
37. Woods, *History*, pp. 69–70.
38. The view of Istanbul in volume six of Georg Braun's *Civitates Orbis Terrarum* (Cologne, 1606–8), locates the 'arsenale' on the Marmara coast just below the mosque of Sokullu Mehmed Pasha in the Old City.
39. The clandestine export of ships' timbers is reported by Thomas Smith's journal of his 1678 voyage to Istanbul in *Miscellanea Curiosa. Containing a Collection of Curious Travels, Voyages, and Natural Histories of Countries, As they have been Delivered in to the Royal Society. Vol. III* (London: for R. Smith, 1708), p. 14.
40. *Kitab Siyahat al-Khoury Ilyas bin al-Qisses Hanna al-Mawsuli*, trans. Nabil Matar, in *In the Lands of the Christians: Arabic Travel Writing in the Seventeenth Century* (London: Routledge, 2003), p. 57.
41. In addition to studies by Peirce and Faroqhi already mentioned, see the illuminating case-studies of women's lives in fifteenth-century Bursa in Faroqhi's *Stories of Ottoman Men and Women* (Istanbul: Eren, 2002), and more generally Mohja Kahf, *Western Representations of Muslim Women: From Termagent to Odalisque* (Austin, TX: University of Texas Press, 1999). In his brief survey

article, 'Turkish Women in the Ottoman Empire: The Classical Age', in Lois Beck and Nikki Keddie, eds., *Women in the Muslim World* (Cambridge, MA: Harvard University Press, 1978), pp. 229–44, Ian Dengler offers some useful generalisations based on summations of accounts by western travellers and other secondary sources, though some of his conclusions regarding the fifteenth, sixteenth and seventeenth centuries rely too heavily on nineteenth-century accounts. More useful for the later period are the essays in Madeline C. Zilfi, ed., *Women in the Ottoman Empire: Middle Eastern Women in the Early Modern Era* (Leiden: Brill, 1997).

42. Joan Kelly-Gadol, 'Did Women Have a Renaissance?', in Renate Bridenthal and Claudia Koontz, eds., *Becoming Visible: Women in European History* (Boston: Houghton Mifflin, 1977). This important essay was recently reprinted in Lorna Hutson, ed., *Feminism and Renaissance Studies* (Oxford: Oxford University Press, 1999), a collection of essays exclusively concerned with European women. The impact of printing on the lives of European women has been examined by Brian Richardson, *Printing, Writers and Readers in Renaissance Italy* (Cambridge: Cambridge University Press, 1999), Floyd Gray, *Gender, Rhetoric, and Print Culture in French Renaissance Writing* (Cambridge: Cambridge University Press, 2000), and most recently, by Gaia Servadio, *Renaissance Woman* (London: Tauris, 2005), who argues that print facilitated women's education, thereby creating both a 'new vision of womanhood' and a 'new' woman.

43. See Peirce, *Imperial Harem*, and Faroqhi, *Subjects*, p. 99.

44. Peirce, *Imperial Harem*, p. 131, and see Ülkü Bates, 'Women as Patrons of Architecture in Turkey', in Beck and Keddie, eds., *Women*, pp. 245–60.

45. On Nurbanu, see Peirce, *Imperial Harem*, and Benjamin Arbel, 'Nur Banu (c. 1530–1583): a Venetian Sultana?', *Turcica* 24 (1992): 241–59.

46. Peirce, *Imperial Harem*, p. 226.

47. Faroqhi, *Subjects*, p. 100.

48. Faroqhi, *Subjects*, p. 121.

49. See Joan Kelly, 'Early Feminist Theory and the *Querelle des Femmes*, 1400–1789', *Signs* 8 (1982): 4–28.

50. Cited in Faroqhi, *Subjects*, pp. 117, 122.

51. Faroqhi, *Subjects*, p. 115.

52. In addition to Servadio, *Renaissance Woman*, see Margaret F. Rosenthal, *The Honest Courtesan: Veronica Franco, Citizen and Writer in Sixteenth-Century Venice* (Chicago: University of Chicago Press, 1993), and Ann Rosalind Jones, *The Currency of Eros: Women's Love Lyric in Europe, 1540–1620* (Bloomington, IN: Indiana University Press, 1990). For Hubbi Hatun, see Faroqhi, *Subjects*, p. 118; for Nisayi, see Walter Andrews, Najaat Black and Mehmet Kalpakli, trans. and eds., *Ottoman Lyric Poetry: An Anthology* (Austin, TX: University of Texas Press, 1997), pp. 82–4, 237–8. The same volume also includes brief biographical accounts of, and translations of poems by, Necati, Mihri Hatun, Zeynep Hatun and Fitnat Hanım.

53. Faroqhi, *Subjects*, p. 118.

54. Faroqhi, *Subjects*, p. 118. On the building of the 'New Mosque', see Lucienne Thys-Şenocak, 'The Yeni Valide Mosque Complex at Eminönü', *Muqarnas* 15 (1998): 58–70.

55. Faroqhi, *Subjects*, pp. 110, 113. Unfortunately, I did not see Suraiya Faroqhi and Christoph Neumann, eds., *Ottoman Costumes: From Textile to Identity*

(Istanbul: Eren, 2004) until it was too late to incorporate the research findings of the various essays in this Introduction; my thanks to Caroline Finkel for the reference to this invaluable work.

56. Faroqhi, *Subjects*, p. 113. Dengler notes that women engaged in retail were often Jewish or Armenian, but that their number also included some ethnic Turkish women, and that beyond textiles, the only other commercial activities available to women in the Ottoman Empire were entertainment and prostitution. Both these latter groups, he observes, were considered to be outsiders and non-Muslims. Prostitutes, Dengler writes, 'represented a category of errant women whose husbands were either unwilling or unable to control them', and cites the legal code of Süleyman that 'set fines for prostitution under the section on adultery', see 'Turkish Women', pp. 231, 233 and notes 12, 27–32.

57. See British Library Ms Cotton Nero B viii f. 124, and f. 204, dated 14 February 1592, which detail the contents of the chests.

58. Susan Skilliter, 'Three Letters from the Ottoman "Sultana" Safiye to Queen Elizabeth I', in S. M. Stern, ed., *Documents from Islamic Chanceries* (Oxford: Clarendon, 1965), pp. 119–57; passages cited on pp. 146, 148.

59. Skilliter, 'Three Letters', p. 43.

60. See Gerald MacLean, *The Rise of Oriental Travel: English Visitors to the Ottoman Empire, 1580–1720* (Basingstoke: Palgrave Macmillan, 2004), epilogue.

61. Nicolas de Nicolay, *The Navigations, Peregrinations, and Voyages, made into Turkie* (Lyons, 1567), English translation by Thomas Washington the Younger (1585); German translation, with hand-coloured plates by Georg Mack, *Der Erst Theil. Von der Schiffart und Raisz in die Türckey und gegen Orient beschriben durch H. N. Nicolay* (Nürenberg: Conrad Saldoerffer, 1572).

62. Unable to gain access to the *harem*, Nicolay comments: 'And therefore to finde the meanes to represent unto you the maner of their apparel I fel familiarly acquainted with an Eunuche of the late Barbarousse called Zaferaga of nation a Ragusan, being a man of great discretion & a lover of vertue, which from his tender age had been brought up within the Sarail, who so soone as he had perceived, that I was desirous to see the fashion of the attire and apparrell of these women, to satisfie my mind, caused to be beclothed two publique Turkish women, with very rich apparrell, which hee sent for the Bezestan whereas there is too be solde of all sortes, by the wich I made the draughts and protractes here represented unto you', p. 53v. See also Clarence Dana Rouillard, *The Turk in French History, Thought, and Literature (1520–1660)* (1940; rpt. New York: AMS, 1973), pp. 212–17, 276–8.

63. I am referring here to the British Library copy that is bound with and catalogued under Melchior Lorichs [sic] et al., *Costumes (1570–83)*, shelfmark 146.i.10. The collection of engravings made after originals by Melchior Lorck, which was assembled by John Evelyn and is now at Stonor Park, Henley-on-Thames, includes some fine examples of Lorck's skill in the genre. The Evelyn collection has been reproduced in Erik Fischer, *Melchior Lorck: Drawings from the Evelyn Collection at Stonor Park, England and from the Department of Prints and Drawings, the Royal Museum of Fine Arts, Copenhagen* (Copenhagen, 1962) and is discussed by Barnaby Rogerson's essay in this book.

64. George de la Chappelle, *Recueil de divers Portraits des Principales Dames de la Porte du Grand Turc, Tireé au natural sur les lieux* (Paris: Antoine Estiene, 1648), British Library copy at shelfmark 146.i.10.

65. I take these examples from BL Add Ms Sloane 5255, a collection of Persian and Turkish costume portraits. On the *bohçacı kadın*, see Faroqhi, *Subjects*, p. 113.
66. Faroqhi, *Subjects*, p. 120.
67. See Joan-Pau Rubiés, *Travel and Ethnography in the Renaissance: South India through European Eyes, 1250–1625* (Cambridge: Cambridge University Press, 2000) for a specialised account of European encounters with the Indian sub-continent and an engaging contribution to the emerging historiography of pre-colonial Orientalism.

1
The Status of the Oriental Traveller in Renaissance Venice

Deborah Howard

Travel lore in its widest sense was an integral part of Venetian culture. Over the centuries, merchant handbooks, ambassadors' reports and pilgrim chronicles had recorded journeys made in the interests of trade, diplomacy and Christian devotion. Within Venice this body of knowledge circulated freely, orally and in manuscript form, but during the sixteenth century its dissemination was to be transformed by ambitious printing initiatives. A new genre, the printed anthology of travel narratives, gave added authority to geographical information and helped to shape the ways in which travellers were perceived.

The accumulation of information about foreign parts was a crucial component of the education of Venice's mercantile nobility, who often travelled abroad at a very young age. For example, from the age of 17 to 22, the diarist Girolamo Priuli traded in London, where he claimed to have met King Henry VII on several occasions.[1] In his youth, Giosafat Barbaro, later to be Venetian ambassador in Persia, traded for 16 years based at Tana on the Black Sea.[2] The young Chioggian merchant Nicolò dei Conti spent 24 years in Cairo from 1415 to 1439, trading on behalf of his father in Egypt, Persia and India.[3] Alvise da Mosto, later a celebrated explorer, began his mercantile career in his teens as agent of the merchant Andrea Barbarigo from 1442 to 1448.[4] As he later explained: 'My whole idea was to spend my youth trading on every possible route, to accumulate *facoltà* [a word comprising both authority and wealth], so that with the experience of the world I would be able to achieve every *perfection of honour*' (emphasis added).[5]

For fifteenth-century Venetian merchants, honour was inseparable from commercial success. In 1421 the future explorer Pietro Querini went to Flanders 'with the aim of acquiring something of what we men of the world crave insatiably, that is *honour and riches*' (emphasis added).[6] Trade was regarded as the perfect training for an honourable career in government and public service. The diarist Girolamo Priuli remarked that since the Venetians had always been involved in commerce, those who knew how to run their businesses properly would be much better qualified to govern and understand the affairs of state.[7]

There was always the risk, however, that too long a period abroad might result in alienation. This was a well-known trope of travel literature since Antiquity; when Homer's Ulysses returned home, dirty and dressed in rags after 19 years of wandering, his wife, Penelope, failed to recognise him. In the same vein, Mafio Priuli, author of a long letter from Coromandel in India written in 1537, feared that since his hair had turned white he would no longer be known if he returned home.[8] Similarly, by tradition, the Polos, on their return from China wearing rough, Tartar-style clothes, had acquired 'something of the Tartar in their faces' and had almost forgotten their native Venetian dialect, so that their family hardly recognised them. According to this story, later recounted by a neighbour of the Polos, Gasparo Malipiero of Sta Marina, they went home and changed into rich textiles, gave presents of cloth to their servants, put on a banquet for their relatives and showed off the jewels sewn into their old travel clothes, which astounded everyone.[9] Interestingly, recent excavations in the foundations of the Teatro Malibran, built over Polo property, have revealed extensive foundations dated by radiocarbon dating to the very time of Marco Polo's return, so it seems that he soon invested some of his profits in building to recover his honour.

The horizons of Venetian travel

For Venetian merchants, the limits of the known world corresponded closely to the lands of the Bible. But their frontiers were determined not by religious study, but by the frequency of trade. Alexandria, Damascus and Aleppo, with their resident colonies, were regarded as so familiar that few Venetian visitors felt the need to describe them. A fascinating set of documents, which I have analysed in two recent articles, reveals 68 named Venetians in Damascus within a mere three-year period, 1455–7.[10] Yet, way beyond the limits of these cities, Venetians were to be found settled and assimilated into local life. On his Scandinavian explorations in 1431, Pietro Querini was surprised to encounter a Venetian called Zuan Franco who was serving as a feudal knight in the castle at Stege in Denmark.[11] At Elefante in India around 1580, the Venetian jeweller Gasparo Balbi came upon a flourishing shipbuilding industry producing both large and small galleys, thanks to the expertise of 'a good master from Venice called Domenico da Castello, who makes them rather well'.[12]

Marco Polo's travels, like those of John Mandeville, were regarded as 'extravagancies', extending into the realms of fantasy.[13] More credence was afforded to the classical texts, especially Ptolemy, Strabo and Pliny. Indeed, some writers suggested that the world had, in effect, contracted again during the Dark Ages and that it was only now through trade that these strange and unknown lands were again becoming familiar. As the publisher Antonio Manutio remarked in 1543, 'the world today owes a great debt to the efforts of merchants' in recovering this knowledge.[14] The big problem, however, was how to match up the new place-names, which he called '*nomi barbari*', in order to marry the knowledge of Antiquity to more recent discoveries.

Even those Venetian travellers who extended the limits of geographical knowledge usually ventured further afield in search of profit, rather than for mere exploration. In 1455 Alvise da' Mosto was the first to discover the Cape Verde islands, but for him this discovery was of little importance because the islands were barren and uninhabited. As a potential place for commercial adventure, the lush green forests of the West African equatorial regions promised far more. There he sold horses, wool and silk in return for slaves and 150 parrots. He hoped that others after him would realise that the West African rulers badly needed supplies of salt, and that merchants could also make money from the slave trade.[15]

Since Venetians had been travelling to the eastern Mediterranean and beyond since at least the ninth century, few redirected their interests westwards, even after 1500. Although the Flanders galleys sailed regularly to the Low Countries and England, via Spain, most Venetians were still far more interested in the traditional routes to Alexandria, Beirut, North Africa and Constantinople. They were slow to realise the potential of western travel. John Cabot, the discoverer of Newfoundland, had to get patronage from England for his voyage of 1496.[16] A letter of 23 September 1497 from a Venetian merchant, Lorenzo Pasqualigo, in London, proudly mentioned that when Cabot set foot in the New World he planted the flag of St Mark together with a crucifix alongside the English flag 'so that our flag stood a long time over there'.[17] Yet his son Sebastian Cabot was twice refused Venetian support for his voyages of exploration in 1522 and 1551.[18]

In August 1499 the diarist Girolamo Priuli mentioned the voyage of Vasco da Gama around the Cape, but with some scepticism: 'This news and its import seems very great, if indeed it is true. However, I don't entirely believe it.'[19] Two years later, people were beginning to fear the worst: 'Those in the know claimed that this [news] brings the greatest possible threat to the liberty of the Venetian Republic.'[20] By 1502 the impact of the discovery of the Cape Route was only too clear. In February of that year, Priuli sadly attributed the lack of spices on the returning Alexandria galleys to the effects of Portuguese competition.[21] Just five years later, in 1507, the first printed anthology of travel writing, published in Vicenza, was to give substance and reality to these new discoveries and to extend the boundaries of imaginable geography beyond the Old World.[22]

Printing travel literature: some preliminary considerations

Before turning to the role of printing in the dissemination of travel information to the Venetian public, a few prior observations are needed. To preface these remarks, we must remember that, even after the invention of printing, numerous manuscripts were still in circulation in the sixteenth century, including the travels of both Marco Polo and Alvise da Mosto. Similarly, handwritten journals continued to be family treasures handed down through the generations. For example, the Venetian merchant Alessandro Magno copied out his travel journals from 1557 to 1562 in an elegant humanist hand, illustrated by his own drawings and bound in vellum for his descendants.[23] Yet, as we shall see, printing changed the public perception of the known world, just at the very time when its frontiers were being extended to hitherto unimaginable limits.

Printing, most importantly, gave the sense of greater authority and authenticity. Traditional merchant handbooks began to appear in printed form, and although these were less easily personalised and updated than their manuscript predecessors, their content had a definitive aspect that added conviction. The conferring of authenticity was always a preoccupation of travel writers, especially when describing their more remarkable experiences. As Alvise da Mosto put it: 'In truth, life and customs in our [familiar] places could be called another world in comparison with the things I have seen.'[24] Giosafat Barbaro echoed this sentiment: 'For those who have never been out of Venice, these things would probably seem like lies.'[25]

A favourite device of travel writers was to give plausibility to foreign places by comparing them with familiar Venetian monuments. In his description of Pegù in Burma in 1583, Gasparo Balbi used the Procuratie Nuove in Piazza San Marco as an analogy for its arcaded streets. He compared the width of the main street to that of the Grand Canal at Rialto and estimated the Pagoda to be the same height as the Campanile of San Marco and the same size as the Doge's Palace, although round rather than square.[26]

Secondly, printed texts reached a wider audience. The preface of the 1548 Italian translation of Ptolemy's *Geography* claimed its usefulness not only to philosophers, theologians, astronomers, medical doctors, lawyers, orators, poets and other scholars, but also to princes, high commissioners (*rettori di republiche*), mercenary generals (*condottieri*), captains, admirals, private navigators, solders, merchants and gentlemen, as well as *gentilissime Madonne*, wanderers and pilgrims.[27] Venetian women rarely travelled abroad – although, interestingly, the Venetian wife and children of John Cabot accompanied him to London, and Nicolò dei Conti's wife and family were with him in Cairo, where she and two of the children died of the plague.[28]

Thirdly, the language of the discourse of travel was drastically modified by printing. In the thirteenth and fourteenth centuries, under the influence of crusading culture, many texts about the East, including the original version of Marco Polo's travels, had been written in French.[29] By the fifteenth century, however, most travel narratives were composed in Venetian dialect, whether in diary form or under subject headings. Merchant handbooks too were written in dialect, using the familiar 'tu' for the reader.[30] The main exception was the odyssey of Niccolò dei Conti, whose travels were written in Latin by the Florentine humanist Poggio Bracciolini, at the request of Pope Eugenius IV. This unusually humanistic context resulted from the historical circumstances of dei Conti's repatriation. On his return from his voyage to the East Indies in about 1439, he had to go to Florence to seek absolution from the Pope for having renounced the Christian faith while abroad in order to save his skin.[31]

During the sixteenth century, by contrast, a more Tuscan version of Italian became the standard language for the printed texts of travel literature. The vernacular was universally adopted, but dialect disappeared even when the text was clearly addressed to active Venetian merchants, such as the account of his travels to the East Indies by the jeweler Gasparo Balbi, published in Venice in 1590.

As Francis Bacon remarked, most people travelling over land write little, whereas on board ship 'where there is nothing to see but sky and sea', many travellers indulge in travel writing.[32] A striking exception was the Venetian ambassador to Persia, Ambrogio Contarini, whose highly readable adventures on his overland journey via Russia and Kiev were widely read in the sixteenth century.[33] It is worth remembering that many

Venetian children learned to read using the vernacular version of the *Lives of the Saints* by St Jerome, rewritten in the fourteenth century by the Dominican friar Domenico Cavalca as a series of racy adventures.[34] Thus the recounting of travel in distant lands was a familiar literary genre.[35] By contrast, diplomats were trained to record their experiences more systematically. Contarini's fellow envoy to the court of Uzun Hasan in 1474, Giosafat Barbaro, wrote up his journey after his return, following subject headings, as recommended for the writing of diplomatic *relazioni*.[36]

The first printed travel anthologies

The printing of travel narratives in Venice began in the fifteenth century.[37] The first printed edition of Marco Polo seems to have been that published in Venice in 1496 and reprinted in 1508.[38] Ambrogio Contarini's travels to Persia were printed in 1476–7, but the extreme rarity of this edition suggests that the print-run was very small.[39] A reprint of 1524 published in Venice was more widely circulated. The title-page lists the profusion of topics to be included:

> notable mountains, rivers, plains, deserts, horrid wildernesses, distances, frontiers, difficult passes, the fertility or otherwise of the lands, merchandise, animals and fish of strange kinds, forms of boats and houses, place names, countries, courts of kings, dukes and lords, the nature, customs, religion and stature of the inhabitants (male and female), and endless other things.[40]

The first proper anthology of travel writing, edited by Fracanzio da Montalboddo, was originally published in Vicenza in 1507.[41] This selection appeared at the very time when the suspicions of Venetians about the long-term impact of Portuguese competition were beginning to sink in. Its emphasis was exclusively westward. The only Venetian traveller to be included was Alvise da Mosto, whose West African voyages open the book. Most of the narratives are concerned with discoveries in the Americas, including those by Columbus and Amerigo Vespucci. The only mention of the East is a little note at the end recording an observation about Christians in India.[42] The dedicatee of the book, Angiolello, was himself a renowned traveller to the East, best known for his period in the service of Sultan Mehmed II from 1474–c.1483.[43] Fracanzio used Angiolello's previous experience to stress the novelty of the publication: 'Because having travelled in almost all of Europe and a great part of Asia you will recognize in the diversity of the things mentioned how marvelous they are.'[44] The language of publication, Tuscan Italian, was quite deliberately chosen, for Fracanzio felt that in any other form, whether 'florid Latin', 'rough dialect' or Portuguese, the narratives would have been overlooked.[45]

A new edition published in Venice in 1517 by the Milanese publisher Giorgio Rusconi seemed to address a more specifically Venetian readership, for the title page is largely taken up by a woodcut of the centre of Venice, stretching from Piazza San Marco with its quay and warehouses ('magageni') to the Rialto market (Figure 1). The importance of this little book lies in the gathering of miscellaneous texts in various languages, including a series of letters collected from Spain and Portugal. Its diversity helps to give conviction to the richness of the experiences related, because of the range of modes of discourse. The anthology format was to prove highly influential, as we shall see.

Once the genre of the anthology of travel writing was established, the idea began to take root. In 1543 Antonio Manutio, heir to the famous publishing house of Aldus Manutius, published a much longer anthology of travel writing called *Journeys from Venice to Tana, Persia, India and Constantinople*, which extended to 180 double-sided pages.[46] Here the emphasis appears to be an attempt to restore the primacy of oriental travel in the Venetian consciousness. In direct contrast to Fracanzio's anthology, the emphasis is exclusively eastward. Indeed, it focuses on all the traditional destinations of Venetian merchants. In his foreword, Manutio stresses their contribution:

> Among all the moderns who have hitherto travelled the world, without any doubt the Venetian nobility [hold the first place]; because of their greatness and power in maritime affairs, both as merchants and as envoys from their most illustrious Republic to various potentates, they have been able to sail to the most remote places, and thus to interact with many barbarous nations ... For the mutual benefit of their descendants they have left faithful accounts.[47]

The collection opens with the two by now celebrated accounts of the missions to Persia of Giosafat Barbaro and Ambrogio Contarini. It continues with Alvise Roncinotto's journeys to India in 1529 and 1532, and a eulogistic account of an anonymous journey to Constantinople in 1533. The final narrative recounts the adventures of a Venetian who was seized in Alexandria and taken on the Ottoman expedition to try to seize Diu from the Portuguese in 1538. Manutio's introduction stresses that the aim of the book is entertainment rather than practical

Paesi nouamente ritrouati per

la Nauigatione di Spagna in Calicut. Et da Alber tutio Vefputio Fiorentino intitulato Mon do Nouo: Nouamente Impreſſa.

Figure 1 Fracanzio da Montalboddo, ed., *Paesi novamente ritrovati*, 2nd edition (Venice: Rusconi, 1517): frontispiece with woodcut view of central Venice showing Piazza San Marco in the foreground and the Rialto market in the background. Photo credit: Biblioteca del Museo Correr, Venice.

usefulness.[48] In other words, the audience is not the active, enterprising Venetian merchant, but the 'universal' reader. Despite the appeals to the Republic's supremacy in trade and travel, these peregrinations thus entered the realm of literature.

The individual contribution of Gian Battista Ramusio

The most celebrated Venetian printing initiative in the realm of travel writing was, of course, that of Gian Battista Ramusio. Ramusio was the son of a famous jurist Paolo Ramusio and nephew of Hieronomo Ramusio, a celebrated physician and Arabic scholar.[49] Ramusio's main aim was neither to draw attention to the importance of the New World (like the Vicenza anthology), nor to seek to restore the reputation of Venetian oriental travel (like Manutio). His goal was a purely scholarly, scientific one. The sole aim was to update the geographical knowledge of Antiquity in every continent, whether east or west, in order to assist mapmakers. Above all, Ptolemy's *Geography* needed supplementary texts in the light of recent voyages of exploration.[50]

There was no desire to privilege Venetians or any other nation. Yet in his preface to volume two, Ramusio mused on whether the Venetian overland explorations were more marvellous than the voyage of Columbus. Putting aside his patriotic instincts, he still concluded that the hardships endured by Venetians such as Marco Polo on land were greater than those suffered on a short sea voyage to the New World.[51] For Venetians, seafaring was just part of normal life. The excitement of the project for Ramusio lay in the sense that the whole surface of the globe was becoming part of the known world, inhabited everywhere by the human race, no matter how cold or hot.[52]

The project seems to have evolved during scholarly conversations with his friends in the villa of the humanist Girolamo Fracastoro above Lake Garda.[53] In an earlier tentative venture of 1534 Ramusio had published a *History of the East Indies*, using material sent from Spain by Andrea Navagero.[54] For decades Ramusio collected texts, using his network of humanist friends and his connections as secretary in the Doge's Palace, first to the Senate and later from 1550 to the Council of Ten.[55] He himself translated all the texts into elegant Italian, including not only those in Latin, Portuguese and Spanish, but also the accounts in Venetian dialect.[56] According to the dedication the intended audience included both scholars and princes.[57] Ramusio was critical of those rulers who were not interested in knowledge for own sake, in contrast to the initiative shown by the kings of Portugal.[58]

The promotion of trade was not the main motivation. None the less, Ramusio's position at the heart of government meant that he was not oblivious to the economic implications of the new information. His Venetian outlook is surely betrayed by his lengthy excursus on the spice trade in volume one. Similarly, in his preamble to da Mosto's text, he hopes that 'reading these voyages, as if to see and touch [the places] with one's own hand, shows how one could open a new trading route to these negro lands, that would be short, easy, convenient and safe'.[59]

The publication was a huge enterprise. The three original massive volumes, published by Tommaso Giunti in Venice, appeared in 1550, 1559 and 1556 respectively. They were dedicated to Fracastoro, author of a well-known work on cosmology, *Homocentricorum* (1538), and of a much-admired Latin poem on syphilis (1530).[60] The second volume was due to appear in 1557, the year of Ramusio's death, but an unfortunate fire in the printer's workshop in that year destroyed the woodblock illustrations, and the book eventually appeared without the intended maps two years later.[61] All three volumes were originally published anonymously, and Ramusio's identity was not revealed until 1563 when the publisher Giunti added a tribute to their late editor in the Foreword to volume one.

Ramusio's three volumes were organised geographically. The first volume included accounts of Africa, India and the East Indies; the second was concerned with Russia, the Middle East and Central Asia; and the third with the New World. His publisher Giunti mentioned, probably in jest, that Ramusio hoped to publish a fourth volume on the Antarctic, in which case 'there would no longer have been any need to read Ptolemy, Strabo, Pliny or any of the other ancient writers on geography'.[62]

Cartography: the role of Ramusio and Gastaldi

The benefits of the enterprise for cartography were explicitly stated, yet it is hard to see how such knowledge could have been applied directly. Most explorers were vague about distances and directions, tending to measure distance by travel time. Pietro Querini, for instance, recognised that his discoveries made Fra Mauro's mid fifteenth-century globe doubtful, but confessed that he had not 'had time to measure or even consider the distances'.[63]

The woodcut maps included in Ramusio's volumes are anonymous, but may have been made by his friend the great cartographer Giacomo Gastaldi, who instructed his young son in geography.[64] The first volume contained only one woodcut map of the Nile and some plans of

Figure 2 G. B. Ramusio, *Navigationi et Viaggi*, vol. 3 (Venice: Giunti, 1556): woodcut map of West Africa attributed to Giacomo Gastaldo. Reproduced from 1563 edition. Photo credit: By permission of the Syndics of Cambridge University Library.

40

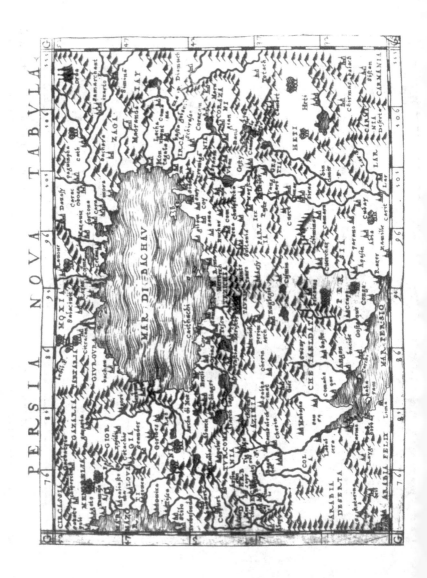

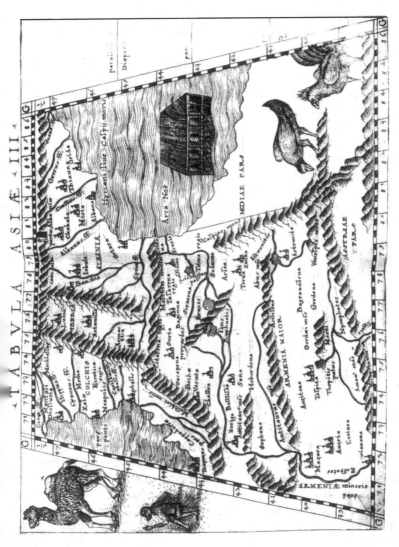

Figure 3 La geografia di Claudio Ptolemeo Alessandrino (Venice: Pedrezano, 1548): woodcut maps by Giacomo Gastaldi, the new map (left) compared with the traditional Ptolemaic version (right). Photo credit: Biblioteca Marciana, Venice.

Ethiopian churches. Volume three included a number of maps of the New World as well as Africa and the East Indies (Figure 2). All the maps show anecdotal details, such as exotic animals and fish, natives with weapons and primitive huts. In addition, there are some small woodcuts of similar features: unfamiliar plants (including cactus, sweetcorn, pineapple and rhubarb), wooden dwellings, near-naked figures and an Indian hammock.

Map publication was a flourishing sector of the sixteenth-century Venetian printing trade, and one cannot doubt that the production was at least inspired by Ramusio's volumes, and vice versa.[65] Indeed, a more systematic series of maps, engraved on copper from maps by Gastaldi, had only recently been published in an Italian translation of Ptolemy's *Geography*, published in Venice in 1548.[66] These modern maps were interleaved with the traditional Ptolemaic versions (Figure 3).

Ramusio himself seems to have been the moving spirit behind a nearly contemporary project to decorate the large Sala dello Scudo in the Doge's Palace with up-to-date maps of the world.[67] Maps were not only decorative, but also invaluable in the formulation of policy, whether in peace or war. The huge maps were painted on canvas by the mapmaker Gastaldi between 1548 and 1553, using as his studio the large space of the near complete Library being erected on the opposite side of the Piazzetta.[68] In the contracts for these maps, Gastaldi was specifically instructed to take full account of travel writings such as those of Alvise da Mosto, Jacques Cartier and Marco Polo.[69]

Explorers as heroic figures: the eighteenth century

By the eighteenth century the condition of the maps in the Doge's Palace had deteriorated, and they were largely repainted by the restorer Grisellini.[70] It was only at this point that it was suggested celebrating individual Venetian travellers, including Marco Polo, Pietro Querini, Alvise da Mosto and Nicolò dei Conti, in the decorative scheme (Figure 4). In a touching recognition of their contribution, the two editors of travel anthologies, Ramusio and Antonio Manutio, were included in this hall of fame. Three overdoors were added to depict famous Venetian voyages. By this time the maps were so obviously out-of-date that they were of historical significance only. Thus they became a public celebration of famous Venetian exploits in travel and exploration. A century later, the stage door of the Teatro Malibran received a commemorative inscription to Marco Polo, while a house in the Via Garibaldi was chosen for a plaque in honour of John and Sebastian

Figure 4 Venice, Palazzo Ducale, Sala dello Scudo, *Map of West Africa* by Giacomo Gastaldi (1548–53): addition of figures and text on the left by Francesco Grisellini (1762) to commemorate Alvise da Mosto's discovery of the Cape Verde Islands. Photo credit: Cameraphoto, Venice.

Cabot. At the time of writing, Alvise da Mosto's house, the venerable Ca' da Mosto on the Grand Canal, is still anonymous and neglected, awaiting its likely destiny as a hotel.

Over the centuries the commercial and political success of the Venetian Republic had depended on travel overseas. Venetian merchants were used to risk and adventure, to the dangers of shipwreck, piracy and disease, and to unfamiliar and uncomfortable experiences. This was normal life, rather than heroism. Even with the dissemination of their adventures in print in the sixteenth century, the achievements of Venetian explorers were not given public recognition. Whereas in Venice the writing of history became increasingly preoccupied with myth-creation, in the age of printing, geography had to be as exact a science as possible. Reliable information about far-away places was an essential part of Venetian education, whoever had made the discoveries. It was only in the last decades of the Venetian Republic in the eighteenth century, when their explorers had become of historical rather than geographical significance, that their contribution was publicly commemorated in the Doge's Palace.

Notes

1. 'molte volte io l'ho veduto et pratichato', Marin Sanudo (Sanuto), *I Diarii*, ed. R. Fulin et al., 58 vols. (Venice: Fratelli Visentini, 1879–1902): 5: col. 9. See R. Fulin, 'Girolamo Priuli e i suoi diarii', *Archivio Veneto*, 22 (anno 11 [1881]): 137–248.
2. Laurence Lockhart, 'Introduction: Giosafat Barbaro', in L. Lockhart, R. Morozzo della Rocca and M. F. Tiepolo, eds., *I Viaggi in Persia degli Ambasciatori Veneti Barbaro e Contarini* (Rome: Istituto Poligrafico dello Stato, 1973), pp. 16–23, on pp. 16–17. See also Angelo Ventura, 'Giosafat Barbaro', *Dizionario Biografico Italiano* (henceforth *DBI*), 6: 106–13.
3. Ugo Tucci, 'Mercanti, viaggiatori, pellegrini nel Quattrocento', in *Storia della cultura veneta, III/II, Del primo quattrocento al Concilio di Trento* (Vicenza: Neri Pozza, 1980), pp. 324–5.
4. Later, after two voyages as a noble *balestriere*, or bowman, on galleys to Alexandria (1451) and Flanders (1452), da Mosto returned to Flanders in 1454 aged 25. See Ugo Tucci, 'Alvise da Mosto', *DBI*, 32: 369–73.
5. 'tutto il pensier mio era di essercitar la mia gioventù travagliando per ogni via possibile, per acquistarmi facultà, accioche poi con la esperientia del mondo in eta possi venir ad alguna perfectione de honore.' Gian Battista Ramusio, ed., *Navigationi et Viaggi, Venice 1563–1606*, intro. R. A. Skelton and George B. Parks, 3 vols. (Amsterdam: Theatrum Orbis Terrarum, 1967–70), 1: 97. All citations from Ramusio's *Navigationi ei Viaggi* will be made from this reprint, which reproduces the expanded editions of 1563, 1583 and 1606 respectively. This was also used as the scheme for the Italian reprint edited by Marica Milanesi, 3 vols. (Turin: Einaudi, 1978–88).
6. 'per desiderio di acquistare parte di quello che noi mondani siamo insatiabili, cioè honore e ricchezze', Tucci, 'Mercanti', p. 325.
7. 'Per essere stato sempre merchadanti, per il qual esercito degno et molto apreziato in la citade, perchè quelli sanno et intendeno bene et governano la facultade, robe et la merchatantia loro, molto meglio saperanno governare et intendere li bisogni et negotti et danari publici', Priuli, *Diarii*, 6: 152v (manuscript in Corver Library, Venice), cited by Fulin, 'Girolamo Priuli', pp. 137–8. The published version of Priuli's diaries is incomplete and does not include this volume of the manuscript: see Arturo Segre and R. Cessi, eds., *I Diarii di Girolamo Priuli 1494–1512*, 3 vols. in *Rerum Italicum Scriptores* 24: 3 (Città di Castello and Bologna, 1912–38).

8. Giuliano Lucchetta, 'Viaggiatori e racconti di viaggi nel Cinquecento', in *Storia della cultura veneta, III/II, Del Primo quattrocento al Concilio di Trento* (Vicenza: Neri Pozza, 1980), pp. 433–89, on p. 446: 'divenuto tanto bianco e canuto che non è uomo che mi conoscesse.'

9. Ramusio, *Navigationi*, 2: 5–5v.

10. Francesco Bianchi and Deborah Howard, 'Life and Death in Damascus: The Material Culture of Venetians in the Syrian Capital in the mid-Fifteenth Century', *Studi Veneziani*, n.s. 46 (2003): 233–300, statistics on p. 298; Deborah Howard, 'Death in Damascus: Venetians in Syria in the mid-Fifteenth Century', *Muqarnas* 20 (2003): 143–57.

11. Tucci, 'Mercanti', p. 325. Since 'borg' means castle, this was probably the historic Danish town of Stege.

12. 'buon maestro da Venetia, chiamato Maestro Domenico da Castello, il qual le fa assai belle', Gasparo Balbi Gioielliero Venetiano, *Viaggio dell'Indie orientali* (Venice: Camillo Borgominieri, 1590), p. 63. For Balbi's journey in a modern edition, see Olga Pinto, ed., *Viaggi di C. Federici e G. Balbi all' Indie orientali* (Rome: Istituto Poligrafico dello Stato, 1962).

13. As Francesco Sansovino remarked, Marco Polo 'wrote the travels of the new world (*mondo nuovo*), being the first before Columbus to discover new countries; however, not believing this account because of its extravagancies (*cose stravaganti*), Columbus added credibility (*credulità*) in the time of our fathers, by discovering the part formerly thought to be uninhabited'. See Francesco Sansovino, *Venetia città nobilissima et singolare* (Venice: I. Sansovino, 1581), p. 25v, my translation.

14. 'Grandissima obligatione veramente ha oggidi il mondo alla industria de Marcatanti', Antonio Manutio, ed., *Viaggi fatti da Vinetia alla Tana, in Persia, in India et in Costantinopoli* (Venice: Manutius, 1543), p. 2.

15. Ramusio, *Navigationi*, 1: 97–111v. In 1463/4 aged about 35, da Mosto returned to Venice to marry and make his career in public service, although he continued to trade in Egypt, Syria, Spain and England. He wrote his narrative between 1460 and 1466. See Ugo Tucci, 'Alvise da Mosto', *DBI*, 32: 369–73.

16. John Cabot sailed from Bristol with a permit from the King but at his own expense. Although authorised to arm five ships, he took only one, probably for lack of sponsorship. See Ugo Tucci, 'Giovanni e Sebastiano Caboto', *DBI*, 15: 702–22, esp. pp. 703–5.

17. '... à impiantato su li tereni à trovato, una gran croxe con una bandiera de Ingeltera e una di San Marcho, per esser lui veneziano; sichè el nostro confalone s'è steso molto in qua', Sanudo, *Diarii*, 1: cols. 806–7.

18. Tucci, 'Giovanni e Sebastiano Caboto', *DBI*, 15: 702–22, esp. pp. 713, 721. See also Alison Sandman and Eric H. Ash, 'Trading Expertise: Sebastian Cabot between Spain and England', *Renaissance Quarterly* 57 (2004): 813–46.

19. 'Questo nova et effecto mi par grandissimo, se l'he vero. *Tamen* io non li presto autenticha fede.' Cited in Giuliano Lucchetta, 'L'oriente mediterranea nella cultura di Venezia tra Quattro e Cinquecento', *Storia della cultura veneta, III/II, Del primo quattrocento al Concilio di Trento* (Vicenza: Neri Pozza, 1980), pp. 375–432, quoted passage on p. 411.

20. 'Intexa veramente questa nova a Venetia, tuta la citade se ne risente grandemente et chadauno ne rimaxe stupefacto. Et fo tenuto questa nova per li sapienti che la fusse la pegior nova che mai la Republica veneta potesse havere havuto dal perder la libertade in fuori.' Cited Lucchetta, 'L'oriente', pp. 411–12.

21. Fulin, 'Girolamo Priuli', p. 165.
22. Francazio da Montalboddo, ed., *Paesi novamente retrovati et Nuovo Mondo da Alberico Vesputio Florentino intitulato* (Vicenza: Enrico da Ca' Zeno, 1507). Vicenza also saw the printing of the important Latin translation by Jacopo Angelo of Ptolemy's *Geographia* (Vicenza: Hermannus Levilapide, 1475).
23. Folger Library, Washington DC, ms. V.A. 239 (1317/1).
24. 'Veramente e il viver e i costumi e i luoghi nostri, in comparatione de le cosse per me vedute et intesse, altro mondo se poteria chiamar', Tucci, 'Mercanti', p. 324.
25. 'a quelli che, per modo de dir, mai fuori di Venetia, forsi parerian busie', Lockhart et al., eds., *Viaggi*, p. 68.
26. Balbi, *Viaggio*, pp. 96–96v.
27. *La geografia di Claudio Ptolemeo Alessandrino, con alcuni comenti & aggiunte fattevi da Sebastiano munstero Alamanno, Con le tavole non solamente antiche e moderne solite di stamparsi, ma altre nuove aggiuntevi di Messer Iacopo Gastaldo Piamontese cosmographo, ridotta in volgare Italiano da M. Pietro Andrea Mattiolo Senese medico Eccellentissimo* (Venice: Gioan Battista Pedrezano, Venice, 1548), Proemio ai lettori.
28. Tucci, 'Giovanni e Sebastiano caboto', p. 703; Nicolò dei Conti, *Viaggi in Persia, India e Giava*, ed. Mario Longhena (Milan: Alpes, 1929), Introduction, p. 23.
29. Deborah Howard, *Venice and the East: The Impact of the Islamic World on Venetian Architecture 1100–1500* (New Haven, CT: Yale University Press, 2000), p. 22.
30. Howard, *Venice and the East*, p. 17.
31. Ramusio, *Navigationi*, 1: 338. For the likely date of this voyage, see Conti, *Viaggi*, p. 34.
32. Francis Bacon, *Essays*, ed. John Pitcher (Harmondsworth: Penguin, 1985), p. 113.
33. F. Cavazzana Romanelli, 'Ambrogio Contarini', *DBI*, 28: 97–104; Lockhart et al., eds., *Viaggi*, pp. 177–232.
34. See Paul F. Grendler, 'What Zuanne Read in School: Vernacular Texts in Sixteenth-century Venetian Schools', *Sixteenth Century Journal* 13:1 (1982): 41–54, reprinted in Grendler, *Books and Schools in the Italian Renaissance* (Aldershot: Variorum, 1995), essay 7. See also Carlo Delcorno, *La traduzione delle 'Vite de' Santi Padri'* (Venice: Istituto Veneto di Scienze, Lettere ed Arti, 2000), pp. 515–25.
35. Nicolò de Ruzino, who died on the Beirut galley in 1457, had a copy of St Jerome's *Vite de Santi Padri* for travel reading in his deck luggage; see Bianchi and Howard, 'Life and Death in Damascus', p. 245.
36. Lockhart et al., eds., *Viaggi*, pp. 67–171; Ugo Tucci, 'Il viaggio di Giosafat Barbaro in Persia', in Michela Marangoni and Manlio Pastore Stocchi, eds., *Una famiglia veneziana nella storia: I Barbaro* (Venice: Istituto Veneto di Scienze, Lettere ed Arti, 1996), pp. 117–32. On the conventions of writing diplomatic *relazioni*, see Howard, *Venice and the East*, p. 44.
37. As a possible precedent, Francesco Sansovino mentions a certain Vincenzo Querini in the time of Doge Foscari (1524–57) who published 'un libro, De singulis conclusionibus omnium scientiarum. Et alcuni commentarii dell'India, et di Colocuth', but this may not have been printed, *Venetia città nobilissima* (1581), p. 244v. On travel literature in early modern Venice, see Lucchetta, 'Viaggiatori e racconti', and Daria Perocco, *Viaggiare e*

raccontare: Narrazione di viaggio ed esperienze di racconto tra Cinque e Seicento (Alessandria: dell'Orso, 1997).

38. Marco Polo, *Delle maravigliose cose del mondo* (Venice: Sessa, 1496), and *Delle meraviglie del mondo* (Venice: Sessa, 1508).

39. The travels of Ambrogio Contarini are mentioned by Francesco Sansovino as taking place during the reign of Doge Andrea Vendramin (1476–8), *Venetia città nobilissima*, p. 239.

40. *Itinerario del Magnifico et Clarissimo messer Ambrosio Contarini, dignissimo Orator della illustrissima Signoria de Venetia, mandado nel anno 1472 ad Usuncassan Re di Persia* (Venice: Francesco Bindoni and Mapheo Pasini, 1524).

41. Francazio da Montalboddo, ed., *Paesi novamente retrovati et Novo Mondo da Alberico Vesputio Florentino intitulato* (Vicenza: Henrico Vicentino and Zammaria suo filo, 1507).

42. This was a comment made by an Indian called Joseph who had joined a Portuguese caravelle.

43. See Franz Babinger, 'G. M. Angiolello', *DBI*, 3: 275–8.

44. 'Si perche havendo tu quasi tutta la europa & gran parte del asia pagiato, in tanta diversità de cose discerne qual diano piu maraviose', Francazio da Montalboddo, ed., *Paesi novamente ritrovati per la Navigatione di Spagna in Calicut. Et da Alberitio Vesputio Fiorentino intitulato Mondo Novo* (Venice: Zorzi de Rusconi milanese, 1517), dedication.

45. Nevertheless, within ten years of the original publication in 1507, the anthology was also translated into both Latin and French. See Lucchetta, 'Viaggatori e racconti', p. 435.

46. Antonio Manutio, ed., *Viaggi fatti da Vinetia alla Tana, in Persia, in India et in Costantinopoli* (Venice: Manutius, 1543).

47. 'tra tutti i moderni che prima & con maggior chiarezza hanno in questa parte giovato al mondo, senza alcun dubbio sono stati i Signori Venetiani; i quali per la loro grandezza & potenza cha hanno havuto nelle cose maritime, et come mercanti & spesse fiate come oratori della loro Illustrissima Republica à diversi Potentati, hanno potuto penetrare navigando in luoghi remotissimi; & cosi tenere commentio con molte barbare nationi ... per comune utilità de loro descendenti, hanno lasciato fedel memoria', Manutio, *Viaggi*, pp. 2–2v.

48. 'per fine principale, piu tosto il giovare universalmente à gli huomini, che al suo privato comodo', Manutio, *Viaggi*, p. 2v. The book is dedicated to Antonio Barbarigo, the Captain of the Alexandria galley from which the writer of the last narrative was seized.

49. Ramusio's uncle Hieronimo, son of Benedetto, was a philosopher and physician, who knew Greek, Latin and Arabic, and who translated both Galen and Avicenna. According to Franceso Sansovino, his manuscript of Avicenna, written in parallel texts in his own hand, was still in the hands of his descendants in Casa Ramusia in 1581. He died in Damascus aged 36 in 1486; *Venetia città nobilissima*, p. 250. Gian Battista Ramusio himself began his career travelling 'dallo havere nella sua giovinezza praticato molt'anni in diversi paesi e provincie, mandatovi per honorati servitii di Questa Eccelentissima Republica'. He went to France 1505 aged 20 in the suite of the Venetian ambassador. See the tribute to Ramusio in the 1563 edition of volume one of his *Navigationi et viaggi*.

50. These editions should be considered in the context of printed editions of Ptolemy's geography: the Latin editions published in Vicenza, 1475 (see above, n. 22) and in Venice by Bernardo Sylvano, 1511, as the Italian translation with new maps by Gastaldi published in 1548 (see above, n. 27).
51. See Ramusio, *Navigationi*, 'sopra il principio del libro del mag. M. Marco Polo all'eccellente M. Hieronimo Fracastoro', preface, 2: unnumbered pagination.
52. 'd'ogni intorno questo globe della terra è maravigliosamente habitato, ne vi è parte alcuna vacua, ne per caldo o gielo priva d'habitatori', tribute to Ramusio by Tommaso Giunti in 1563 edition of volume one, unnumbered pagination.
53. Ramusio's dedication to Girolamo Fracastoro in volume one says that the idea originated in discussions with Count Raimondo della Torre, who died in 1541; see Skelton's introduction to *Navigationi*, 1: ix. In his discourse on the spice trade in volume two, Ramusio particularly remembers 'un grande, & ammirabile ragionamento, che io udi questi mesi passati, insieme coll'Eccellente Architetto M. Michele da San Michele, nell'ameno, & dilettevol luogo dell'Eccellente messer Hieronimo Fracastoro detto CAPHI, posto nel Veronese, sopra la sommità di un lago che discopre tutto il lago di Garda'; *Navigationi*, 2: 373.
54. Skelton, Introduction to *Navigationi*, 1: viii.
55. Lucchetta, 'Viaggiatori e racconti', pp. 482–6.
56. Perocco makes a detailed comparison between the original Venetian dialect of Ambrogio Contarini and Ramusio's Italian translation; see *Viaggiare e raccontare*, pp. 9–10.
57. 'dotti & studiosi', also 'i Signori & Principi'. Ramusio, preface to Fracastoro, in *Navigationi*, 1: unnumbered pagination.
58. Lucchetta, 'Viaggiatori e racconti', p. 489.
59. 'leggendoi queste navigationi, veder & tocchar con mano, come se potria aprir un nuovo viaggio a detti regni de Negri per mare, che saria breve, facile, commodo & sicuro', Ramusio, preface to Alvise da Mosto, in *Navigationi*, 1: 96.
60. On Fracastoro, see E. Peruzzi, 'Girolamo Fracastoro', *DBI*, 49: 543–8; Spencer Pearce, 'Fracastoro on Syphilis: Science and Poetry in Theory and Practice', Pierpaolo Antonello and Simon A. Gilson, eds., *Science and Literature in Italian Culture from Dante to Calvino* (Oxford: Legenda, 2004), pp. 115–35.
61. Skelton, Introduction to *Navigationi*, 1: xii–xiii.
62. 'non havesse fatto più di bisogno leggere, ne Tolomeo, ne Strabone, ne Plinio, ne alcun'altro de gli antichi scrittori intorno alle cose di Geografia', Tommaso Giunti, preface to *Navigationi* (1563), 1: unnumbered pagination.
63. He had not 'habuto tempo de mesurar over pur considerar questa distantia', Tucci, 'Mercanti', p. 325.
64. Skelton, Introduction to *Navigationi*, 1: xii. Two of the maps were very similar to maps by Gastaldi in the 1548 edition of Ptolemy's *Geography* cited note 27 above.
65. Eugenia Bevilacqua, 'Geografi e cosmologi', *Storia della cultura veneta, III/II, Del Primo quattrocento al Concilio di Trento* (Vicenza: Neri Pozza, 1980), pp. 355–74, esp. pp. 356–60.

66. *La geografia di Claudio Ptolemeo Alessandrino*, see note 27 above.
67. Rodolfo Gallo, 'Le mappe geografiche del Palazzo Ducale di Venetia', *Archivio Veneto*, 5th series, 32/33 (1943): 47–113. This was the first room in the private apartments of the Doge, to which the new Scala d'Oro, erected in 1555–9, would give almost direct access. See Francesco Sansovino, *Venetia città nobilissima et singolare*, ed. Giovanni Stringa (Venice, 1604), p. 222v. This passage is not in the original 1581 edition, but was added by Stringa.
68. Gallo, 'Le mappe geografiche', p. 60.
69. Gallo, 'Le mappe geografiche', pp. 60, 62–3.
70. Gallo, 'Le mappe geografiche', pp. 79–80.

2
St George between East and West

Jerry Brotton

The connection between St George and Englishness is firmly rooted in most discussions of the iconography of nationalism. It stretches from Shakespeare through to the recent revival of the red-cross flag as the defining symbol of England in the wake of political devolution in Scotland and Wales. The history of the saint's migration from eastern Christian and Ethiopian traditions in late Antiquity into England during the Crusades and development into a national patron saint has attracted much broad historical discussion.[1] But relatively little critical attention has considered the ways in which this cultural transmission mediated specific tensions between Christian European and Islamic cultures to the east of Europe during one of their most competitive periods of artistic and intellectual engagement, from the late fifteenth century onwards. This is partly because cultural historians and literary scholars have only recently started to consider such cultural exchanges as meaningful to the wider development of the European Renaissance.[2] I want to suggest that this renewed sensitivity to the ways in which icons and images circulated between Christian Europe and the predominantly Islamic communities to its east offers a different perspective on the ways in which St George signified to various communities, both Christian and Muslim, and that the nationalist perspective is just one, somewhat anachronistic dimension of the saint's significance which tends to limit our understanding of the way such figures looked eastwards and westwards in the global early modern world.

If, as I am suggesting, St George is a figure who mediates religious and imperial relations between eastern and western cultures, it is first of all important to situate this cultural mediation within a broader symbolic economy of exchanges between what can at least initially be called East and West. As recent critics in the fields of art history, architecture, history, anthropology and literary studies are beginning to appreciate, there was a variety of intellectual, material and aesthetic exchanges between East and West during the fifteenth and sixteenth centuries that have been occluded or marginalised within established accounts of the development on the European Renaissance.[3]

Traditional Renaissance historiography practised by the likes of Jacob Burckhardt, Paul Oskar Kristeller and Erwin Panofsky tended to focus on the rise of the Italian city-states from the late fourteenth century, paying scant attention to the diplomatic, architectural and commercial exchanges that took place throughout the Mediterranean world during this period, and that witnessed the rise to power of the Egyptian Seljuk Empire and the Turkish Ottoman Empire. Although the more economically-driven approach of scholars like Fernand Braudel in *The Mediterranean World* (1949; trans. 1972) addressed the idea of a shared economic world between Christian and Muslim communities, these approaches had little impact on the more cultural and philosophical understanding of the development of the Renaissance, which was represented as centring almost exclusively on Italy and migrating northwards from the late fifteenth century onwards.

From a different approach, the critique of European Orientalism that developed out of various currents within poststructuralism, and which culminated in Edward Said's classic study *Orientalism* (1978), were almost too successful in arguing that the East was either a fantasy or simply an omission in the early European literary and artistic imagination. For critics like Said, the myth of the Orient was always already there in European writings on the East, from Dante's representation of Muhammad in the *Divine Comedy* to the Orientalism of Gustave Flaubert and Ernest Renan. If there is an historical dimension to the rise of European Orientalism within this approach, then it begins in the eighteenth century and culminates in the ideology of nineteenth-century European Imperialism. Within this conspectus, the fifteenth and sixteenth centuries are elided as lacking any meaningful encounters with and responses to the regions and cultures to the east of Europe.

However, more recently, partly in response to the impact of postcolonial theory and history, scholars from a variety of different disciplines have started to revise this narrative by investigating a range of cultural exchanges between Europe and its eastern neighbours that have been overlooked or simply dismissed as irrelevant or anomalous. Much of this attention has focused on the role of the Ottoman Empire as a key player in the structure of Renaissance politics and courtly life. In a series of important articles, Julian Raby has pointed to the significant patronage of Mehmed the Conqueror between the fall of Constantinople in 1453 and his death in 1481.[4] Mehmed's patronage included the invitation of several Italian painters and architects to Constantinople to refashion it in Mehmed's image, and included the Venetian artist Gentile Bellini. Gülru Necipoğlu has expanded on Raby's work in her analysis of both Mehmed's creation of a cosmopolitan architectural style, as well his successor Süleyman the Magnificent's appropriation of papal iconography in his campaigns through central Europe in the late 1520s.[5]

What these recent studies suggest is that Christians and Muslims, in particular members of the Ottoman court in Istanbul, were involved in a series of competitive exchanges of commercial, artistic and intellectual ideas and objects, in which both sides learnt from each other. This is not to idealise such exchanges. As Necipoğlu shows in her account of Süleyman's display of Venetian regalia as he marched on Vienna in 1529, such displays served the interest of political power and imperial might, often within the context of military confrontation. But the point is that both sides appreciated and understood the impact of exchanging ideas and objects in a way that classic Orientalist attempts were reluctant to accept. It is our loss in the Anglo-American world that, until recently, such transactions were no longer legible or deemed significant to the wider narrative of the European Renaissance.

In what follows, I will suggest that the figure of St George fulfils a similar function in mediating religious tensions and imperial conflicts between East and West, and that representations of the saint shift and mutate according to the political and religious pressures it experiences, but which invariably acknowledge a connection between Christian and Islamic cultures, a connection which has usually been written about in western accounts of St George.

Most accounts of the complex history of the story of St George concede that he was a figure that looked east as well as west, and possessed spiritual significance not just for the eastern and western branches of Christendom, but also for African and Arab cultures. The story of George's life first emerges in Coptic and Ethiopian texts written in the fourth century AD, in which George is born in either the Nubian kingdom of Nobatia or Cappadocia in central Turkey around AD 270. As a Christian officer in the Roman army, he is asked by a pagan ruler to make a sacrifice to the Roman gods. George refuses, and in most versions of the story he turns into an iconoclast and destroys the idolatrous icons in the temples of Apollo. As a feared icon of Christian militancy, George was then dismembered but miraculously resurrected, before finally being decapitated and martyred. His pagan adversary dies shortly after George's martyrdom, which leads to a series of converts to Christianity.

Eastern Christianity developed and refined the account of George's life, but this archetypal story of the trial and martyrdom of a militant believer was not limited to Christianity. In Islam, George is associated with Al Khidr, 'The Verdant One', a key figure in Sufism, and another religious warrior who some sources claim to have been a senior officer in the army of Alexander the Great. Like St George, it was believed that Al Khidr was resurrected after his death at the hands of a pagan king. As William Dalrymple has pointed out, the shared East–West genealogy of George and al Khidr can still be seen in the spectacle of the Christians and Muslims who continue to revere the saint's tomb in the Palestinian town of Lod (ancient Lydda), southeast of Tel-Aviv.[6]

Sixteenth-century Christian commentators were aware of George's Islamic provenance, as the Flemish ambassador Ghiselin de Busbecq revealed in his account of a diplomatic embassy to the Ottoman court of Sultan Süleyman the Magnificent in 1555. Breaking his trip in central Anatolia in April 1555, Busbecq stayed at a dervish lodge founded by a Sufi master. The ambassador's hosts regaled him with stories of the saintly figure of Hızır-Ilyas, whose slaying of a dragon had taken place in central Anatolia. Busbecq's response is immediately to see the saintly figure, which he refers to as 'Chederle', as a Turkish version of St George:

Here is a famous establishment of Turkish monks, whom they call Dervishes, from whom we learnt much about a hero called Chederle, a man of great physical and mortal courage, whom they declare to be identical with our St George and to whom they ascribe the same achievements as we ascribe to our saint, namely, that he rescued a maiden by the slaughter of a huge and terrible dragon. They add many other stories and invent them according to their own pleasure, saying that he used to wander to distant climes and at last reached a river whereof the water gave immortality to those who drank it. They could not say in what part of the world this river was; it should probably be placed in No-man's-land ... [he] rides to and fro on a splendid horse ... They say that he takes pleasure in battle and comes to the assistance of the righteous cause in the fight and of those who have implored his help, whatever their religion ... they declare that he was one of the companions and friends of Alexander the Great![7]

Busbecq was also intrigued by the ways in which the Ottomans openly appropriated the figure of St George from Byzantine Greek iconography, particularly frescoes. He observed 'that the Turks are much amused at the pictures of St George, whom they declare was their own Chederle, in the Greek churches'.[8] Later in his account he returned to the figure of St George, reflecting on the impact that frescoes of the saint in Byzantine churches had upon the Ottomans:

> When they [the Turks] enter a church, the presence of images of the Virgin Mother, St Peter, St Paul, and the other saints has but little interest for them; but there is always one picture for which they look, that of St George on horseback, and before this they prostrate themselves in adoration and imprint kisses all over it, not omitting even the horse's hoofs. St George, they declare, was a man of might, a famous warrior, who often in single combat fought with the Evil Spirit on equal terms and was victorious, or at least left the field unbeaten.[9]

The dervishes conflated the character of the legendary Hızır-Ilyas with their own thirteenth-century Sufi master and spiritual father, Baba Ilyas. Busbecq concluded that what he had heard was an Islamicised version of the cult of St George. What the ambassador had encountered was a multilayered cultural web of narrative and myth surrounding the figure of George which had been appropriated in different ways by eastern Christian, Arab, Anatolian and Islamic folklore. George's origins probably went back even further into pagan fertility myths. These origins do not particularly concern me here. What does is the way in which, from the Crusades through to the late sixteenth century, St George was an openly shared and often contested figure between eastern and western cultures.[10]

In terms of its dissemination within Christianity, the story of St George is a familiar one. His image was widely circulated throughout the Crusades, when the slaying of the dragon and rescue of the princess first emerged as a crucial dimension of the story. It was this version that gained common acceptance thanks to the *Golden Legend* (c.1260). During the Crusades George was officially adopted as the patron saint of soldiers after stories began to circulate that he appeared as the Redcross Knight before the Christian army in the midst of their victory at the Battle of Antioch in 1098. George's reputation as a slayer of Moors and Saracens can be seen in the German artist Marzal de Sas's Valencia altarpiece (c.1400). This shows George violently spearing a Moorish soldier through the face. Here is George the militant Christian, slaying the symbolic dragon of Islam. Subsequent Italian representation of George by Donatello, Pisanello and

Raphael reinforced his symbolic status as a militant Christian holding the line against Islamic military expansionism.[11]

Vittore Carpaccio's paintings of St George, commissioned for the Scuola di San Giorgio in Venice and completed in 1504–7, were designed to celebrate the valiant struggle of the Knights of St John against the Turks in Dalmatia. The Knights were eventually defeated, but in Carpaccio's paintings St George undergoes a subtle but significant transformation, recognisably shaped by events in Dalmatia. The slaying of the dragon in *The Triumph of St George* takes place within a Libyan setting identified by its exotic Arab architecture and onlookers attired in oriental dress. In the final painting, *The Baptism of the Selenites*, the Christian saint baptises the non-believers, who lay aside their turbans as they prepare to be received into the faith. In Carpaccio's paintings, the reality of Christian defeat at the hands of Ottoman forces is sublimated into the fantasised victory of the Christian St George over the (Muslim) non-believers.[12] At this point in a particularly close but violent confrontation between Christians and Muslims to the east of Venetian territory, the saint is used to mediate Christian anxieties at Ottoman expansion; but if Busbecq's acknowledgement of Ottoman appropriations of the saint's image is correct, then it is possible to see Carpaccio's paintings as representing a tussle over possession of St George at a particularly fraught moment in Mediterranean imperial politics. In other words, the figure of St George is being broadcast west *and* east, legible to both Christian and Muslim communities.

George is the patron saint of many places, including Georgia, Palestine, Moscow, Istanbul and Catalonia, but he is most readily identifiable with England. George was transplanted from the East into England in the aftermath of the Crusades when, in 1348, Edward III adopted him as patron saint of his chivalric Order of the Garter, rededicating the chapel at Windsor Castle in George's honour. In 1399 the clergy decreed that 'the feast of Saint George the Martyr, who is the spiritual patron of the soldiery of England, should be observed throughout England as a holiday', which was fixed as 23 April – St George's Day. St George's stature rose even further thanks to Henry V's intense identification with the crusading saint in his early fifteenth-century campaigns in France. Henry offered oblations to the saint before his departure for France in 1415, and once Harfleur was captured, the French standard was replaced with the banner of St George. Henry VIII took up George and the Order of the Garter with added enthusiasm as a way of rivalling the older Burgundian Order of the Golden Fleece, an international chivalric order then more closely associated with Henry's Habsburg rival, the Emperor Charles V.

If one particularly significant recreation of St George took place in the face of the rapid expansion of Ottoman power in the Mediterranean at the end of the fifteenth century, arguably the next most important shift in the iconography of St George took place during the Lutheran Reformation. In England, the impact of the Reformation led to a dramatic reduction in George's iconic status. In 1550 the Protestant king Edward VI publicly ridiculed the cult of St George at the Order of the Garter ceremony held at Windsor.[13] The following year he redrafted the statutes of the Order as well as its regalia, excising all images of and references to St George, and banning the celebration of St George's Day in 1552. The Protestant radical John Foxe also castigated the worship of saints, claiming in his *Acts and Monuments* that, 'if God have determined his own Son only to stand alone, let not us presume to admix with his majesty any of our trumpery. He that bringeth St. George or St. Denis, as patrons, to the field, to fight against the Turk, leaveth Christ, no doubt, at home.'[14] The reference to the Turks here is noticeable and would recur in subsequent Protestant discussions of St George that initially seem more concerned with questions of Christian religious observance than Islam.

Foxe's condemnation of the likes of George and Denis closely echoed John Calvin's own rejection of intercession in his *Institutes of the Christian Religion* (1536) where he argued:

> Beside, it is evident that this superstition has arisen from a want of faith, because they either were not content with Christ as their intercessor, or entirely denied his glory. The latter of these is easily proved from their impudence; for they adduce no argument more valid to show that we need the mediation of the saints than when they object that we are unworthy of familiar access to God. Which indeed we acknowledge to be strictly true; but we thence conclude, that they rob Christ of everything, who consider his intercession as unavailing without the assistance of *George* and Hippolytus, and other such phantasms.[15]

For Calvin and Foxe, recourse to the intercession of saints like George diminished Christ's role as the mediator between man and God. It was one of the ironies of George's fate in the early years of the Reformation that after beginning life as a militant iconoclast destroying the idols of paganism in early Christian versions of the story, he became a victim of the crusading zeal of the Protestant reformers in England.

However, the Calvinist rejection of the mediation of saints was not accepted in Lutheran communities throughout Europe. In many

German cities facing the might of the Catholic Habsburg Empire, St George remained a potent image of Protestant militancy, an iconoclast breaking down the idolatrous symbols of Rome. In an engraving of *St George and the Dragon* dated 1552, the Lutheran Peter Gottland represents George as the infant Christ spearing the dragon besides the ruins of the Roman Church. The dying dragon appears to represent the Catholic Church, with the Pope at its head, wearing a papal tiara. However, the dragon has another head – that of a Turk. In this militant Lutheran image Roman Catholic and Islamic Ottoman are conflated as equally antithetical to the new Protestant religion. Here the figure of St George gives way to the figure of the infant Christ, a highly effective way of drawing on residual beliefs to reinforce the message of the new Lutheran Church. George's title as defender of the faith and champion of Christendom had taken on an even more militant and literal significance – but for only one side of the religious divide in sixteenth-century Europe.

This conflation of Catholic and Islamic – specifically Ottoman – tyranny found its most eloquent voice in Luther himself. As early as 1518 Luther made an explicit identification between the papacy and the Ottomans, claiming that 'the Roman Curia is more tyrannical than any Turk'. He subsequently modified his position, but continued to argue:

> Antichrist is at the same time the pope and the Turk. A living creature consists of body and soul. The spirit of Antichrist is the pope, his flesh the Turk. One attacks the Church physically, the other spiritually. Both however are of one lord, the devil, since the pope is a liar and the Turk a murderer.[16]

Luther's conflation was partly spiritual, but also politically strategic. As the threat of Ottoman military expansionism across central Europe continued to distract the Habsburgs from crushing the rise of Lutheranism, it made political sense to push the Catholic powers into a military confrontation to the east, rather than a theological one in Germany. Erasmus adopted a similar attitude in his 1530 treatise 'De bello turcico',[17] in which the Turks were seen as a punishment from God visited upon a divided Christianity. While Erasmus was careful to distance himself from Luther's more polemical statements on the figure of the Turk, Erasmus retained a belief in the Turk as a psychic projection of Christianity itself, which could only be defeated through an internal reformation of the schisms that were threatening to split the Church forever.

However, a similar kind of conflation also emerged in Catholic-sponsored art and iconography that responded to the Lutheran crisis, which explicitly appropriated the figure of St George to make its point. These Catholic counterattacks deployed George as a figure crushing all forms of belief that rejected the Church of Rome. The Hapsburg Empire sponsored most of these images with the tacit endorsement of its ruler Charles V, whose title was, after all, 'Holy Roman Emperor' and 'Defender of the Faith'. The religious and political rhetoric of the 1520s repeatedly responded to Luther's rhetoric by identifying his followers as 'Turks', conflating this new manifestation of theological 'unbelief' with the more established and identifiable version represented by the Ottoman Empire. In 1523 the Papal nuncio and Hapsburg supporter based in Nuremberg wrote that 'we are occupied with the negotiations for the general war against the Turk, and for that particular war against that nefarious Martin Luther, who is a greater evil to Christendom than the Turk'.[18] In England in 1529, Thomas More published his *Dialogue Concerning Heresies* (1529), in which he attacked 'the pestilent sect of Luther and Tyndale', which he saw as an 'infiltrating, foreign enemy', worse than 'all the Turkes / all ye Sarasyns / all the heretykes'.[19] In 1530 Cardinal Campeggio provided another dimension to this conflation of different versions of unbelief, writing to Charles that Luther's 'diabolical and heretical opinions ... shall be castigated and punished according to the rule and practice observed in Spain with regard to the Moors'. For Campeggio and Charles one way to understand and respond to the rise of Lutheranism was to launch the kind of *reconquista* that Charles's Castilian forebears had practised towards the end of the fifteenth century, when Jews and Muslims were officially expelled from the Iberian Peninsula.

Such sentiments were given their most compelling visual form in Titian's dramatic equestrian portrait of *Charles V at the Battle of Mühlberg* (1548). Titian's painting celebrates the Hapsburg victory over the German Protestants in 1547. Aretino had originally advised Titian to portray the vanquished heretics being trampled under the horse's hooves, but the artist rejected such suggestions in favour of a more ambiguous but no less aggressive image. Erwin Panofsky argued that Titian portrayed the Emperor as a conflation of St James and St George. St James was a particularly suitable figure with which to identify Charles V, since he was officially known as the patron saint of the Habsburg expedition against the Ottomans at Tunis in 1535, and better known by his Spanish name of *Matamoro* – killer of the Moors. In Charles's subsequent triumphal procession through Italy, arches, banners and statues repeatedly portrayed him on horseback as a conflated St George/St James, crushing the decapitated bodies of Turks and Moors beneath his horse's hooves. This, alongside the fact that the horse Charles controls is recognisably an Andalusian, a hybrid of Spanish and North African bloodstock, suggests that the viewer is invited to 'see' both Protestant and Muslim crushed beneath the hooves of Titian's horse. The image was reworked and distributed in paintings of the Emperor as St George/St James, circulated throughout Europe in an attempt to establish Charles as the triumphant victor over the twin heresies of Protestantism and Islam.[20]

Having mediated tensions between a unified Christianity and an ascendant Islamic Ottoman imperialism in the late fifteenth century, St George now defined Lutheran–Catholic conflicts over religious observance. These appropriations of St George by both sides suggest just how potent and overdetermined the saint became within theological disputes and visual iconography of the mid-sixteenth century. The impact of the Reformation allowed Catholicism to appropriate George as a crusading figure of the true Church, whilst Protestantism claimed him as a more ambivalent hero, an iconoclast purging the Church of its idolatrous worship of images and icons. In both cases the trace of George's eastern provenance allowed Catholics to conflate Lutherans with heretical Muslims, and Protestants to conflate Catholic imperial supremacy with Ottoman military power. In both cases this is a defensive gesture, a way of struggling to come to terms with the sudden but profound schism in Christian belief. As a result, the figure of St George was a troubling but evocative way of coming to terms with religious and political differences both East and West and within a divided Christianity.

One of the consequences of this renewed and highly aggressive resurgence of interest in St George was the development of an increasingly hostile representation of the figure of the Turk, a representation that actually mediated the political and religious conflict between Rome and Luther, rather than simply the Christian West and Islamic East, as was the case in Carpaccio's pre-Reformation paintings of St George in Venice. This might also lead us to ask to what extent the discourse of the demonic, despotic 'Turk' – which has been subject to such revision recently – may have its roots not in what Said has called the 'flexible positional superiority' of the western Orientalist imagination, but in the religious antagonism and ideological disarray of a radically divided early sixteenth-century Christianity.

And what of early modern England's own highly ambivalent relationship towards St George? With the accession of Elizabeth I, the Garter ceremonies abandoned under her brother Edward's reign were reintroduced and found their most resonant affirmation in the figure of the Redcross Knight in Spenser's *Faerie Queene* and Shakespeare's *Henry V* (1599–1600), with the King's rallying cry before Harfleur, 'Cry god for Harry, England and St George!' Elizabethan explanations of the saint's history were poised between providing a specifically English genealogy for the saint and acknowledging his eastern provenance, inflected by the more recent Reformation accounts discussed above.[21]

Richard Johnson's *Famous History of the Seven Champions of Christendom* (c.1596) provided George with the English origins Spencer's *Faerie Queene* evokes but never fully develops. Johnson's *History* claimed 'the famous cittie of Coventrie was the place wherein the first Christian Champion of England was borne'. In a picaresque rewriting of the story, Johnson sends George from Coventry to Persia, where he confronts the 'Soldan's court' on the day 'when the Persians solemnly sacrificed to their Gods Mahomet, Apollo, Termigaunt, which unchristian Procession so moved the impatience of the English Champion, that he tooke the ensignes and streamers whereon the Persian Gods were pictured, and trampled them under his feete'.[22] In Johnson's account, George is redefined as the iconoclastic Protestant martyr, destroying the fictional symbols of Islamic idolatry.

Just five years later, in 1601, Gerard de Malynes took Johnson's claims a step further and made the connection between Islam and George's dragon explicit in his more recognisably nationalistic revision of the saint's life, *St George for England*. In moving towards a more allegorical version of the dragon, Malynes gave George's adversary a very specific provenance:

> Here you may behold this hideous monster, swelling every month bigger one than another, with his fierie flaming eyes, seeming to cast fire at every moment, by the means of his tridented tongue like unto a Turkish dart ... his taile nimble, & continually wavering & inconstant, for therein consisteth his greatest strength & activity, to the commonwealth's destruction: and the same is marked with the new Moon of the Turkes, like unto the letter C.[23]

Throughout the retelling of the story of St George, the dragon functioned at various moments as quite literally the demonic Other. By the late Elizabethan period, one strand of this demonisation saw the dragon as Islam, and more specifically Ottoman imperial expansion. For Malynes, through an oblique process of displacement, the dragon is represented as explicitly Turkish, and the conquering knight as English.

In his later account of *The Martyrdome of St George of Cappadocia: Titular Patron of England, and of the Most Noble Order of the Garter*, published in 1614, Tristram White developed this more figurative approach to George and his adversary, an approach broadly in line with the Lutheran attempts to appropriate the saint's symbolism as an iconoclast. White argued that 'the ordinary Picture of S. George on horse-backe, killing a Dragon, is but Symbolicall and figurative, learned men on all sides seeme to consent … Martin Luther affirmes it'.[24] In White's account, George's origins were located in 'a Province in the lesser *Asia*, now under Turkes, and called *Natolia*'.[25] This trace of Turkish influence also emerges in White's description of the scene of George's martyrdom:

> That sumptuous Temple at Diospolis,
> Which Asian Lydda also called is
> (Place first of Martyrdome, then of his Shrine)
> Time hath to rubbish turn'd, since Christian signe
> By Turkes prevailing hath beene throwne to ground:
> But neither Turkes nor Time shall quite confound
> The memorie thereof.[26]

For White, like many early humanist scholars, the fact that the Turks effectively controlled the territory that produced the great texts of the classical and biblical world was a source of profound consternation. But like travellers like Busbecq, White responded by claiming a shared heritage between Christian and Turkish identifications with the figure of St George:

> That even the Sects of cursed *Musulmen*
> Honours S. *George*, whose Countryes they Possesse,
> Nor simply honour, but their speech addresse
> In reverent formes which special attributes …
> And though the Turkes his Faith doe disavow,
> Yet to his Vertues they the full allow;
> Admiring his great minde (well worth admiring)
> As men to fame though by false parts aspiring.[27]

Like many other Elizabethan writers, White struggles to reclaim George as an English saint through the fog of Calvinist rejections of saintly intercession and his recognisably shared East–West history. Like Johnson and Spenser, White effects a clumsy manoeuvre to claim that George is 'transplanted to the Westerne States', in the process slaying the unbelieving Turk in a fantasy Crusade carried out in the name of Protestant England.[28] White's account has affinities with Carpaccio's attempt to turn military defeat into religious victory in his series of Venetian paintings of St George. Like Venice, Elizabethan England's diplomatic relations with the Ottoman Empire bore little resemblance to these fantastical accounts of imperial victory and theological triumphalism. England's close diplomatic and commercial ties with the Ottoman Porte only throw into starker relief the symbolic contortions that St George is asked to perform as writers struggled to accommodate England's alliance with the Ottomans with a confident, expansionist vision of Elizabethan England.

This approach to Elizabethan accounts of St George also transforms our understanding of Shakespeare's *Henry V* as a play about the performance of an early version of English national identity, exemplified by Henry as a personification of St George.[29] In reading *Henry V* alongside this broader tradition of Reformation responses to George, it is noticeable that Shakespeare's deployment of the saint throughout his history plays is a bold and potentially controversial recuperation of an icon that had been downgraded in the calendar of popular and religious festivity. However, this recuperation was broadly in line with Elizabeth's conservative attempts to retain many of the elements of Mary Tudor's brief Catholic reign and her father's strategic religious position. Elizabeth retained the Garter ceremonies which had been revived by Mary, simply deleting the more explicitly Catholic elements of the religious observances. Those closest to the queen enthusiastically embraced the Order and zealously observed its terms every year. In 1599 the Earl of Essex celebrated St George's Day whilst campaigning in Ireland, an event recorded in *A new ballade of the tryumpes kept in Ireland uppon Saint Georg's day last, by the noble Earle of Essex and his followers*. Elizabeth is celebrated as 'that renownéd mayden', whilst the ballad's refrain is a virtual paraphrase of Henry's cry before Harfleur: 'Now God and S[ain]ct George for England!' This sheds new light on the debate over Essex's appearance in the play's final Chorus, 'the General of our gracious Empress', returning from Ireland 'Bringing rebellion broached on his sword'. It is clear that Essex is here represented as St George slaying the dragon of Irish rebellion. Iconically, the image does not allow for the possibility that Essex is fermenting or 'broaching' rebellion, as some critics have suggested.[30]

Shakespeare's St George lacks an explicit eastern identification, but there is a strange oblique fascination with eastern and particularly Turkish issues which runs throughout the Henriad. At the end of

Henry IV Part I, Hal reassures his brothers that 'This is the English not the Turkish court; / Not Amurath an Amurath succeeds, / But Harry Harry',[31] a reference to Murad III who killed his brothers after his accession in 1574. At the close of *Henry V* the King proposes to Catherine that they will 'compound a boy, half-French half-English, that shall go to Constantinople and take the Turk by the beard' (V.ii.194–6). When St George is evoked before Harfleur, there is no eastern dimension, simply the by now familiar call to arms:

> I see you stand like greyhounds in the slips,
> Straining upon the start. The game's afoot:
> Follow your spirit; and, upon this charge
> Cry God for Harry, England and St George!
> (III.i.31–4)

However, the repeated identification of the French forces with 'hot-blooded' horses – in other words, of Arab bloodstock – does make a significant link between the French and Muslim forces. Just as the trace of confrontation with Islam permeates the paintings of Carpaccio and Titian, so it seems to reappear in Shakespeare's play, where the 'crusade' against the French is obliquely seen as a victory over a fantasised Islamic foe.

Throughout this chapter I have sought to question the secure basis upon which we read St George as a nationalist icon, whose Englishness is firmly secured by the time that Shakespeare completes *Henry V* at the end of the sixteenth century. On the contrary, I would argue that the period is still struggling with the ways in which St George is a contested figure between eastern and western cultures, although hopefully the complex nature of this contestation reveals the inadequacy of these terms 'East' and 'West'. If we want to locate a moment at which St George is finally and seamlessly appropriated as part of the discourse of Englishness, it is surely with the publication of Elias Ashmole's *The Institution, Laws and Ceremonies of the Most Noble Order of the Garter* (1672), which recasts the Stuart dynasty, and Charles I in particular, as the quintessential St George, the tragic martyr portrayed on horseback by Van Dyck and cut down by his own people. By the later seventeenth century, England and Europe's most fruitful confrontation with Islam, personified by the Ottoman Empire, had faded; St George was needed to build bridges across a divided England, rather than between East and West.

Notes

1. See most recently Samantha Riches, *St George: Hero, Martyr and Myth* (Gloucester: Sutton, 2000).
2. For a new approach to such exchanges, see Lisa Jardine and Jerry Brotton, *Global Interests: Renaissance Art between East and West* (London: Reaktion, 2000).
3. See, for instance, Deborah Howard, *Venice and the East: The Impact of the Islamic World on Venetian Architecture 1100–1500* (New Haven, CT: Yale University Press, 2000), and Julian Raby, *Venice, Dürer and the Oriental Mode* (London: Sotheby, 1982).
4. Julian Raby, 'East and West in Mehmed the Conqueror's Library', *Bulletin du Bibliophile* 3 (1987): 297–321, and 'Pride and Prejudice: Mehmed the Conqueror and the Italian Portrait Medal', in J. Graham Pollard, ed., *Italian Medals* (Washington, DC: National Gallery of Art, 1987), pp. 171–84.
5. Gülru Necipoğlu, *Architecture, Ceremonial and Power: The Topkapı Palace in the Fifteenth and Sixteenth Centuries* (Cambridge, MA: MIT Press, 1991), and 'Süleyman the Magnificent and the Representation of Power in the Context of Ottoman–Habsburg–Papal Rivalry', *Art Bulletin* 71 (1989): 401–27.
6. See William Dalrymple, *From the Holy Mountain: A Journey in the Shadow of Byzantium* (London: HarperCollins, 1997). Al Khidr, the patron of travellers in Turkish folklore, is often linked with the servant of Allah whose encounter with Moses is described in the Qur'an (18: 64–81); see F. W. Hasluck, *Christianity and Islam under the Sultans*, 2 vols. (Oxford: Clarendon Press, 1929), 1: 319–36, and Katib Chelebi, 'The "Life" of the Prophet Khidr', in *The Balance of Truth*, trans. Geoffrey Lewis (London: Allen and Unwin, 1957), pp. 33–7.
7. Edward Seymour Forster, ed., *The Turkish Letters of Ogier Ghiselin de Busbecq* (1927; rpt. Oxford: Oxford University Press, 1968), pp. 54–5. I am grateful to Oya Pancaroğlu for drawing this reference to my attention.
8. Busbecq, *Turkish Letters*, p. 56.
9. Busbecq, *Turkish Letters*, p. 131.
10. On links between St George and the Khirgiz epic-hero Manas, and the characterisation of General Monk with the 'Cappadocian knight' at the Restoration of Charles II in 1660, see Gerald MacLean, 'The Sultan's Beasts: Early English Encounters with the Fauna of the Ottoman Empire', in Matthew Birchwood and Matthew Dimmock, eds., *Cultural Encounters between East and West, 1453 to 1699* (Cambridge: Cambridge Scholars Press, forthcoming 2005).
11. For a reproduction and discussion of this image see Jerry Brotton, 'Saints Alive: the Iconography of Saint George', in Bruno Latour and Peter Weibel, eds., *Iconoclash: Beyond the Image Wars in Science, Religion, and Art* (Cambridge, MA: MIT Press, 2002), pp. 155–7.
12. Jardine and Brotton, *Global Interests*, pp. 18–20.
13. See Roy Strong, 'Queen Elizabeth I and the Order of the Garter', in *The Tudor and Stuart Monarchy: Pageantry, Painting and Iconography, II Elizabethan* (London: Boydell, 1995), pp. 55–86.
14. John Foxe, *The Acts and Monuments of John Foxe*, ed. George Townsend, 8 vols. (1834–49; rpt. New York: AMS, 1965), vol. 4, part 1, p. 19.

15. John Calvin, *Institutes of the Christian Religion*, ed. John Allen, 2 vols. (London: Thomas Regg, 1844): 2: 94–5.

16. Quoted in Kenneth M. Setton, 'Lutheranism and the Turkish Peril', *Balkan Studies* 3 (1962): 133–68, cited pp. 144, 151.

17. Reproduced in Erika Rummel, ed., *The Erasmus Reader* (London: University of Toronto Press, 1990), pp. 315–33.

18. Quoted in Setton, 'Lutheranism', p. 147.

19. See *The Yale Edition of the Complete Works of Thomas More*, vol. 6: *A Dialogue Concerning Heresies*, ed. Thomas M. C. Lawler, Germain Marc'hadour and Richard C. Marius (New Haven, CT: Yale University Press, 1981), pp. 2–236. I am grateful to Matthew Dimmock for bringing this reference to my attention. See Dimmock's *New Turkes: Dramatizing Islam and the Ottomans In Early Modern England* (Aldershot: Ashgate, 2005).

20. On Titian's painting, see Jardine and Brotton, *Global Interests*, pp. 178–83. On Charles's triumphal entries following the victory at Tunis, see Roy Strong, *Art and Power: Renaissance Festivals 1450–1650* (London: Boydell, 1973), pp. 75–97, illus. 61. On the reproduction of the painted image of Charles as St George/St James crushing 'unbelievers' of a specifically Islamic provenance see H. Janson, 'A Portrait of Charles V', *Worcester Art Museum Annual* 1 (1935–6), pp. 19–31.

21. I have quoted Shakespeare from Stanley Wells and Gary Taylor, *The Oxford Shakespeare: The Complete Works* (Oxford: Oxford University Press, 1999).

22. Richard Johnson, *The Famous History of the Seven Champions of Christendom* (c.1596), p. 23.

23. Gerard de Malynes, *St George for England* (1601), p. 57.

24. Tristram White, *The Martyrdome of St George of Cappadocia: Titular Patron of England, and of the Most Noble Order of the Garter* (1614), sig. A2r.

25. White, *St George*, sig. A2r.

26. White, *St George*, sig. C4v.

27. White, *St George*, sig. D2v.

28. White, *St George*, sig. Dv.

29. In what follows, I indicate potential approaches to the play, which I hope to develop at greater length in subsequent publications.

30. See Annabel Patterson, *Shakespeare and the Popular Voice* (Oxford: Blackwell, 1989), pp. 71–92.

31. *Henry IV, Part I*, V.ii.47–9.

3
Mummy is Become Merchandise: Literature and the Anglo-Egyptian Mummy Trade in the Seventeenth Century

Philip Schwyzer

> Yet in those huge structures and pyramidal immensities, of the builders whereof so little is known, they seemed not so much to raise sepulchres or temples to death, as to contemn and disdain it, astonishing heaven with their audacities, and looking forward with delight to their interment in those eternal piles ... Yet all were but Babel vanities. Time sadly overcometh all things, and is now dominant, and sitteth upon a sphinx, and looketh unto Memphis and old Thebes, while his sister Oblivion reclineth semisomnous on a pyramid, gloriously triumphing, making puzzles of Titanian erections, and turning old glories into dreams. History sinketh beneath her cloud. The traveller as he paceth amazedly through those deserts asketh of her, who buildeth them? and she mumbleth something, but what it is he heareth not.[1]

In Thomas Browne's 'Fragment on Mummies', Egypt is represented as both ancient and amnesiac, quite incapable of giving any good account of herself or her former glories. The quoted passage couples a general meditation on the entropic power of Time with a specific comment on the state of Egyptian civility in the seventeenth century. As a meditation, it echoes and bears comparison to Browne's *Hydriotaphia*, and some readers have held it in no less esteem. As a comment on Egypt, it is typically 'Orientalist' in the sense of the term developed by Edward Said. The 'mumbling', senile East cannot articulate, much less represent itself;

it must be interrogated, deciphered, transformed into an object of knowledge by the (presumably) European 'traveller' who 'paceth amazedly' in the shadow of the pyramids. 'Egypt itself is now become the land of obliviousness and doteth.' Oriental forgetfulness serves as the starting point for an English project of selfless scholarly recovery that will eventually be used in turn to justify colonial rule.[2]

If the image of Egypt in Browne's 'Fragment on Mummies' accords so easily with the assumptions of nineteenth- and twentieth-century Orientalism, there is a good reason for this. The 'Fragment' is in fact a nineteenth-century forgery. Its first appearance, at the dawn of Victoria's reign, was as a document in the handwriting of James Crossley, who passed it to his friend George Wilkin, claiming to have lost track of the manuscript from which he transcribed it.[3] The text was duly included in Wilkin's 1836 edition of Browne and quickly garnered admiration. Referring to the paragraph quoted above, Ralph Waldo Emerson declared: 'It would not be easy to refuse to Sir Thomas Browne's *Fragment on Mummies* the claim of poetry.'[4] Although its shadowy provenance, coupled with some lexical peculiarities, soon led to doubts, Crossley to the end of his life would do no more than hint coyly at his culpability; and though the proofs offered against its authenticity in the twentieth century were all but definitive, the 'Fragment' still appears in the standard edition of Browne's works, lying in wait to mislead the occasional researcher.[5]

Crossley's command of Browne's eccentric style and the characteristic movement of his imagination are little less than brilliant. His grasp of English attitudes towards Egypt in the seventeenth century is somewhat less secure. The 'traveller' in the 'Fragment' who interrogates the silent pyramids owes more to Shelley's 'traveller from an antique land' than to any early modern voyager. For the denunciation of Egypt as 'the land of obliviousness', one could not easily find a seventeenth-century parallel.[6] Rather than scorning superannuated civilisations, early modern minds habitually venerated Antiquity, and the more of it the better. For Browne and most of his contemporaries, the lifecycles of cultures consisted of just two stages, youth and maturity. It was thus seen as natural for civil-isational 'children', such as the natives of the New World, to be ruled over by Europeans *in loco parentis*.[7] But the notion that some civilisa-tions might age to the point of senility, and have to come under the pro-tection of younger, more energetic peoples, would have made little sense to Browne or his contemporaries – nor, indeed, was there much need for such a notion until the domination of ancient civilisations in the Near and Far East became a practical possibility.

When the English did take notice of Egypt's pyramids and their contents in the seventeenth century, it was not generally in the guise of disinterested scholars, much less as imperial overlords in waiting. Of the small number of English people who visited Egypt and toured its ancient monuments, the majority were merchants. Trading in Egypt was a difficult business; merchants were subjected to semi-systematic harassment and found themselves with little to offer that Egyptians might want – certainly not England's chief export, woollen cloth.[8] Egypt, on the other hand, offered much that English consumers desired, both spices brought in from further east and certain highly valued domestic products. One of these products lay within the ancient tombs themselves. To put it simply, when the English went to the pyramids in the seventeenth century, they were looking for something to eat.

The plain facts of the case are conveyed fairly accurately in the forged 'Fragment on Mummies'.

> That mummy is medicinal, the Arabian Doctor Haly delivereth and divers confirm; but of the particular uses thereof, there is much discrepancy of opinion. While Hofmannus prescribes the same to epileptics, Johan de Muralto commends the use thereof to gouty persons; Bacon likewise extols it as a stiptic: and Junkenius considers it of efficacy to resolve coagulated blood. Meanwhile, we hardly applaud Francis the First, of France, who always carried Mumia with him as a panacea against all disorders; and were the efficacy thereof more clearly made out, scarce conceive the use thereof allowable in physic, exceeding the barbarities of Cambyses, and turning old heroes unto unworthy potions. Shall Egypt lend out her ancients unto chirurgeons and apothecaries, and Cheops and Psammiticus be weighed unto us for drugs? Shall we eat of Chamnes and Amosis in electuaries and pills, and be cured by cannibal mixtures? Surely such diet is dismal vampirism; and exceeds in horror the black banquet of Domitian, not to be paralleled except in those Arabian feasts, wherein Ghoules feed horribly.[9]

Saturated with the spirit of the Gothic, the final sentence betrays the real origins of the 'Fragment' more nakedly than any other passage. 'Vampirism' and 'ghoul' – from the Arabic *ghūl* – entered the English language no earlier than the late eighteenth century, the latter via the masterpiece of oriental Gothic, William Beckford's *Vathek* (1786). Nevertheless, in its exposition of a central fact about early modern medicine, the 'Fragment' is unsettlingly accurate. In Browne's age, 'mummy' was a coveted pharmaceutical. Throughout the seventeenth century, as for centuries before, physicians routinely prescribed small portions of the embalmed corpses of ancient Egyptians as a cure for a variety of ailments, notably excessive bleeding and internal bruising caused by falls. Browne himself conducted experiments with *mumia* and, as a practising physician, may well have prescribed it.

Crossley probably took the hint for this passage (and perhaps for the whole of his forgery) from just two sentences in *Hydriotaphia*: 'The Ægyptian Mummies, which Cambyses or time hath spared, avarice now consumeth. Mummie is become Merchandise, Miszraim cures wounds, and Pharaoh is sold for balsoms.'[10] This brief passage is typical of Browne's style, at once powerful and paradoxical, stately and elusive. Reading Browne, one is struck again and again by the feeling that no one could have said it better – a sense followed a moment later by the realisation that 'it' is something both stranger and more complex than one had initially understood. (Crossley, by contrast, captures the balance and grandeur of Browne's style admirably well; but he betrays himself by telling us too often what we expect to hear.) In the passage from *Hydriotaphia*, Browne is no more approving than Crossley of the medical consumption of mummies. Surprisingly, however, what appears to trouble him is not the fact of cannibalism, which he does not even address, but something else. As I shall discuss below, both of the qualities notable in Browne's remark – the identification of mummy-eating as a problem and the refusal to identify that problem as cannibalism – are typical of seventeenth-century references to the mummy trade, and shed light on a period of dramatic cultural and economic transition.

'The flesh was turned to drugge'

For more than 3,000 years, from at least the period of the Old Kingdom (c. 2649–2152 BC) to the advent of Islam in the seventh century, the Egyptians mummified their dead.[11] The most elaborate and successful method of mummification, practised on the bodies of Pharaohs and elite individuals in the second and first millennium BC, involved the removal of the internal organs, followed by a prolonged process of dehydration in natron, anointment with oil and resins, and carefully wrapping in layers of linen. Access to mummification gradually extended to the middle classes, and later, in the Ptolemaic period (from 332 BC), to wider sectors of society. The mass production of mummies led inevitably to a decline in standards; eviscerated bodily cavities were hastily stuffed with a range of materials, including mud, molten resin, broken pottery and the black, pitchy substance known as bitumen.

From the moment they were interred, Egyptian mummies faced the threat of having their rest disturbed by tomb-robbers. By the twelfth century, they faced a new and unanticipated danger – from European cannibals. Medieval scholars discovered in the *Qanun* of Avicenna and in other Arabic medical treatises reference to a substance called *mumia*, effective in curing a range of disorders, notably internal bleeding and epilepsy.[12] *Mumia*, or *mumiya* in Arabic, in fact refers to naturally occurring mineral pitch, pissasphalt or bitumen. There are several sources of bitumen in the eastern Mediterranean region, including the Dead Sea, from whose depths large hunks occasionally rise to the surface – this appears to have been the chief source of the bitumen used in the mummification process during the Ptolemaic era.[13] The substance was nevertheless relatively rare and difficult to come by. One readily available substitute, however, noted by the Baghdad physician Abd Allatif in the early thirteenth century, lay 'in the hollows of corpses of Egypt'.[14] Here was an apparently elegant solution to the problem of sourcing bitumen – the same mineral substance that had once been used to preserve the dead could be recycled from their corpses to preserve the living. An alternative but related view, proposed by Latin redactors of Arab medical treatises in and after the twelfth century, was that the congealed liquids exuded by embalmed Egyptian corpses – whether or not the embalming process had involved bitumen – constituted a form of *mumia*.[15] It was not long before, by a further misunderstanding (or shortcut), the embalmed bodies themselves came to be defined as that *mumia* which, in pitchy or powdered form, could be taken medicinally.

From Avicenna's prescription of mineral pitch or asphalt, European medicine arrived with remarkable speed and complacency at the licensed consumption of mummified human flesh. It is difficult not to see this as a case of almost wilful mishearing, of managing to hear what one has been both dreading and longing to hear all along. Yet it would be misleading to describe the emergence of mummy as medicine as an example of the return of the repressed. After all, in medieval western Christendom, the desire to take life from dead human flesh was not exactly repressed. The ritual of the mass centred on the consumption of Christ's real human body – as Caroline Walker Bynum has demonstrated, the cannibalistic implications of this rite were as apt to be graphically celebrated as glossed over.[16] The veneration of saints and their relics would also have worked to make mummy-eating seem less outlandish; like mummies, saintly corpses might be miraculously preserved, and their body parts or bodily products were efficacious in healing the sick. From the tombs of St Nicholas of Myra and of St Catherine of Alexandria flowed oils that were in demand throughout Europe for their healing properties.[17] The latter miracle in particular, taking place on Egypt's Mount Sinai, suggests a context into which the acquisition and medicinal consumption of mummified Egyptians could have fitted not uncomfortably.

It seems to have been possible for some Catholic observers not only to acknowledge implicitly but also to accentuate and celebrate the links between mummy-eating and eucharistic devotion. A post-medieval example is found in Fray Luis de Urreta's history of Ethiopia (1610–11), which describes the Ethiopian method of manufacturing *mumia*, differing from that of the Egyptians:

> they take a captive Moore, of the best complexion; and after long dieting and medicining of him, cut off his head in his sleepe, and gashing his bodie full of wounds, put therein all the best spices, and then wrap him up in hay, being before covered with a seare-cloth; after which they burie him in a moist place, covering the bodie with earth. Five dayes being passed, they take him up againe, and removing the seare-cloth and hay, hang him up in the sunne, whereby the body resolveth and droppeth a substance like pure balme, which liquor is of great price: the fragrant sent is such, while it hangeth in the sunne, that it may be smelt (he saith) a league off.[18]

The echoes of mystical writings focusing on Christ's body and wounds are very clear. Just as the burial and exhumation of the Moor mirror Christ's three-day sojourn in the tomb, so the fragrant balm resolving out of the wounds in the hanging body parallels the divine blood and water gushing from the wound in the side of the crucified Christ (often depicted in medieval art as flowing directly into the cups or mouths of worshippers).

The account of Luis de Urreta brings us near to the era of Thomas Browne. Browne, however, lived and wrote in a dramatically different spiritual context. Seventeenth-century English Protestant culture recoiled phobically from the very aspects of medieval Christianity that might conceivably have allowed mummy-eating a comfortable niche. Gone was the real presence of Christ in the host; gone were the fleshly, efficacious relics of saints. Not gone, perhaps, but severely diminished were the reverence and honour traditionally paid to the dead: 'For of all ostentations of pride', wrote the Puritan William Perkins, 'that is most foolish, to be boasting of a loathsome and a deformed corpse'.[19] At least one seventeenth-century writer made the link between Catholic idolatry and mummy-eating explicit, referring satirically to 'How dead Saints Relicks cure the gout and ptisick, / And are like Aegypts mummy us'd for physick.'[20] Vigilance against popery combined with other historical factors to make seventeenth-century England unprecedentedly and unusually alert to the multiple levels of abomination entailed in mummy-eating. English colonial ideology rested to a large degree on the absolute distinction between civilised Europeans and New World 'cannibals', a distinction which domestic mummy-eating threatened to undermine entirely.[21] Emergent notions of biological race, moreover, with the fear of miscegenation, would surely have counselled against the English accepting the bodies of non-Europeans into their own, thereby mingling their flesh with flesh that was not only dead but, by all accounts, black.[22] For English Protestants in Browne's age, mummy-eating entailed not just scandal but a surplus of scandal, a super-scandal.

Yet in spite of these overwhelming grounds for abhorrence – abhorrence that, as we shall see, found full expression in contemporary writing – the medicinal consumption of mummy remained a common practice in seventeenth-century England. If anything, for reasons I will come to shortly, mummy was more readily available and more widely in request in this period than ever before. Thomas Browne was undoubtedly familiar with its use and pharmaceutical preparation. We cannot know if he personally prescribed it, but he certainly had access to it and even conducted experiments upon it; thus he is able to conclude in *Pseudodoxia Epidemica* that in common with other bitumens it has no electrical properties, 'although we have tried in large and polished pieces'.[23] Browne's admirer Sir Kenelm Digby was a firm believer in mummy's efficacy, including half an ounce of the substance in his 'Experimented Vulnerary Potion or Wound-Drink', together with handfuls of comfrey, mugwort, several other herbs and white wine. (This potion, of which 'a little glassful' should be taken before breakfast, had reputedly cured a friar of the stone and a gentlewoman of an ulcer in the loins.)[24] Equally convinced was Browne's arch-opponent Alexander Ross, the great detractor of *Religio Medici*, who extolled mummy's virtues against a different set of ailments:

And as dead bodies embalmed with spices, are preserved from corruption; so by the same dead bodies, men are oftentimes preserved alive: for that stuffe which proceeds from them, called by the *Arabians Mumia*, is an excellent remedy against diseases arising from cold and moisture. *Francis* the first carried always some of it about him. It was found in the Tombs of those Princes who had been imbalmed with rich spices.[25]

One powerful indicator of the persistence of mummy-eating is the extraordinary number of references to the practice in seventeenth-century literature. This phenomenon is entirely unprecedented. References to mummies in medieval and early Tudor English literature are rare indeed, outside of medical treatises. The Elizabethan period offers a small handful of references; the subsequent century, an explosion. Among those who write of mummy in this period are Shakespeare, Donne, Jonson, Webster, Fletcher, Middleton, Dekker, Shirley, Bacon, Browne, Marvell, Cavendish, Congreve and Dryden – together with dozens if not hundreds of other less well-known poets and playwrights. That the references to mummy in non-medical works are almost invariably negative – ranging in tone from wry, tutting disapproval to vehement disgust – makes it seem all the more remarkable that they should be so numerous.

Several factors contributed to the English public's new awareness of and interest in mummies in this period. One was the spread of Paracelsian medical theory. Paracelsus and his followers notoriously praised human bodies and bodily products as the best remedy for human ailments – not only mummy but also human blood, excrement, sweat, milk and hair were employed. The early American poet Edward Taylor, who was also the town physician and a Paracelsian, included all these items in his 'Dispensatory'.[26] Yet while the legacy of Paracelsus divided English physicians into opposing camps in the seventeenth century, the efficacy of mummy was a point on which both sides were able to agree. If for Paracelsians mummy was a repository of vital human spirits trapped within the flesh, for others it remained an accessible and accepted source of medicinal bitumen.

Perhaps more significant than trends in medical science was the unprecedented penetration of English merchants into the eastern Mediterranean during the later sixteenth century. The Turkey Company was founded in 1581, merging with the Venice Company in 1592 to become the long-lived Levant Company. In 1583 the Company set up a consulate in Cairo. The establishment of formal trading links opened the possibility of a steady stream of mummified flesh flowing out of the tombs of Memphis into the apothecaries' shops of London. In 1584, the merchant William Barret, writing from Aleppo, listed among the goods he traded in 'Momia from the great Cairo'.[27] Two years later John

Sanderson, an apprentice to the Turkey Company stationed in Egypt, tracked the 'momia' to its source – the mummy pits of Memphis.

> The Momia, which is some five or six miles beyond [the pyramids] are thousands of imbalmed bodies, which were buried thousands of yeeres past in a sandy cave, at which there seemeth to have bin some citie in times past. We were let down by ropes, as into a well, with waxe candles burning in our hands, and so walked upon the bodies of all sorts and sizes, great and small, and some imbalmed in little earthen pots, which never had forme: these are set at the feet of the greater bodies. They gave no noysome smell at all, but are like pitch, being broken. For I broke of all the parts of the bodies to see how the flesh was turned to drugge, and brought home divers heads, hands, armes, and feet, for a shew. Wee brought also 600 pounds for the Turkie Companie in pieces; and brought into England in the Hercules, together with a whole body. They are lapped in above a hundred double of cloth, which rotting and pilling off, you may see the skin, flesh, fingers, and nayles firme, onely altered blacke. One little hand I brought into England, to shew, and presented it to my brother, who gave the same to a doctor in Oxford.[28]

Sanderson went to the mummy pits in search of profits, and also no doubt in search of thrills (being lowered with a candle into a cave full of corpses may have constituted an early form of adventure tourism). He was no archaeologist – he has little notion of or interest in the antiquity of the site – though he did take time to observe and record the state of the wrappings and the presence and positioning of the small earthen pots, which he seems to think contain embalmed foetuses (in fact, they were presumably canopic jars, containing the internal organs of the deceased). Reverence for the dead is not prominent in Sanderson's account, as he tramples on the bodies, sniffs them and snaps them apart in his hands. If Sanderson did sense that there was something unwholesome or sordid about the trade in which he was engaged, he was quick to pass the stigma on to his Egyptian trading partners. 'It is *contrabanda* to sell of them, but by friendship, which William Shales had among the Moores, he having their language as perfect as English, with words and money the Moors will be entreated to anything.'[29] The Arabs are so pliable and so mercenary, in other words, that they will sell their deceased countrymen to the cannibals.

Since the tactic of shifting blame will emerge as pervasive in discussions of mummy, it is worth noting that the efforts of the Egyptian authorities to stamp out the trade were long-standing and apparently sincere, if inevitably ineffective. As early as 1424, a number of Egyptians were imprisoned for boiling mummies with the aim of selling the oil to European merchants.[30] A sixteenth-century French surgeon, Louis de Paradis, reported that the people of Egypt considered 'that Christians are unworthy of eating their dead bodies ... [I]f they are taken out of the country, it is by means of some Jews, who ... pack them with their merchandise.'[31] Even the elements reputedly conspired to thwart this illicit trade; ships carrying contraband *mumia* from Alexandria would be wracked by storms, which would subside only when the offending material was dumped into the sea.[32]

'Sell him for mummia, he's half dust already'

The 600 pounds of mummy Sanderson brought back, sufficient for the preparation of many thousands of vulnerary potions, would presumably have been sufficient to stock the shelves of apothecaries in the capital for many years.[33] It is not clear how regular or safe the trade was in later years. English merchants in Egypt complained of extortion and poor profits, and the Levant Company's attempts to establish a consulate in Cairo were frustrated (the first consul disappeared; the second defected to the French and was hanged for intriguing with the Spanish; the third converted to Islam).[34] Around 1641, the German Paracelsian Johann Schroeder complained that genuine mummy was proving impossible to source, advising apothecaries to make do with the easily embalmed bodies of executed criminals. Yet the trade clearly did not cease entirely. In 1612 the Scottish traveller William Lithgow visited the same mummy pits explored by Sanderson, from which he reported, 'whole bodies, hands, or other parts ... by merchants are now brought from thence, and doth make the mummia which apothecaries use'.[35] And in 1638, Lewes Roberts noted that in Egypt *mumia* was sold by the same measure as cardamom, cinnamon and nutmeg, among other spices.[36] While the importation of actual Egyptian mummies was always irregular, and probably grew more so over time (that what passes for *mumia* in the present is an inferior or counterfeit product is a common complaint),[37] it remained throughout the seventeenth century a fixed feature of the popular imagination. The English public firmly believed that ships of the Levant Company returned from Alexandria laden with the powdery or pitchy remains of ancient pharaohs – and this notion, true or not, told them something important about the society and the world in which they lived. Mummy had

indeed become merchandise; more than that, it had become a nego-
tiable literary coin, capable of evoking or encapsulating ideas about
race, sexuality and the changing economy, along with love, death and
immortality.

Mummy in seventeenth-century literature is a powerful and flexible
trope, typically signifying something rotten in the household or the
state, but otherwise malleable (like the substance itself) in the hands of
the poet or playwright. The simplest version of the trope takes mummy
as the extreme example of degraded, disintegrated flesh. Particularly in
Restoration comedy, characters not infrequently threaten to beat each
other into mummy – that is, into a pasty or pulpy substance, like that
sold in apothecaries' shops.[38] An early and unusually graphic example is
found in John Webster's *White Devil* (1612), where mummy is imagined
as what is left when all individuating physical features have been
brutally excised:

> To dig the strumpets eyes out, let her lie
> Some twenty months a-dying, to cut off
> Her nose and lips, pull out her rotten teeth,
> Preserve her flesh like mummia, for trophies
> Of my just anger![39]

A variation on the trope of mummy as degraded flesh is the description
of a living person, male or female, as so aged and decrepit that he or
she could be mistaken for *mumia*. Counselled to marry an old man, a
young woman in Maidwell's *The Loving Enemies* (1680) retorts, 'I don't
intend to embalm matrimonial mummy, to spoile the Apothecary's
trade'.[40] In Cavendish's *The Sociable Companions* (1668), an old woman
is said to have 'been in such passions, as she is almost transform'd to
mummy', to which another character retorts 'that she was before'.[41]
And when Sir Francis Kinnaston attempts to dream up an appropriate
'Mistresse for his Rivals' (1642), he imagines a woman so decrepit that
she could be mistaken for 'mummy, stolne from Egypts partched
sand'.[42] At the extreme end, Dryden imagined the possibility of
necrophiliac sex with mummies themselves, to 'make love to 'em, the
Aegyptian way'.[43]

Another common type of reference is to mummy as a means of
immortalisation, usually contrasted negatively with the power of
language. Mummy, in other words, provides the vehicle for a variation
on Shakespeare's theme: 'Not marble nor the gilded monuments / Of
princes shall outlive this powerful rhyme.'[44] Thus we find Thomas

Philipot asserting in 1652 that:

> When a Poet dies,
> His Sheets alone winde up his Earth, they'l be
> Instead of Mourner, Tomb, and Obsequie;
> And to embalm it, his own Ink he takes:
> Gumme Arabick the richest Mummy makes.[45]

A similar note is struck by James Howell in 1663 with reference to the power of History:

> Which dost Brave Men embalm, and them conserve
> Longer then can Arabian Gums or Spice:
> And of their Memories dost mummy make,
> More firm then that hot *Lybia's* Sands do cake.[46]

A further set of references, relatively rare but including some of the most well known to readers today, involve the association of mummy with witchcraft or the supernatural. The famous sibyl-sewn and strawberry-spotted handkerchief in *Othello*, to which are ascribed some ominous magical properties, is said by Othello to have been 'dyed in mummy, which the skilful / Conserved of maidens' hearts' (III.iv.72–3). In *Macbeth* 'Witches' mummy' (IV.i.23) forms part of the weird sisters' brew, along with other human and animal members and excretions. And John Donne concludes 'Love's Alchemy', in which the lover is compared to an alchemist seeking the true elixir but winding up at best with 'Some odoriferous thing, or medicinal', with the teasingly ambiguous couplet: 'Hope not for mind in women; at their best / Sweetness and wit, they are but mummy, possessed.'[47] Here the jocular misogyny that views women in the act of sex ('possessed') as bodies pure and simple ('mummy'), jostles with the equally misogynistic but darker idea of women as corpses possessed by supernatural forces.

Finally, there is the type of reference of which Browne's own 'mummy is become merchandise' is an example, that is, the depiction of mummy as a commodity – more specifically, as the commodity that anyone might become. This is among the best represented ways of describing mummy, especially in the drama, and the most intriguing.[48] The tone in the plays is almost invariably satirical. Sometimes the satire is sombre, as when Bosola tells the Duchess of Malfi: 'Thou art a box of worm-seed, at best but a salvatory of green mummy.'[49] More often it is street-smart and wisecracking, as in James Shirley's *The Bird in the Cage* (1633), where

Rolliardo boasts that if he fails in his task, 'Make Mummy of my flesh and sell me to the Apothecaries.'[50] In Jonson's *Volpone*, Mosca ponders what to do with the aged Corbaccio and suggests, 'Sell him for *mummia*; he's half dust already.'[51] And in Field and Fletcher's *The Honest Man's Fortune* (performed 1613), the servants hope their mistress will not marry a merchant, because 'hee'l sell us all to the Moors to make mummy'.[52] On the grimmer side, a villain who has been cheated in *The Honest Lawyer* (1616) cries out 'Oh I could wish my nailes turn'd Vultures talons / That I might teare their flesh in mammocks, raise / My losses from their carcases turn'd mummy.'[53] Here too we might mention Falstaff in the *Merry Wives of Windsor*, who complains that if he were to drown he would swell to 'a mountain of mummy' (III.v.15); in the quarto edition of 1602, however, the line reads 'a mountain of money'. This is doubtless a compositor's error, but we should not dismiss the possibility of a buried pun, in this and perhaps other cases.

The link between mummification and commodification is one I will return to. What requires emphasis at this point is that almost all of these literary versions of mummy seem to carry with them some implication of blame or of crime. This is present even in the blandest type, when a character threatens to beat another into mummy, and it is felt more sharply in the others. Mummy tends to be invoked in – and to evoke – an atmosphere of sin, criminality and double-dealing. The mummy-dyed handkerchief in *Othello* is not only a piece of exotic fabric; it is also, as far as its magical properties are concerned, a fabrication – the story of its manufacture is a lie designed by Othello to entrap and expose Desdemona in a greater lie. Similarly, from the cauldron containing 'Witch's mummy' arise visions that will entice, mislead and betray Macbeth. In Webster's *White Devil*, mummy is invoked as a metaphorical explanation for the revoking of allegiances: 'Your followers / Have swallowed you like mummia, and, being sick / With such unnatural and horrid physic / Vomit you up i' th' kennell.'[54] In a less sinister context we might notice how the mistress Kinnaston imagines for his rivals is made to resemble not merely mummy but 'Mummy, *stolne* from Egypts partched sand'. Dryden too, when he imagines sex with mummies, is also talking about a kind of theft: plagiarism, by those who 'Dare with the mummeys of the Muses play'.[55] Intimations of crime and deception seem to creep in almost unbidden whenever mummy is mentioned.

Oddly enough, however, though mummy is frequently associated in literature with crime and transgression, the transgression in question never seems to be the obvious one: cannibalism. Poets and playwrights found many reasons to disparage mummy in the seventeenth century, but they rarely if ever did so for what might seem the best reason – that in taking *mumia* as medicine, people were eating people. Instead, while the very mention of mummy conveys the insinuation that someone somewhere is doing something very wrong, that someone almost always turns out to be somewhere else. English writers, in short, are passing the buck; blame for the transgression is being shifted further up the chain. Sometimes it settles on the medical practitioners who insist on prescribing such a horrible substance – a traveller in Hakluyt declares with disgust: 'these dead bodies are the Mummie which the Phisitians and Apothecaries doe against our willes make us to swallow.'[56] Often the blame is passed further off, to the Moors who so shamelessly sell the bodies of their own ancestors, and above all to the Jews, who both control the illicit mummy trade and flood the market with inferior imitations. As the load of blame that mummy seems to bear with it settles on the Jew, mummy becomes associated not so much with cannibalism as with the archetypal Jewish sin, usury.

Mummy seems to have become associated with Jews in the Christian imagination at least by the sixteenth century and possibly earlier.[57] If there was a burden of shame attached to the mummy trade – and almost everyone acknowledged that there was – the Jews were most fit to bear it. Ephraim Chambers, an eighteenth-century sceptic as to mummy's medicinal properties, blamed the origins of its false reputation as a remedy on 'the malice of a Jewish physician'. Chambers went on to complain, somewhat inconsistently, that one could not get genuine mummy nowadays; that which was sold in shops was 'factitious, the work of certain Jews, who counterfeit it by drying carcasses in ovens after having prepared them with powder of myrrh, caballin aloes, Jewish pitch, and other coarse or unwholesome drugs'.[58]

While earlier generations may not have shared Chambers' confidence that mummy was of no medicinal use, the charge that Jews were responsible for manufacturing and selling false mummies was a familiar one. Ambroise Paré, the great French surgeon of the sixteenth century and himself an early sceptic, recounted a story told him by a friend who had visited Egypt:

> Guy de la Fontaine being at Alexandria in Egypt, went to see a Jew in that city, who traded in mummies, that he might have ocular demonstration of what he had heard so much of; accordingly, when he came to the Jew's house, he desired to see his commodity or mummies, which he having obtain'd with some difficulty, the Jew at last open'd his magazine, or store-house, and show'd him several

bodies pil'd one upon another. Then after a reflection of a quarter of an hour, he asked him what druggs he made use? And what sort of bodies were fit for his service? The Jew answer'd him, that as for the dead he took such bodies as he cou'd get, whether they dy'd of a common disease or some contagion; and as to the druggs, that they were nothing but a heap of several old druggs mix'd together, which he apply'd to the bodies; which after he had dry'd in an oven, he sent into Europe; and that he was amaz'd to see the Christians were lovers of such filthiness.[59]

The sudden twist at the end, shifting the blame or taint onto the Christian consumer, shows that the attempt to scapegoat the Jews over the matter of mummy was not without tensions; tensions familiar from present-day campaigns against the production of heroine and cocaine – substances which indeed bear a number of similarities to *mumia*. Nevertheless, the association of mummy with Jewish underhand dealing stuck in the English imagination. In Robert Daborne's play *A Christian Turn'd Turke* (1612), a Jewish servant tells his Jewish master, 'If you gull me now, Il'e giue you leave to make mummy of me.'[60] (The master does shortly go on to gull and murder him, though not to mummify him.)

Alexandrian Jews presumably did play a role in the export of mummy, and possibly also in the manufacture of counterfeit products (around 1625 the Egyptian and Syrian authorities reputedly cracked down on Jews involved in the trade).[61] Yet the association of Jews with mummy-making, mummy-selling and mummy-eating is obviously overdetermined. First of all, in the anti-Semitic imagination, Jews were and are frequently associated with cannibalism.[62] They thus provided ideal scapegoats for any Christian anxieties about the consumption of *mumia*. To put this a little differently, to associate *mumia* with Jews provided a covert way of acknowledging that mummy-eating was indeed cannibalism. Yet it must also be borne in mind that the common charge of Jewish cannibalism was itself frequently a trope – a way of literalising and demonstrating the abhorrent nature of Jewish financial practices, such as usury. Rather than producing or creating anything of value, the Jew is perceived as an economic 'bloodsucker', a 'vampire', a 'parasite on the body of other peoples' (the particular phrases are Hitler's).[63] Behind the Jewish mummy-dealer stands the Jewish cannibal, but behind the Jewish cannibal stands the Jewish usurer. It is possible, then, that English writers associated mummy-eating with Jews not, or not simply, because they knew in their hearts that it was cannibalism, but because they saw in it a form of usury, or more broadly, sin of an economic nature.

The repeated association of mummy-eating with mercenary Moors and double-dealing Jews may look like straightforward projection, a desperate attempt to avoid recognising the real guilty party as well as the real nature of the crime. The very mention of mummies seems at times to prompt a compulsive outward gesture, a flinging off of the taint. The quip in *The Honest Man's Fortune* that the merchant will 'sell us all to the Moors to / make mummy' is a clear example of this reflex. (Obviously, if the merchant had a domestic source of mummy to hand, he would not need to expose himself to the risk and expense of trading with the Moors.) Such determination to pin the scandal on another (and an Other) is reminiscent of the repeated efforts of Captain Cook and his crew in the eighteenth century to feed human flesh (which they had broiled) to their Maori hosts.[64] English sailors themselves were not infrequently driven to acts of 'survival cannibalism': there is nothing like the threat of being branded a cannibal oneself to make one desperate to discover and expose genuine cannibalism somewhere – anywhere – else.

Nevertheless, there is good reason to resist the conclusion that the English in the seventeenth century were either 'in denial' about their participation in cannibalism or desperate to cover it up. The sheer number and frankness of the references to mummy-eating would seem to militate against this. While it is true that the burden of scandal is often ascribed to foreigners, such as Jews, this does not necessarily represent an intention to dodge responsibility by scapegoating. For as Marlowe and Marx both knew, the figure of the transgressive Jew can be used not to displace but rather to focus and lay bare the sins of a Christian society.[65] It is significant that, like Marlowe's *Jew of Malta*, Paré's anecdote of the Alexandrian Jew concludes with the devastating revelation of Christian hypocrisy. Here it is not so much a matter of flinging away the taint as of transmitting it along a circuit, passing through the Levantine Jew before returning to the European. I would argue that in raising the matter of *mumia*, English writers are often attempting to get to grips with something unsavoury in their own culture – but their efforts to get at the problem of Englishness are typically routed through images of the alien or exotic before completing the circuit. The taint goes out, and it comes home.

The actual mummy trade, to whatever extent it existed, did indeed involve a circuit, with ships of the Levant Company travelling back and forth between England and Alexandria. Yet several writers manage to imply that mummy was in some sense already on board when the ships left dock. Thus John Hagthorpe describes how avarice draws men:

> to the burning line,
> And *Affricks* desarts drie,
> Where many thousands pine,
> And perish wilfully;
> Where by the sunne and wind,
> They mummey doe become.
> Yet we, with this in mind,
> To th' same misfortunes run.[66]

The greedy quest for *mumia* draws merchants to the Egyptian desert where, meeting with mischance, they become the very commodity they set out to find – and thus become the object of desire for the next wave of greedy Europeans, bent on recovering what are in fact true English mummies. A still briefer circuit is completed in Motteux's *Love's a Jest* (1696), when an Englishman catches a gypsy picking his pocket and taunts him: 'You shall be trust up next assizes, hang'd in chains, and shewn for a right Egyptian mummy.'[67] Although routed through the body of the gypsy transgressor, 'Egyptian mummy' is here revealed paradoxically as a product of English manufacture.

Thus, even where it is apparently displaced onto derogatory images of alien peoples, mummy-eating provides a way of gesturing to the sins of English society. Above all, mummies offer writers a way of thinking through the cultural ramifications of an emergent market economy. Mummy becomes the emblem of an economy out of control. This is at stake most obviously in the many biting references to mummy as a commodity, including that from Browne's *Hydriotaphia*: 'The Ægyptian mummies, which Cambises or time hath spared, avarice now consumeth. Mummie is become merchandise, Miszraim cures wounds, and Pharaoh is sold for balsoms.' Strikingly, Browne here admits that mummy is being eaten, but not by English people, possibly including his own patients. It is not the English who are consuming mummies, cannibalistically, but rather avarice that is consuming them, capitalistically.

The metaphorical linkage of capitalism with cannibalism is as old as capitalism itself, and the trope has been deployed in disparate, sometimes contradictory ways. Sometimes, as in anti-Semitic discourse, it is the banker who is depicted as a cannibal; for Marx it is the primitive accumulator or ruthless industrialist, eating up his own labour force in the drive for absolute profit.[68] But in those seventeenth-century texts concerned with mummy-eating, the focus is less on the financial system or the mode of production than, appropriately enough, on consumption. The trade in mummified flesh comes to stand for a society in which nothing is exempt from commodification, in which no form of value other than exchange value stands secure.[69] It gestures, moreover, towards the dim beginnings of what we now call globalisation. When 'Pharaoh is sold for balsoms', three traditional barriers to the absolute dominion of the marketplace, barriers of hierarchy, geography and morality, are being broken down simultaneously. An English person is consuming an Egyptian; a commoner is consuming a king; a human being is consuming a human being.

The mummy trade serves as a remarkably apt figure for the market economy not simply because it suggests its ruthless quest for limitless extension (even our bodies are not exempt, even cannibal tastes will be catered to), but because mummy, in its physical form, literalises the collapse or disintegration of all values into a single (exchange) value. Mummy, as a paste or powder, is the human body reduced to an undifferentiated and formless mass, stripped not only of life but also of particularity and context, of external features and internal complexity. (There would be no way even of knowing whether the half-ounce of mummy in one's vulnerary potion came from a single dead Egyptian or from many.) If market forces have the power to reduce every established value and social barrier to so much dust, then mummy's potency as a figure for these forces is enhanced by the fact that it is, in at least one of its manifestations, nothing but dust.

In the seventeenth-century imagination, mummies stood not for the potential of the human body to achieve an embalmed immortality, but rather for the body's destined dissolution into pure commodity. The nightmare of corporeal disintegration, which lurks behind so many of the references to mummy explored in this chapter, is captured most vividly in Robert Howard's *The Blind Lady* (1660), in which an amorous old woman is wooed by a young scoundrel:

> I have heard
> Of a dead body that has long been so,
> And yet retain its form, but when once toucht
> Crumbles to dust; for ought I know she may do so too,
> And I be hang'd for embracing mummie.[70]

In an instant, the individual – or rather, what masqueraded as the individual – gives way to the commodity, and the lover who sought a stolen embrace winds up with stolen goods (for the possession of which he risks execution). As the exotic (Egyptian mummies) collapses into the domestic (four shillings a pound), so individual value collapses into exchange value. 'All that is solid melts into air.'[71] All that is human crumbles to mumia.

Notes

1. 'Fragment on Mummies', in Geoffrey Keynes, ed., *The Works of Sir Thomas Browne*, 2nd edition (London: Faber and Faber, 1964), 3: 472.
2. As Arthur James Balfour told Parliament in 1910, justifying Britain's role in Egypt: 'We know the civilization of Egypt better than we know the civilization of any other country. We know it further back; we know it more intimately; we know more about it. It goes far beyond the petty span of the history of our race, which is lost in the prehistoric period at a time when the Egyptian civilization had already past its prime.' Cited in Edward Said, *Orientalism: Western Perceptions of the Orient* (New York: Vintage Books, 1978), p. 32.
3. For a description of the manuscript and a demolishment of its pretensions, see Robert J. Kane, 'James Crossley, Sir Thomas Browne, and the *Fragment on Mummies*', *RES* 9 (1933): 266–74.
4. Quoted in Kane, 'James Crossley', p. 273.
5. The 'Fragment on Mummies' appears as the end-piece of volume three of Browne's *Works* in Keynes' edition, with no other note than that it is '*From a copy in the handwriting of J. Crossley, Esq.*', p. 469. Almost 500 pages later, at the close of the 'Editor's Preface', Keynes acknowledges the manuscript's very dubious origins, and leaves it to the reader 'to judge whether Browne would have owned to its verbal extravagances, or would even have gusted so irreverent a pleasantry', p. xvii. Not every scholar has taken (or noticed) the warning. As recently as 2002, an article in a respected scholarly journal quoted extensively from the 'Fragment' as Browne's own work.
6. While the genuine Thomas Browne did indeed ask, in *Hydriotaphia*, 'Who can but pity the founder of the Pyramids?', Keynes, ed., *Works*, 1: 167, he was not pointing to the specific failure of Egyptian memory, but rather to the inevitable failure of all memorials, even the most magnificent, in an amnesiac and impermanent world. Similarly, when Richard Verstegan demanded, 'What moste excellently learned men, & great doctors of the Churche, hath Africa brought forth, and with what learned men is Africa in our tyme acquainted?' his point was not that nations have lifecycles and grow old like human beings, but simply that learning is not an immutable characteristic of ethnic groups. See Verstegan, *A Restitution of Decayed Intelligence in Antiquities* (Antwerp, 1605), p. 51.
7. In his poetic 'Prophecy Concerning the Future State of Several Nations', Browne playfully imagines what will happen when the colonies grow up: 'When the new World shall the old invade, / Nor count them their Lords but their fellows in Trade', Keynes, ed., *Works*, 3: 104.
8. See Alfred C. Wood, *A History of the Levant Company* (London: Oxford University Press, 1935), pp. 33, 234–5.
9. 'Fragment on Mummies', in Keynes, ed., *Works*, 3: 470.

10. Browne, *Hydriotaphia*, in Keynes, ed., *Works*, 1: 168.
11. Rosalie David, 'Mummification', in Paul T. Nicholson and Ian Shaw, eds., *Ancient Egyptian Materials and Technology* (Cambridge: Cambridge University Press, 2000), pp. 372–89.
12. On the medical history of *mumia*, see Karl H. Dannenfeldt, 'Egyptian Mumia: The Sixteenth-Century Experience and Debate', *Sixteenth Century Journal* 16 (1985): 163–80.
13. Margaret Serpico, 'Resins, Amber and Bitumen', in Nicolsaon and Shaw, eds., *Ancient Egyptian Materials*, pp. 430–74, see esp. pp. 454–5. Serpico notes some recent evidence that bitumen may have been used occasionally in the mummification process in earlier periods, when it was certainly used as a varnish, p. 466.
14. Quoted in Dannenfeldt, 'Egyptian Mumia', p. 167.
15. See Dannenfeldt, 'Egyptian Mumia', pp. 164–5. As one of the original Arabic medical treatises has been lost, it is not clear whether the Latin translators had any genuine authority for their view of *mumia* as an exudate. The difference between the predominant Arab view (*mumia* as embalming material which might be extracted from corpses) and the Christian view (*mumia* as an exudate of embalmed human flesh, or the flesh itself) is significant, as the former could, at least technically, be ingested without cannibalism, while the latter obviously could not. The actual extent of mummy-eating among Arabs is unclear. Johann Helfrich, who went looking for mummies in Egypt in 1565, reported that 'Some of the Arabs eat them out of curiosity'. Dannenfeldt, p. 168.
16. Caroline Walker Bynum, *Holy Feast and Holy Fast: The Religious Significance of Food to Medieval Women* (Berkeley, CA: University of California Press, 1987).
17. See Bynum, *Holy Feast*, pp. 123, 273. There is indeed a specific term, 'myroblyte', for saints whose bodies exude miraculous oils after death.
18. Samuel Purchas, ed., *Purchas his Pilgrimage*, 3rd edition (1617), p. 849.
19. William Perkins, *The Golden Chaine* (1600), quoted in David Cressy, *Birth, Marriage, and Death: Ritual, Religion and the Life-Cycle in Tudor and Stuart England* (Oxford: Oxford University Press, 1997), p. 415.
20. John Oldham, *Babylon Blazon'd, or, The Jesuit Jerk'd* (1681), p. 5.
21. See Peter Hulme, *Colonial Encounters: Europe and the Native Caribbean, 1492–1797* (London: Methuen, 1986), and Francis Barker, Peter Hulme and Margaret Iversen, eds., *Cannibalism and the Colonial World* (Cambridge: Cambridge University Press, 1998).
22. See, e.g., William Lithgow, *The Totall Discourse of the Rare Adventures* (1640), p. 311. The blackness of mummified flesh was sometimes ascribed to the presence of bitumen, but a racial resonance could hardly be avoided.
23. Browne, *Pseudoxia Epidemica*, Bk. 2, Ch. 4, in Keynes, ed., *Works*, 2: 118.
24. Sir Kenelm Digby, *Choice and Experimented Receipts in Physick and Chirurgery* (1675), p. 68.
25. Alexander Ross, *Arcana Microcosmi* (1652), p. 97.
26. Karen Gordon-Grube, 'Evidence of Medicinal Cannibalism in Puritan New England: "Mummy" and Related Remedies in Edward Taylor's "Dispensatory"', *Early American Literature* 28 (1993): 185–221; see also Dannenfeldt, 'Egyptian Mumia', 173–4.
27. Richard Hakluyt, *The Principal Navigations, Voyages, Traffiques and Discoveries of the English Nation* (1599), 2: 277.

28. Samuel Purchas, ed., *Purchas his Pilgrimes* (1625), Part 2, Bk 9, Chapter 16, p. 1616. See the detailed analysis of this passage in Iman Hamam, 'Disturbing Western Representations of Ancient Egyptian Mummies', unpublished DPhil dissertation (University of Sussex, 2002).
29. Purchas, ed., *Purchas his Pilgrimes*, p. 1616, marginal note. The marginal notes in *Purchas* do not appear in William Foster's edition of Sanderson's manuscript, *The Travels of John Sanderson* (1931; rpt. London: Hakluyt Society, 1967), but these notes appear to be Sanderson's own additional contributions.
30. Dannenfeldt, 'Egyptian Mumia', p. 167.
31. Cited in Dannenfeldt, 'Egyptian Mumia', p. 170.
32. Jean Bodin, cited in Dannenfeldt, 'Egyptian Mumia', pp. 169–70. The tradition is repeated by Crossley in the 'Fragment on Mummies'.
33. The marginal notes in Purchas, ed., *Purchas his Pilgrimes*, p. 1616, specifies that 'The 600 pounds ... were sold to the London Apothecaries'. With the price of mummy running at 4 shillings a pound in 1582, the sale probably brought in about £120 for the Turkey Company.
34. Wood, *History*, pp. 32–5. After the dismissal of the third consul in 1601, the post remained vacant for more than 50 years, and those who claimed the title later in the seventeenth century lacked the support of the Levant Company.
35. Lithgow, *Totall Discourse*, pp. 310–11.
36. Lewes Roberts, *The Merchants Map of Commerce* (1638), p. 108.
37. Thus Alexander Ross: 'He [Bacon] tells us, That *Mummy hath a great force in stanching of blood.* But I wish he could tell us where we may find it: For the true mummy which was found in the Tombes of the Ægyptian Kings, which were embalmed with divers pretious liquors and spices, are spent long agoe, so that the mummy now in use is only the substance of dried karkasses digged out of the sands, being overwhelmed there, in which there is no more vertue to stanch blood, then in a stick.' *Arcana Microcosmi*, p. 263.
38. See, e.g., John Dryden, *Sir Martin Mar-All*, in *The Works of John Dryden, Volume 9*, ed. John Loftis (Berkeley, CA: University of California Press, 1966), 4.1.508; Thomas D'Urfey, *The Fond Husband* (1677), pp. 27, 40; John Leanerd, *The Rambling Justice* (1678), p. 8.
39. John Webster, *The White Devil*, 2.1.247–51, in David Bevington, ed., *English Renaissance Drama* (New York: Norton, 2002).
40. Lewis Maidwell, *The Loving Enemies* (1680), p. 23.
41. Margaret Cavendish, *Plays* (1668), p. 85.
42. Sir Francis Kinnaston, 'To Cynthia, On a Mistresse for his Rivals', in *Leoline and Sydanis* (1642), p. 126.
43. John Dryden, 'Prologue to *Albumazar*', in *The Works of John Dryden, Volume 1: Poems 1649–1680*, ed. Edward Niles Hooker and H. T. Swedenborg, Jr. (Berkeley, CA: University of California Press, 1956), p. 142.
44. William Shakespeare, Sonnet 55, in Stephen Greenblatt, ed., *The Norton Shakespeare* (New York: Norton, 1997), p. 1941. All references to Shakespeare's works are to this edition.
45. Thomas Philipot, 'For the Renowned Composer', in Edward Benlowes, *Theophila* (1652), sig. C3v.
46. James Howell, 'Historiae Sacrum', in *Poems on Several Choice and Various Subjects* (1663), p. 9.

47. John Donne, 'Love's Alchemy', in A. J. Smith, ed., *The Complete English Poems* (London: Penguin, 1986), p. 65, lines 10, 23–4.
48. Louise Noble argues that these references point to the genuine existence of a domestic mummy industry – embalming the bodies of executed criminals for pharmaceutical use. Such an expedient might have been readily acceptable to Paracelsians, but not to the majority of physicians. See Noble, ' "And Make Two Pasties of Your Shameful Heads": Medicinal Cannibalism and Healing the Body Politic in *Titus Andronicus*', ELH 70 (2003): 677–708.
49. John Webster, *The Duchess of Malfi*, 4.2.122–3, in Bevington, ed., *English Renaissance Drama*.
50. James Shirley, *The Bird in the Cage* (1633), sig. C1r.
51. Ben Jonson, *Volpone*, 4.4.14, in Bevington, ed., *English Renaissance Drama*.
52. *The Honest Man's Fortune*, ed. Johan Gerritsen (Gröningen: Wolters, 1952), 5.3.23–4.
53. S. S., *The Honest Lawyer* (1616), sig. E2r.
54. John Webster, *The White Devil*, 1.1.15–18, in Bevington, ed., *English Renaissance Drama*.
55. John Dryden, 'Prologue to *Albumazar*', p. 142.
56. Hakluyt, *Navigations*, 2: 201.
57. See Dannenfeldt, 'Egyptian Mumia', p. 170.
58. Chambers, *Cyclopaedia* (1738), cited in Albert S. Cook, 'Shakespeare, *Oth.* 3.4.74', *Modern Language Notes* 21 (1906), p. 248.
59. Paré's anecdote is repeated in *A Complete History of Druggs, written in French by Monsieur Pomet* (1712), cited in Cook, 'Shakespeare', p. 249.
60. Robert Daborne, *A Christian Turn'd Turke* (1612), sig. I1v.
61. See Dannenfeldt, 'Egyptian Mumia', p. 171.
62. See Jerry Phillips, 'Cannibalism qua Capitalism: The Metaphorics of Accumulation in Marx, Conrad, Shakespeare, and Marlowe', in Barker, et al., eds., *Cannibalism*, pp. 195–203.
63. Cited in Phillips, 'Cannibalism', p. 201.
64. Gananath Obeyesekere, ' "British Cannibals": Contemplation of an Event in the Death and Resurrection of James Cook, Explorer', *Critical Inquiry* 18 (1992): 630–54; Peter Hulme, 'Introduction: The Cannibal Scene', in Barker et al., eds., *Cannibalism*, pp. 21–4.
65. See Stephen Greenblatt, 'Marlowe, Marx and Anti-Semitism', in *Learning to Curse* (London: Routledge, 1990), pp. 40–58; Phillips, 'Cannibalism'.
66. John Hagthorpe, *Divine Meditations* (1622), p. 72.
67. Peter Anthony Motteux, *Love's A Jest* (1696), p. 47.
68. See Crystal Bartolovich, 'Consumerism, or the Cultural Logic of Late Cannibalism', in Barker et al. eds., *Cannibalism*, pp. 204–37.
69. These texts thus anticipate by three centuries Peter Greenaway's professed aim in his film *The Cook, the Thief, his Wife and her Lover* (1989): 'I wanted to use cannibalism not only as a literal event but in the metaphorical sense, that in the consumer society, once we've stuffed the whole world into our mouths, we'll end up eating ourselves', cited in Bartolovich, 'Consumerism', p. 205.
70. Robert Howard, *The Blind Lady*, in *Poems* (1660), pp. 92–3.
71. Karl Marx and Frederick Engels, *The Communist Manifesto* (New York: International Publishers, 1948), p. 12.

4
A Double Perspective and a Lost Rivalry: Ogier de Busbecq and Melchior Lorck in Istanbul

Barnaby Rogerson

The double perspective offered up by a pairing of artist and writer can leave a transfixing legacy. Take Restoration London as an example. It is almost impossible to visualise the city without viewing it through the engravings of Wenceslaus Hollar and the diaries of Samuel Pepys. As Hollar depicts London Bridge decorated with the decapitated heads of traitors, it also comes alive as the place where the naval secretary Pepys took his brief pleasure with prostitutes. Similarly, eighteenth-century Venice is forever caught by the accidental double-act of Canaletto and Casanova, rural nineteenth-century Russia by that of Ilya Repin and Leo Tolstoy, while arguably the befogged nineteenth-century London conjured up by both Turner and Charles Dickens still dominates our perception of that city.

If Pepys is firmly set in the English literary constellation, Hollar, despite his equivalent brilliance, is less convincingly sung. This Prague-borne artist, loyal servant to both Charles I and Charles II as their 'King's Scenographer', would die in poverty and neglect. The bailiffs seized his sole remaining possession, his bed, as he lay dying in 1677.[1]

The combined vision of artist and writer also possesses our perception of other another great city: Constantinople-Istanbul of the sixteenth century. The capital of the Ottoman Empire is caught in all its magnificent, turbulent, restless creativity in the writings of Ogier de Busbecq and the drawings of Melchior Lorck. Their names are not familiar; indeed, they seem deliberately obtuse, like a pair of scholarly footnotes celebrating obscurity. However, as we will see, their influence is just as powerful as that of Pepys and Hollar over London. No history of the Ottoman Empire, no critique of Istanbul, no biography of Süleyman the

Magnificent can escape using Busbecq and Lorck.[2] They are vital sources, prisms through which the past is perceived. Busbecq and Lorck, like Pepys and Hollar, were courtiers; men of talent attracted to the dangerous bright flame of royal patronage.

There is also an intriguing mystery about their relationship. For Ogier de Busbecq and Melchior Lorck maintain a deathly silence about each other, despite the four years they spent packed together in the same embassy compound in Istanbul and despite their great fame in Europe as 'Turkish travellers'. Their careers are comparatively well documented, though the official papers no more than hint at the strong passions involved. For all their shared immersion in High Renaissance culture and their shared loyalty to the Hapsburg dynasty, they were clearly very different characters. They seem like Herman Hesse's Narziss and Goldmund, where the career of the passionate artist is set against the foil of the reflective scholar.[3] Melchior Lorck could have screen-tested for the role of the restless artist. He was beautiful, well known, well travelled and highly regarded by the society of both the princely courts and the ancient free cities. He was extraordinarily versatile. He could by turns be labelled an explorer, architect, poet, surveyor, artist, etcher, jeweller and engineer. His *View of Constantinople* (c.1559–62) was hung in one of the most revered sites of intellectual Europe, the Great Hall of the University Library of Leiden.[4] In modern terms, it was the smash hit movie of the day.

Nor was he shy of celebrity. Lorck depicts himself in the dead centre of the *View*, his head turned to show a handsome profile, his cap rakishly slanted on the back of his head, his torso swathed in a fetching cloak to reveal puffed shoulders and perfect cuffs.[5] His arms are extended with casual grace, whilst his attenuated fingers dip a sliver of a pen into a crystal goblet of ink held out for him by the sort of forbidding bearded, be-turbaned Turk that frightened the hell out of Christendom. He portrays himself with a careless ease that is in complete contrast to the meticulous research, draughtsmanship and technical brilliance of his view of the 'enemy' citadel. For his audience it was all the more thrilling in that the power of the Ottomans was dreaded throughout Europe. To pile conceit on conceit, Lorck based his picture on that of the Emperor Charles V standing before Ingolstadt. Lorck was a star.

Melchior Lorck was born into a large, noble family in 1526. They lived in Flensburg within the Danish-ruled Duchy of Schleswig-Holstein and his father was sufficiently well respected to receive the Danish monarch when he passed through the city. Lorck was proud of his noble birth but equally of his urban identity, signing all his pictures MLF, Melchior Lorck Flensburgensis. He was apprenticed to a master goldsmith in the great neighbouring Hanseatic city of Lübeck, from whence, in the course of his training, he travelled through the other trading cities of the Baltic. Clearly this apprenticeship, like that of Albrecht Dürer, was about design, drawing and composition as well as the casting, carving and mixing of precious metals.

By the time he was 20 he was set on his own course. At the Diet of Augsburg in 1547 he met such useful patrons as the Count Palatinate and the Prince-Bishop of Augsburg. His earliest surviving work, an etched portrait of Martin Luther, was made the following year. In 1549 King Christian III decided to foster this home-grown talent and provided funds for Lorck to finish his artistic education with an extended Grand Tour. The idea was for Lorck to return to the court of Denmark after four years. From the cities of the Netherlands the young Lorck travelled to Nuremberg and then south to Vienna, Bologna, Florence and the artistic apogee of Rome. The life, the light, the art were all together far too good. The young artist failed to return to Copenhagen and Christian was irritated enough to interfere personally and put a restraint on a legacy that Lorck was due to inherit.[6]

Thereafter Lorck's trail goes faint, though no doubt he was moving from court to court and from commission to commission, before being dispatched to Istanbul on an artistic commission by the Hapsburg Archduke Ferdinand. The official embassy was travelling down across the Balkans from Vienna. How Lorck reached Istanbul we do not know, though a small body of surviving sketches suggests that he took the sea route from Venice, perhaps with the Danubian navy, skirting the Greek coast on his way to Istanbul.

He probably arrived in Istanbul at the end of 1555 where, by his own account, he stayed for four and a half years. There may have been some sort of a row over his exact role and status at the embassy. This would certainly explain a curious document issued by the Hapsburg Court in February 1564, which retrospectively and explicitly states that Lorck had been 'ordered to Turkey', as well as codifying and renewing his coat of arms and noble status.[7] It is easy to imagine that the talented, free-spirited Lorck might have found the enclosed life of the embassy compound in Istanbul stifling. The Hapsburg or Imperial Embassy was under the command of Ogier Ghiselin de Busbecq.

Busbecq was two years older than Lorck. The Ottoman capital could be a dangerous posting: the health of Malvezi, the previous Hapsburg ambassador, had been broken by imprisonment in Istanbul. It was also an important posting: only the best men were up to the job and Busbecq was one of those. Born in Flanders, educated at the universities of

Louvain, Padua and Venice, he spoke seven languages fluently. He was an intelligent, hardworking, scholarly civil servant, who was happy to confess that he found books 'my companions and the joy of my life'. He was also a private man, travelling with his own bed 'which I always carried with me',[8] and when faced with the curiosity of other travellers in a caravanserai he used to retire to the seclusion of a tent or a carriage. He plainly adored animals, was generous to his servants and cheerfully distributed wine to those that liked it – like his Ottoman guards. Even in Istanbul he made a habit of receiving guests in the embassy grounds, entertaining and interviewing the many travellers that passed his door rather than venturing out into the city. He liked tennis, archery, fishing and the company of a few handpicked and likeminded friends. This may well have been the natural working of a studious nature, but it was also a social defence mechanism. For Busbecq had a problem: he was a bastard. For all his talents he stood outside the charmed circle of nobility, that indispensable network of cousins, patrons and legally enforced privilege. True, his father, George Ghislain II, lord of the manor of Busbecq outside Lille in Flanders, was a gentleman, but Ogier had been officially recognised only when he was 27 years old. Busbecq was born with a chip on his shoulder, but that is exactly what made him such a good observer. He appreciated the classlessness of Muslim society, its innate good manners, the equality amongst believers, the respect for education and that the Ottoman Empire was run on meritocratic grounds.

He had entered the service of the Holy Roman Emperor's brother, the Archduke Ferdinand, in 1552. Two years later, having just returned from England where he had officially witnessed the marriage of Mary Tudor and Phillip II of Spain in Winchester Cathedral, Ogier was summoned post-haste to Vienna. There he was given the task of patching up a truce with the Ottoman Empire and explaining why his master had annexed Transylvania and assumed the title King of Hungary. In particular, the exact status of Siebenburgen needed sorting out. He was given twelve days in which to pack and brief himself for the new mission before leaving for the border. Busbecq was informed that he would be travelling with Anton Wranczy (Antonius Verantius), Bishop of Erlau (Eger in Hungary), and Franz Zay, commander of the Danubian navy. The archduke, however, failed to inform him which members of his entourage might be involved in espionage or working on 'parallel negotiations'. With the benefit of hindsight we know that one of the chief Hapsburg secret agents in Istanbul was Michael Cernovic, the son of a local ropemaker who ostensibly worked as dragoman to the Venetians.

It must have come as a surprise for Busbecq to find that Melchior Lorck, the young Danish artist, had also been sent on a mission to Istanbul by the archduke. Lorck may have been in Istanbul for Busbecq's first visit in 1555, but was most certainly in the city for Busbecq's second mission from 1556 to 1562, for we have a series of drawings clearly dated 1556, 1557 and 1558. They spent nearly four years together in a caravanserai courtyard that was converted into an embassy compound. We have Busbecq's eloquent description of this compound, complete with his delight in the sea view, his Arab horses, his five she-camels and a fabulous menagerie of exotic pets. We also have a completely enchanting drawing of the view from the roof by Lorck.[9] It is a beautiful composition, a masterful exercise in perspective with the long, sagging flight of roof tiles punctuated by a distant mosque, minaret, the stump of the Arcadius Column and the sea. It is complete with a very Lorck-like detail, a couple making love on a rooftop verandah in the stillness of the afternoon siesta. It is intriguing, therefore, that Busbecq in his *Turkish Letters*, describes the embassy cellarman, how much he liked his apothecary, the company of his erudite doctor, how he enjoyed his professional rivalry with the French, how well he got on with one of the viziers, what the Spanish prisoners-of-war were like, but of Lorck – nothing.

Clearly, the dashing, young, well-connected Danish nobleman-artist and the Flanders scholar-diplomat did not get on. There is just one possible oblique reference, when Busbecq mentions that he owns a 'drawing of the column of Arcadius' which we know Lorck drew many times.[10]

Melchior Lorck was no slouch in Istanbul. For not only was he working on his famous panorama of the city, he was also filling sketchbook after sketchbook with intimate details of Ottoman life: weddings, funerals, naked prostitutes, uniforms, buildings, ships and antiquities. He had a fine eye for detail and returned again and again to the totemic power of the Ottoman horsetail battle standards. He was also granted sufficient access to a harem to draw convincing scenes of everyday life as well as making portraits of Busbecq, Franz Zay, the Persian ambassador, Roxelana and some Turkish dignitaries. Busbecq's own audiences with the great Sultan were brief, formal affairs but, on 15 February 1559, Lorck had a sufficiently long audience to create a half-length portrait. He must also have charmed his way into being allowed to make such a detailed sketch of the city's harbour and defences for the *View of Constantinople*, his chosen vantage point being the walls and towers of Galata.

By 1560 Lorck was back in Vienna, writing his travels and working up his sketches into finished engravings, woodcuts, portraits and of course his celebrated panorama. Honours and flattering dedications were heaped upon him. Busbecq meanwhile was still locked in intractable and dangerous negotiations in Istanbul and may have been envious that some of his thunder as Turkey expert and traveller had been stolen. Maximillian, King of the Romans, Frederick III of Denmark and the Duke of Schleswig-Holstein were all delighted to add Lorck's exotic oriental portraits to their collections and responded with grants of arms, patents of nobility, pensions and new commissions. In these years Lorck confidently turned his hand to anything; surveying the Elbe, designing three triumphal gates for the new Emperor Maximillian or a new gate for the city of Hamburg. But his Turkey sketchbooks remained an inspirational goldmine. Over decades he used them to create 128 Turkish images, contributing them to anthologies, dictionaries and frontispieces, as well as in his own dedicated Turkey book, finally printed in Antwerp in 1574.[11] Lorck eventually retired in some honour and estate to the Danish court at Copenhagen, where he received a pension. This was withdrawn in 1583, the same year that he produced an engraving of a woman of the Gambia.[12] Though his royal portrait of Frederick II – finished the previous year – should have kept him in good standing at court, it is popularly supposed that he again angered the Danish king by deserting the court in favour of more travels. It is playfully suggested (though entirely unproved) that at the Copenhagen docks he had jumped on an English or Portuguese ship and was off to test the charms of Araby or Barbary Coast.

Most of his best work – to the modern eye – comes direct from the sketchbooks and not from the finished images, though in their day these were widely sold and collected as useful source material by such painters as Rembrandt and Poussin. There would be a retrospective edition planned in 1619 though this was only finally realised with the Hamburg edition of 1626 and 1646. This volume became an essential item in any library – happily, William Beckford's old copy is available for inspection in the British Museum Prints and Drawings Department. But for the acquisitive and discerning eye of the English diarist and antiquarian John Evelyn, who collected the remnants of Lorck's drawings in 1641, very few of the original sketches would have survived. These would pass into the library at Stonor Park.[13] There was a renewed flurry of publication in the 1680s when the siege of Vienna created a fever for images of Turkish men. Lorck's portraits would be happily attributed to a whole new cast of contemporary Ottoman characters by unscrupulous publishers in need of illustrations.

Busbecq, loaded down with wagonloads of books, manuscripts, ancient coins and scholarly notes, finally trundled back to Vienna in

1562. The truce he had laboriously negotiated did not outlast his absence for more than two years.

His work as a scholar would, however, last forever. Amongst his bales of books were 240 Greek and Roman manuscripts, the first transcription of Augustus' boastful *Res Gestae* from an inscription in Ankara and Europe's first tulips and lilacs. He remained a valued and trusted servant of the Hapsburgs and, by 1574, was well established outside Paris with the remunerative but easy task of managing the estates of the Hapsburg Dowager Queen of France. Here he had time for his books and his scholarly friends and the leisure to polish his Ottoman notes. In 1589, a time when Lorck was well and truly out of the picture, a Latin edition of Busbecq's *Turkish Letters* was published in Paris.[14] The *Turkish Letters* have remained as fresh, charming, funny and informative as the day they were first printed. They take the literary form of four letters from Turkey to a friend, the fellow countryman and fellow Hapsburg diplomat Nicholas Michault, and the reader is flattered by being included within the circle of these two perfect Renaissance correspondents, who could quote Pliny, Polybius, Strabo and Plautus with the perfect assurance that his correspondent also knew well these cherished friends, and would also be able to appreciate the delicacy of his comparisons between Ottoman and Spanish domestic architecture and share his fury at the destruction of anything 'antique' – even if they be but copper coins – as well his delight in making fine copies of any inscriptions he passed on his travels. The letters were of course no more than a literary convention. It was, however, one that clearly had multiple uses. By inference there appears to be a series of missing letters between letters 2 and 3. The third letter is dated June 1560, and Busbecq writes in the first line, 'my colleagues have left me a long time ago ... with whom you are acquainted from my former letters' – no we are not! – but what a supremely elegant way of airbrushing away any unwanted memories. The whole long period when Lorck was in Istanbul from 1556 to 1559 is avoided by the pretence of missing letters from the set of correspondence.

The book was eventually translated into every major European language, cited as a role model by generation after generation of ambassadors, and mined by historians and travel-writers.[15] I was introduced to *Turkish Letters* by a living Busbecq, an English diplomat of high esteem though modest public rank, a connoisseur of Sung porcelain and alabasters from pre-Islamic southern Arabia. The last known copy of Lorck's Turkey book was destroyed during the British bombing of Hamburg in the Second World War. An English edition of Busbecq's *Turkish Letters* was recently reprinted in 2001.

Notes

1. See Graham Parry, *Hollar's England: A Mid-Seventeenth-Century View* (London: Russell, 1980).
2. See Edward Seymour Forster, trans., *The Turkish Letters of Ogier Ghiselin de Busbecq Imperial Ambassador at Constantinople, 1554–1562* (1927; rpt. Oxford: Clarendon, 1968), and J. M. Rogers and R. M. Ward, *Süleyman the Magnificent* (New York: Tabard, 1988).
3. Herman Hesse, *Narziss and Goldmund*, trans. Geoffrey Dunlop (Harmondsworth: Penguin, 1971).
4. For discussion of the date of composition, see Erik Fischer, *Melchior Lorck: Drawings from the Evelyn Collection at Stonor Park, England, and from the Department of Prints and Drawings, the Royal Museum of Fine Arts, Copenhagen.* (Copenhagen: Royal Museum, 1962), p. 24. See also Erik Fischer, 'Melchior Lorck, a Dane as Imperial Draughtsman in the 1550s', in *The Arabian Journey*, exhibition catalogue (Arhus: Prehistoric Museum Moesgard, 1996), and Peter Ward-Jackson, 'Some Rare Drawings by Melchior Lorichs', *Connoisseur* (March 1955), pp. 83–93. The *View* is also discussed and reproduced in a series of plates in Eugen Oberhummer, *Konstantinopel unter Sultan Süleyman dem Grossen Aufgenommen im Jahre 1559 durch Melchior Lorichs aus Flensburg* (Munich: Oldenbourg, 1902).
5. Reproduced in Oberhummer, *Konstantinopel*, plate XI.
6. See Fischer, *Melchior Lorck*, pp. 13, 17.
7. See Fischer's account of this document and Lorck's visit to Istanbul, *Melchior Lorck*, pp. 23–5.
8. Philip Mansel, ed., *The Turkish Letters by Ogier de Busbecq* (London: Sickle Moon, 2001), p. 4. My subsequent comments here on Busbecq are indebted to Mansel's historical introduction, and to the same author's *Constantinople: City of the Worlds Desire* (Harmondsworth: Penguin, 1997).
9. Reproduced in Fischer, *Melchior Lorck*, p. 82.
10. Mansel, ed., *Turkish Letters*, p. 36.
11. *Itinera Constantinopolitanum et Amasianum ab A. G. B … Ejusdem Busbequii De acie contra Turcam instuenda consilium* (Antwerp, 1574).
12. Reproduced in Fischer, *Melchior Lorck*, p. 127.
13. See Fischer, *Melchior Lorck*, pp. 7–9.
14. Augerius Gislenius Busbequii, *Legationis Turcicae Epistolae Quatuor* (Paris, 1589).
15. See Mansel's introduction to *Turkish Letters*.

5

The French Renaissance in Search of the Ottoman Empire

Philip Mansel

The Renaissance owed much to the influence of Greeks from Istanbul, who helped western Europeans rediscover the Greek classics – in particular the works of Plato – and other works, such as Ptolemy's geography, the base of all European maps of the Near East until the eighteenth century.[1] The Renaissance's debt to another group of people from Istanbul, namely European diplomats and travellers living there in the sixteenth century, is the subject of this essay.

Istanbul was one of the earliest and most important centres of European diplomacy: Venice and Genoa had permanent representatives there before 1453. Tuscany, Poland, Muscovy and the Holy Roman Emperor regularly sent envoys to the Ottoman Sultan in the sixteenth century. Far more than the republic of Turkey today, since the Ottoman Empire covered all the Balkans as well as most of the Middle East, it was a European power; unlike Ankara, the Ottoman capital of Istanbul was one of the great capitals of Europe.

The most important embassy in Istanbul was the French. For three centuries, from the arrival of the first ambassador, Jean de La Forest, in 1535, it functioned as Europe's window on the Islamic world. At first this might have seemed unlikely for no country had a stronger crusader tradition than France. The crusader states were largely founded by knights from France and Louis VII of France had gone on crusade in 1147. The hero of the French monarchy, Saint Louis, went to Jerusalem on one crusade and died on another in Tunis. Charles VIII had entered Naples in 1494 determined to prolong his victorious march through Italy by conquering the Ottoman Empire: he had bought hereditary rights to the Byzantine Empire from surviving Byzantine princes and had in his entourage the Ottoman claimant Djem, brother of Bayezid II. After his death in 1498, his successor, Louis XII, continuing the crusading tradition, sent a fleet to the Aegean and took the island of Lemnos in 1512.

However, centuries of French crusading tradition ended in a decade. Between 1515 and 1521, Charles of Austria, ruler of the Netherlands, inherited the thrones of Castile, Aragon, Naples and Sicily and was elected Holy Roman Emperor. Henceforth France was surrounded by a hostile world power. At the battle of Pavia in 1525, the Emperor Charles V captured Louis XII's successor, François I. Threatened on all sides by the House of Austria, François I turned to Süleyman the Magnificent. Messengers travelled between the court of France and 'the asylum of the universe'. In 1526, probably in response to a plea from the King's mother, Süleyman attacked Hungary, defeating its king at the battle of Mohaçs. The arrival of the first French ambassador in Istanbul in 1535 marked the beginning of the Franco-Ottoman alliance, which, until Bonaparte's invasion of Egypt in 1798, would be the only fixed point in the unending struggle for territory and hegemony between the different powers of Europe.

Some of the critical events in European history were influenced by what one French ambassador in Istanbul called 'the union of the lily and the crescent'. For example, Lutheranism was able to spread in the Holy Roman Empire partly because the Emperor Charles V was occupied in defending it from Ottoman attacks. William III was able to land in England in November 1688, because French armies, which might have helped James II or attacked William's base in the Netherlands, were attacking the Holy Roman Empire in order to relieve its armies' pressure on the Ottoman Empire after the failure of the siege of Vienna in 1683.

France and Spain swapped roles. Despite Philip II's purchase of Arab manuscripts for the library of the Escurial and use of Moorish decoration in his royal palace in Seville – proof that artistic tastes are often at odds with political views – the Spanish replaced the French monarchy as Europe's leading crusader. Spain was constantly at war with Muslim powers in North Africa, occupying Melilla, Oran and Tunis. It maintained a tax called the *cruzada*, and did not establish diplomatic relations with the Ottoman Empire until 1784. When Spaniards wrote travel books about the Ottoman Empire, they were generally traditional Christian accounts of a pilgrimage to Jerusalem.[2]

The French embassy in Istanbul, in contrast, concentrated on power and trade, not God. In 1543–4 and 1551–3, when France was at war with Charles V in Europe, the French embassy helped organise joint Franco-Ottoman naval operations in the Mediterranean. In 1543 part of the Ottoman navy wintered in the French port of Toulon. The French ambassador, Gabriel du Luels sieur d'Aramon, perhaps the most brilliant of the many nobles from Provence who filled this post, accompanied and gave military advice to the Sultan while he was on campaign against Persia between May 1548 and January 1550. The French tradition of political reporting, or propaganda, was already so well established that these events were commemorated in print. *Discours du Voyage de Venise à Istanbul, contenant la querele du Grand Seigneur contre le Sophy*, was written by Jacques Gassot, a *commissaire ordinaire des guerres du roi* in the entourage of the French ambassador, allegedly in Aleppo on 5 December 1548, and published in Paris in 1550. Anticipating and no doubt inspiring the great Austrian ambassador the Baron de Busbecq, who repeated some of Gassot's remarks in his own letters ten years later, Gassot particularly praised the discipline of Süleyman's army.[3]

Like many future western ambassadors in Istanbul, such as Lords Ponsonby and Stratford de Redcliffe in the nineteenth century, the French ambassador Aramon was more belligerent than the Ottoman government, even under Süleyman the Magnificent. He tried to provoke wars and to use Ottoman power to conquer Sicily for France. He wrote to Henri II after the Spaniards took the fort of Mahdiya near Tunis: 'Et pour toujours mieux acheminer les affaires je leur ai donné des nouvelles de la prise d'Afrique en la même sorte que les Imperiaux l'ont publié en estampe et leur ai fait voir ladite stampe pour les provoquer à entreprendre quelque vengeance.' In 1552 his desires were fulfilled when the Ottoman navy sacked Messina: however, due to difficulties of logistics and coordination, Franco-Ottoman naval cooperation never became truly effective.[4] Aramon's brilliant embassy to the Sublime Porte was long remembered in France. The famous Renaissance writer Brantôme later wrote: 'quelle gloire pour cet ambassadeur et pour sa nation française de tenir tel rang auprès du plus grand monarque du monde!'[5]

In addition to its role in politics and commerce, the French embassy was equally predominant in intellectual exploration. The French embassy helped make France, although geographically more distant, far better informed about the Ottoman Empire than its two neighbours, Venice and Poland. Between 1480 and 1609 France published twice as many books and editions of books on the Ottoman Empire as on the newly discovered continent of America – and more than on most Christian regions of Europe, except Italy.[6]

In general, French books analysed the Ottoman Empire as a great power rather than as a Muslim enemy.[7] This was due not only to the Franco-Ottoman alliance but also to a tradition of political commentary already well established in France. The French monarchy had inspired the first great secular, non-moralising political work in Europe, the memoirs of Philippe de Commynes, an adviser of Charles the Bold, Duke of Burgundy, who needed to justify his switch of loyalties to King Louis XI. They were published in Paris in 1524 – eight years before Machiavelli's *The Prince*.

Another reason was the growing intellectual curiosity characteristic of the Renaissance. The French traveller Nicolas de Nicolay wrote: 'la raison veut et la nature semble commander à l'homme de chercher, visiter, enquerir, savoir et connaître tous les êtres, toutes les parties et maisons de son universelle habitation.' He saw it as his purpose to describe 'les formes et les habitudes des personnes estranges', and to follow as a geographer in the footsteps of Plato, Strabo and Ptolemy.[8] Another French traveller, Pierre Belon, called his book, published in 1553, *Observations de plusieurs singularités*. Philippe du Fresne-Canaye referred to 'la honte de rester au logis' as one reason for his journey to Istanbul in 1573.[9]

Other French travellers who published books on the Ottoman Empire before 1580 included Jean Thenaud, who went there in 1530; Bertrand de La Borderie, who published *Discours du voyage de Constantinople* in Lyon in 1542; Antoine Geuffroy, whose 1542 *Description de la cour du Grand Turc* was translated into Latin, German, English and Spanish;[10] and the priest Jerome Maurand, who arrived in Istanbul in 1544. Perhaps the most unusual of these travellers was Guillaume Postel, who travelled in the Ottoman Empire in 1535 and 1549–50. Having returned with classical and Arabic manuscripts for the library of François I, his reward was an appointment as a *lecteur royal* in the Collège de France in 1538. A prolix and unreliable mystic, he thought of himself as a new prophet, believed that the Greek and Latin languages derived from Hebrew and advocated the reunion of Muslims, Jews and Christians under the aegis of the King of France.[11] Even this eccentric, however, was well informed about the Ottoman Empire. He noted that Turks hated the name of Turk and never used it in public acts; he praised the modesty, silence and reverence of Turks in mosques compared to Christians, who behaved like brigands in their churches. The Ottomans' attitude to dress was based on identity rather than fashion; 'et la chose qu'ils trouvent la plus étrange chez nous c'est que nous changeons si souvent d'habits différents'.[12]

It might seem strange that so many diplomats and travellers were able to wander around the Ottoman Empire, almost as easily as in Italy. One reason was the law and order maintained by the Ottoman authorities; another was the welcome they extended to foreigners. Postel explains how the system of interaction between foreigners and the Ottoman authorities functioned: 'il vous faut aussi exposer toutes les raisons au sanjak qui est capitaine du pays ou vous vous trouvez en lui faisant bonne révérence et quelque present; il vous donnera sauf conduit pour aller ou vous voudrez sans que quiconque vous en empêche.' Ottomans were suspicious of foreigners, but if you were a subject of a country allied to the Empire, it was easy to travel there.[13]

Pierre Belon travelled in part in the suite of two French ambassadors, Aramon and Fumel, leaving Venice in early 1547 and returning there in 1549. He visited the ruins of Troy and Nicomedia, Mount Athos – where he found 6,000 monks – Rhodes, Egypt, Jerusalem, Damascus, Lebanon and Konya, and published a book titled *Les Observations de plusieurs singularitez et de choses memorables observées en Grèce, Asie, Judée, Egypte, Arabie et autres pays estranges* in 1553. Constantly referring to Greek and Latin authors such as Herodotus, Strabo and Arrian, his book was an attempt at demystification. He wrote of Turks: 'Ils ne font plaisir sinon pour argent comptant et sont tyrants à l'argent plus que autres gens au monde', but also praised their modesty, cleanliness, sobriety and valour. His book, which had three editions in three years and was later republished in Antwerp, provided an encyclopaedic catalogue of the Ottoman Empire's trees, fruit, herbs, gardens, fish, birds, wild animals – including giraffes and chameleons – food, drink, music and antiquities.[14] Belon was later called the father of French zoology. Like many subsequent travellers he sang for his supper and praised the hospitality of his ambassador, Monsieur d'Aramon, whose house was open to all, including Turks. They appreciated French wine, according to Belon, 'd'autant plus doucement qu'il leur est etroitement proihibée et defendu par leur loi'.[15]

For Belon, Ayasofya was finer than the Pantheon and the site of Istanbul was incomparable: 'La ville de Istanbul est située en un lieu le plus à propos pour la grandeur d'un prince que nulle autre ville de tout le monde.' Also, like Gassot, he praised 'la grande continence et obéissance des gens de guerre du Turc'.[16] The author of one of the first works on the pyramids, published in Paris in Latin in 1553, Belon wrote: 'ne deplaisent aux ouvrages et antiquiteés romaines elles ne tiennent rien de la grandeur et orgueil des pyramides.'[17] He recorded the career mechanisms of the Empire, the frequency with which *sanjaks* and pashas were changed, and the absence of nobility or hereditary property: 'le plus grand honneur et bien que puisse avoir un homme en Turquie c'est de s'avouer esclave du Turc.' He also wrote, generally scornfully, on the Qur'an, Muhammad's views on hell and paradise, wives, slaves, circumcision and schools.[18]

Another French writer who travelled with the ambassador d'Aramon to Istanbul in 1547, partly in order to find manuscripts for the King's library, and wrote the finest account of the destruction of the classical antiquities of Istanbul, monument by monument, under the Ottomans, *De topographia Constantinopolis*, was Pierre Gilles. In all, he stayed eight years; for a time, by his own account, he even served in the Ottoman army. He based his work on a description of the Bosphorus by Denis of Byzantium, which he had discovered; he also discovered the *Notitia dignitatum*, listing the offices of the Byzantine Empire. His account was much imitated by subsequent writers, including Du Fresne-Canaye and Pietro della Valle. Gilles was a dedicated classicist, lamenting both the destructive violence of the barbarians, i.e. the Turks, and the passive ignorance of the Greeks.[19]

Probably sent by the King to study Ottoman fortifications, Nicolas de Nicolay travelled in the Ottoman Empire between July 1551 and July 1552, and after his return to France was named *géographe ordinaire du roi*. In Lyons in 1567–8 he published, with some of the first semi-accurate illustrations of Ottoman costumes, *Les quatre premiers livres des navigations et pérégrinations orientales*. His book contains lengthy descriptions of Algiers, Malta, Tripoli, Cythera and Chios – where, anticipating many subsequent writers, he wrote women were 'plutôt nymphes ou déesses que femmelles ou filles mortelles'.[20] In Istanbul he described both low life and the power structure: eunuchs, baths, pederasts, lesbians, women's clothes, the slave market, doctors, lascivious Sufis, the ambassadors 'qui font la residence tant pour entretenir les ligues et confederations d'amitié qu'ils ont avec le Grand Seigneur que pour le trafique et commerce de marchandise qu'ils exercent là et par toutes les autres parties du Levant'.[21]

Janissaries, he noted, like the Praetorian guards of the Roman emperors, wanted to 'seigneurer leur maître'. Representing the security angle of the interaction between Ottomans and Europeans, Janissaries guarded, and were paid by, foreign ambassadors in order to protect them from *l'insolence turque*. In quarrels between Ottomans and westerners, the Ottoman government often sided with foreign ambassadors rather than with their own officials. One *sanjak* who insulted the French ambassador's son was dismissed.[22] Belon had found Jews established wherever there were Turks, and used them as interpreters:[23] Nicolay, however, hated Jews – although he noted that in Istanbul they were allowed to print books in every language except Arabic and Turkish.[24] Like many travel writers, Nicolay often used previously published books rather than his own observations as sources for his text. Although he was in Istanbul in 1551, he mentions none of the magnificent mosques built since 1530, no doubt because none of the books he was gutting did so. French authors spread information about the Ottoman Empire in Europe as well as France: by 1580 there had been two French re-editions of Nicolay, and translations into German, Italian, Flemish and English.

By the time of the publication of Nicolay's work, certain *topoi* or clichés about the Ottoman Empire had entered the mainstream of western travel writing. All say that an open purse was the key to success in the Ottoman Empire. Travellers and diplomats should close their purses only when they leave.[25] At the same time, travellers also, in contradiction, admit that the hospitality of the khans built along the main trade routes was free and admirable.[26] By the regularity of the daily calls to prayer, it was generally agreed, muezzins served as human watches; most travellers found no difficulty in visiting mosque interiors.[27] Turks' love of baths and cleanliness aroused admiration and surprise.[28] Local Christians were generally despised as hypocritical, decadent and drunk.[29] Turks were brutal, grasping and inflexible.[30] Reflecting their impregnation by classical literature, western travellers constantly refer obliquely to Plutarch, Livy and Herodotus.[31] Nicolay gives three times more space to the past than the present of the island of Cythera.[32] Travellers often repeat the same errors, for example about the decoration of obelisks in the hippodrome, because they rely on classical authors rather than their own eyes.[33]

The long tradition of hypocritical lust with which western travellers regarded eastern bodies had already started. Gassot and Nicolay describe with envious precision naked female slaves and their inspection by prospective purchasers.[34] Nicolay lamented lesbians' practices in the *hammam* and Persians who 'sont tellement adonnés au détestable péché contre nature qu'ils ne la tiennent à honte ni vergogne' and had special places for its practice. Michel Baudier, in *Histoire générale du serail et de la cour du grand seigneur* of 1624, said that 18 out of 20 Ottoman sultans abandoned themselves to the love of boys and used them as women.[35]

A more authentic travel book – although it too relied a lot on Pierre Gilles – was Philippe Du Fresne-Canaye's account of his *Voyage du Levant* in February–June 1573, probably written soon after his return.[36] He was a Huguenot who preferred to stay away from France after the Massacre of Saint Bartholomew's Eve – although this did not prevent him travelling with one of the most successful of all French ambassadors, the Bishop of Dax. (In the sixteenth century, though not later, it was possible for a Catholic bishop to be ambassador to the Ottoman Sultan.) The bishop had secured Ottoman support for the King of France's brother to become King of either Algiers or Poland, and a guarantee of 200 Ottoman ships for French wars against Spain: at times, the Ottoman government appears less as the terror of Christendom than as the auxiliary of France. Du Fresne-Canaye was more concerned with power and ceremony than his predecessors. He describes caravans; the route from Dubrovnik to Istanbul; the conditions of diplomatic life; the *pompe merveilleuse* of the Turks; their silence in the palace, which was even more impressive than their costumes; the women of Pera; Turks' love of flowers; the Bosphorus; the hippodrome; the bazaar; the Orthodox patriarchate; the arsenal and the departure of the Ottoman fleet, sped on its way out of the Golden Horn by weeping wives and lovers.[37] Selim II is described as a hopeless drunk: 'les joues gonflées et gâtées par la boisson'.[38] The Ottoman Empire was judged with revolted admiration: 'le Turc est un destructeur et un devastateur non seulement des empires et des couronnes antiques mais aussi des lois, usages, coutumes et même des noms des peuples soumis. Il sera gouverné non par des idées philosophiques mais au moyen d'une discipline tel que jamais elle n'a été observée que par des turcs ... et il gouverne de telle façon tant de peoples si divers de langue, de religion et de costume qu'il semble que tout son empire ne soit qu'une seule et meme cité, tant est grande la paix et l'obéissance qui règne dans toutes ses parties.'[39]

That same year as Du Fresne-Canaye's visit, Antoine Regnaut published his *Discours du voyage d'outre mer* (1573), a traditional account of a pilgrimage to the Holy Land. Written from a completely different point of view, it pours scorn on those who wrote travel books out of exaltation, to win respect.[40] With this exception, until Chateaubriand's famous *Itinéraire de Paris à Jerusalem* of 1811, other French travel books described Turks, Greeks, Arabs, Egyptians and different provinces of the Empire, such as Armenia or Trebizond,[41] at much greater length than the Holy Land. Jerusalem, if visited, was a stop on the journey, not its destination. André Thevet, who had also travelled in the entourage of the French ambassador, and wrote *Cosmographie du Levant* (1554), openly stated that he preferred to go to Istanbul than to Jerusalem. Ambassador d'Aramon's secretary, Jean Chesneau, who later converted to Protestantism, in a book partly culled from Gassot, even says, 'il n'est point besoin d'aller en Jerusalem pour trouver Jesus Christ'. Power marginalised pilgrimage.[42]

Indeed, the power of the Empire and the splendour of the city of Istanbul dominate these works. Even more than in accounts of the Spanish conquests of Mexico or Peru, across barriers of language, race, religion and distance, Europeans and Ottomans spoke a common language of monarchy. Süleyman the Magnificent was often represented as the paradigm of the virtuous and successful sovereign: his habit of inspecting ships or the city of Istanbul in disguise was considered especially praiseworthy.[43] The magnificence and majesty, the 'bel ordre et silence', of his Friday procession to prayers were described at length by Thevet and Du Fresne-Canaye, as the *selamliks* of subsequent sultans would be by all European visitors until the fall of Abdulhamid in 1909.[44] No one denied that the Ottoman Empire could put on a good show. Belon, Chesneau, Postel and Busbecq all praise the discipline and order in the Ottoman army – which had 'la meilleure police et obéisance du monde'.[45] The great Austrian ambassador Ogier Ghiselin de Busbecq – whose letters, though written to his masters in Vienna, were published in Paris – praised the Ottoman Empire as a means to criticise the social structure of his own country. Transforming the Ottoman Empire into a vision of meritocracy, at times he sounds like Robespierre making a speech in the French National Assembly:

> Dans toute cette troupe de courtisans l'on ne connaissait personne que par ses virtus et ses belles actions. La naissance n'y apportait point de différence, parce que tout le monde y est honoré par la considération de la charge qu'il exerce ... C'est donc dans cet Etat ou les dignités et les charges sont les justes recompenses des mérites; et que la lacheté, l'injustice et tous les vices étant déshonorés toutes choses fleurissent et les frontières de leur Empire s'étendent tous les jours plus avant; au lieu que dans nos royaumes les moeurs sont tous corrompues ; la vertu ne trouve plus personne qui la considère et la naissance passe pour l'unique règle de la distribution des honneurs.[46]

Such praise – with which few Ottoman witnesses of the infanticides and civil wars of the 1550s within Süleyman the Magnificent's court and family, would have agreed – has rather more to do with Latin rhetorical traditions, Renaissance debates over virtue and merit, and Busbecq's equivocal status as a bastard within his own society, than with Ottoman realities. Another sign of the close association of the Ottoman Empire and power was that Spaniards called Muslims *turcos* rather than *Moros* – although they had Muslim Arabs as neighbours, living among them until 1609. The power of the Ottoman Empire outweighed the proximity of Muslim Arabs.[47]

In the sixteenth century French travellers found it particularly easy to use the language of monarchy, since most were in the personal service of the King of France and his family. André Thevet travelled in the Ottoman Empire under the protection of the Cardinal de Guise.[48] Like Nicolas de Nicolay, Charles Richer, author of *Des coutumes et manière de vivre des Turcs*

(Paris, 1540), was a *valet de chambre* of François I, to whom he dedicated his book.[49] The two ambassadors, Aramon and Fumel, were both *gentil-shommes de la chambre du roy*.[50] Gassot had been in the service of François I's second wife, Eleanor. Jean Chesneau became *premier maître d'hotel* and *intendant* of Renée de France, Duchess of Ferrara, a daughter of Louis XII.[51] Postel was a protégé of François I and his sister, the poet queen Marguerite of Navarre. Jean Palerne wrote an account of his travels in the Ottoman Empire in 1581, published in Lyons in 1606, as *Pérégrinations ... où il est traité de plusieurs singularitez et antiquités, remarqués et provinces d'Egypte, Arabie deserte et pierreuse, Terre Saincte, Surie, Natolie, Grece, et plusieurs isles tant de de la mer mediterranée que Archipelague. Avec la manière de vivre des Mores et Turcs, et de leur religion. Ensemble un bref discours ... à Istanbul.* He was a secretary of the most anti-Spanish member of the French royal family, King Henri III's brother the Duc d'Anjou, to whom, for his part, Postel dedicated *Des histoires orientales*, saying that Anjou came from the first blood in the world, the oldest and noblest family except that of Jesus Christ, connected to Noah and the old Etruscans.[52] Thus one of the most resplendently Christian monarchies in Europe, whose king, crowned and anointed at Rheims, considered himself the *fils ainé de l'Eglise*, was a pro-Ottoman and even pro-Islamic institution – certainly more so than the Third, Fourth or Fifth French Republics.

In conclusion, thanks to books and politics, the Ottoman Empire became more familiar in France than most of Christian Europe. The French Renaissance had its own dynamic, powered by the political needs and cultural interests of the French monarchy. It was not only independent of the Italian Renaissance but, at least in the domain of research into the Ottoman Empire, it is superior. In comparison to the French books which have been discussed – which are only the tip of the iceberg[53] – Italy produced relatively few works: for example, Spandugino's *Petit Traité de l'origine des Princes des Turcqz* (Paris, 1519); Giovio's *Commentario delle cose de Turchi* (Florence, 1529); Bernardo Ramberti's *Libri tre delle cose de Turchi* (Venice, 1539); Menavino's *Trattato de costumi e vita de Turchi* (Florence, 1548). The French political and literary interest in the Ottoman Empire helps explain why, by 1620, French trade with the Ottomans had become, as it long remained, a third of all French maritime trade: in the 1660s the Chevalier d'Arvieux, French consul in Saida, called the Levant 'our Indies'. The French–Ottoman relationship was so stable that until 1914 – with the exception of the interlude 1798–1806 following Bonaparte's invasion of Egypt – France consistently worked for the protection of the Ottoman Empire against Austria and Russia.

The role of French writers in celebrating the French–Ottoman alliance shows that, at least in this case, the pen rather than being mightier than the sword was its servant. It was a Frenchman, Antoine Galland, who had stayed in the *Palais de France* in Istanbul, who was the first to translate the *1001 Nights* into a European language – long before the first French translation of Shakespeare. And it was prints and pictures by Jean Baptise Vanmour, an artist in the service of the French ambassador, the Comte de Ferriol, that were the source for all the *turqueries* of Europe in the eighteenth century. The French Foreign Minister, the Comte de Vergennes, himself a former ambassador in Istanbul, and Louis XVI advocated a plan of regeneration for the Ottoman Empire in the 1780s and sent it its first foreign military and naval instructors; the printing press of Louis XVI's brother, the Comte de Provence, published the greatest of all foreign works on the Ottoman Empire, the *Tableau général de l'Empire Ottoman* in three volumes (Paris, 1787–1820).

The French alliance with the Ottoman Empire helps explain why Paris, long the centre of Arabic and Turkish studies, was the site of Europe's first school of oriental languages, established on earlier foundations in 1796, and of its first Asiatic Society, founded in 1822, and why Paris received the first students from the Muslim Middle East – Greeks had long attended the University of Padua – at the Egyptian educational mission in 1826. In Europe the demands of the balance of power were more important than the division between Christianity and Islam.

Notes

1. Alexandra Merle, *Le Miroir Ottoman: Une image politique des hommes dans la literature géographique espagnole et français (XVIe–XVIIe siècles)* (Paris: Sorbonne, 2003), p. 36.
2. Merle, *Miroir*, p. 55.
3. Merle, *Miroir*, p. 171; and see Philippe Du Fresne-Canaye, *Le Voyage du Levant* (Paris, 1986), p. 127.
4. Throughout, I have quoted Nicolay's *Navigations* from Stéphane Yerasimos, ed., *Dans l'empire de Soliman le Magnifique* (Paris, 1989), pp. 14–17; hereafter cited as Nicolay, *Navigations*.
5. Cited by Frédéric Tinguely, *L'écriture du Levant à la Renaissance. Enquête sur les voyageurs français dans l'empire de Soliman le Magnifique* (Geneva: Droz, 2000), p. 19.
6. Merle, *Miroir*, p. 39.
7. Merle, *Miroir*, p. 54.
8. Merle, *Miroir*, pp. 61, 65.
9. Du Fresne-Canaye, *Voyage*, p. 1.
10. Merle, *Miroir*, p. 249.

11. Tinguely, *L'écriture*, p. 210; Guillaume Postel, *Des histoires orientales*, ed. Jacques Rollet (Istanbul, 1999), pp. xx, xxv.
12. Postel, *Histoires*, pp. 40, 125–6.
13. Postel, *Histoires*, p. 127.
14. Pierre Belon, *Voyage au Levant 1553*, ed. Alexandra Merle (Paris, 2001), pp. 35–7, 121, 130, 322, 386, 506.
15. Belon, *Voyage*, p. 179.
16. Belon, *Voyage*, pp. 221, 259.
17. Belon, *Voyage*, pp. 280, 310.
18. Belon, *Voyage*, p. 466.
19. Tinguely, *L'écriture*, pp. 28n, 97, 98n, 103, 105, 111.
20. Nicolay, *Navigations*, p. 108.
21. Nicolay, *Navigations*, pp. 138, 144.
22. Nicolay, *Navigations*, pp. 158, 160; Du Fresne-Canaye, *Voyage*, pp. 80, 83.
23. Belon, *Voyage*, pp. 215, 234.
24. Nicolay, *Navigations*, p. 33.
25. Merle, *Miroir*, pp. 173–4.
26. Tinguely, *L'écriture*, pp. 250–1.
27. Du Fresne-Canaye, *Voyage*, pp. 99, 101n; and see Tinguely, *L'écriture*, p. 159n.
28. Merle, *Miroir*, p. 204.
29. Tinguely, *L'écriture*, pp. 181–3.
30. Merle, *Miroir*, pp. 187–8.
31. Tinguely, *L'écriture*, p. 94.
32. Merle, *Miroir*, p. 112.
33. Tinguely, *L'écriture*, p. 131.
34. Tinguely, *L'écriture*, p. 172.
35. Nicolay, *Navigations*, p. 215; Tinguely, *L'écriture*, pp. 199, 207.
36. Du Fresne-Canaye, *Voyage*, p. xii.
37. Du Fresne-Canaye, *Voyage*, pp. 59–60, 64, 87, 105, 108, 136, 141.
38. Du Fresne-Canaye, *Voyage*, pp. 127–8.
39. Du Fresne-Canaye, *Voyage*, pp. 31, 147.
40. Tinguely, *L'écriture*, p. 56.
41. Tinguely, *L'écriture*, pp. 71, 75.
42. Tinguely, *L'écriture*, pp. 37, 41n, 45, 47, 66.
43. Merle, *Miroir*, pp. 115, 191; Tinguely, *L'écriture*, p. 186.
44. Tinguely, *L'écriture*, pp. 137, 230.
45. Tinguely, *L'écriture*, pp. 230–1, 234–5.
46. Merle, *Miroir*, p. 214.
47. Merle, *Miroir*, p. 201.
48. Tinguely, *L'écriture*, p. 61.
49. Merle, *Miroir*, p. 255.
50. Belon, *Voyage*, p. 229.
51. Tinguely, *L'écriture*, pp. 19n, 20.
52. Postel, *Histoires*, pp. 3, 5.
53. See, for instance, the extensive but by no means exhaustive 'Bibliography of Pamphlets relating to the Turks, 1481–1660', which appears as an appendix to Clarence Dana Rouillard, *The Turk in French History, Thought, and Literature (1520–1660)* (Paris: Boivin, 1940), pp. 646–65.

6
Petrarch and 'that Mad Dog Averroës'

Robert Irwin

In 1994 the Egyptian filmmaker Yusuf Chahin released the film *al-Muhajir* (The Emigrant). It presented a lightly disguised version of the story of Joseph in Egypt and, since Joseph is a prophet of Islam, Egypt's Islamists promptly attacked Chahin for blasphemy and accused him of pro-Zionism. The film was banned and Chahin was prosecuted. He was found innocent, but it was a close-run thing. 1994 was also the year that Naguib Mahfouz was stabbed in the neck by an Islamist – an act of violence that effectively ended his long writing career.

Chahin's next film, *Destiny* (1997), was a reply to the Islamists and a denunciation of fundamentalist intolerance. Set in twelfth-century Cordova, the film portrays the attempts of a sinister, killjoy group of Islamists to murder Averroës, the famous philosopher and commentator on Aristotle, and to destroy all his writings. The film ends with Averroës vindicated and bigotry defeated. The Sultan recognises that Averroës was right all along, and, though this happens too late to stop the bonfire of the philosopher's books this hardly matters, as ideas can never be killed. Cordova's golden age, which depends on tolerance and openness to new thoughts and discoveries, has been prolonged a little longer.[1] The action scenes and the deliver-a-message-about-hope-and-tolerance scenes are happily interspersed with song-and-dance episodes, giving *Destiny* something of the feel of a musical. The not-so-stuffy Averroës enjoys a good knees-up as much as anyone.

It had seemed natural to Chahin to choose Averroës – or more correctly in Arabic, Ibn Rushd – as the philosopher of free thought and free speech. This image of Averroës as the champion *par excellence* of such things was widespread throughout the nineteenth- and early twentieth-century Arab world. The belated cult of Averroës was a feature of the *Nahda*, or renaissance, that took place at that time. This cult depended heavily on Ernest Renan's famous *Averroes et l'Averroism* (1861). This was later translated into Arabic by Farah Antun (1874–1922), a well-known Lebanese writer and translator. Antun also wrote an essay on Averroës, arguing that 'Islam had destroyed the philosophic spirit'.[2] Renan was long regarded in the Arab world as the European spokesman for science and secularism and hence as being at the height of modernity. I shall come back to Renan's influential book later.

The historical Averroës had no time for song-and-dance acts. It is said that he took only two days off from philosophy in his life – the day he got married and the day his father died. Averroës was born in Cordova in 1126 and died in Marrakesh in 1198. He wrote commentaries on all Aristotle's major works except the *Politics*, but as a substitute for the missing book he produced a commentary on Plato's *Republic*. In general, he defended the role of philosophy in the understanding of religion. He reserved philosophical reasoning for an intellectual elite, whereas the myths of religion were directed at the understanding of the masses. The Prophet Muhammad was himself a philosopher, though one who made use of myth and legend to speak to the simple among his followers. The high status that Averroës accorded to reason was attacked by the famous theologian and Sufi al-Ghazali in *Tahafut al-falsafa*, to which Averroës replied with *Tahafut al-tahafut*.[3]

In his translations and commentaries, he made partially successful attempts to free Aristotle of his Neoplatonic accretions, in particular the essences and the Platonic hierarchy of emanations with which Ibn Sina (or Avicenna) had lumbered his version of Aristotle. Averroës was also largely successful in distinguishing the authentic works of Aristotle from the pseudepigrapha.

After the death of his Almohad patron, Abu Yaqub Yusuf (d.1184), Averroës had indeed been persecuted and his books were burnt in the public square. Contrary to the suggestions of Chahin's film, the campaign of persecutions seems to have been pretty successful and Averroës had few or no heirs in the Islamic world. The great tradition of philosophy in Andalusia and the Maghrib just about came to an end at the end of the twelfth century and there were no first-rate philosophers at the later Nasrid court in Granada. And considering the Mashriq, or eastern Islamic world, neither Averroës or Ibn Rushd even rated a mention by Ibn Khallikan in his great biographical dictionary. Very few people read Averroës's books. There was no Averroist movement in the thirteenth-, fourteenth- or fifteenth-century Islamic world.

But there was what looks like an Averroist movement in medieval Christendom during those centuries. Michael Scot's translations into

Latin were instrumental in popularisation of Averroës. He was being studied in Paris by the 1230s and 1240s. By the thirteenth century various leading philosopher-theologians, including Albertus Magnus and Aquinas, had attacked certain errors, even blasphemies in Averroism. In 1277 Averroism was included in a long list of dangerous doctrines that were condemned by the Chancellor of the University of Paris. Averroists were accused of believing in the eternity of the world (i.e. that it had never been created). The soul was similarly eternal. Also they believed, or rather were accused of believing, in the unity of all human intellect (monopsychism) and denied the existence of demons. They claimed that it was possible to achieve perfect happiness in this world. They espoused the notion of the double truth – that is, that a thing could be philosophically true but theologically false, and vice versa. The Averroists were deemed to be free thinkers, even secret atheists.[4] Averroës himself was later libelled by being described as the author of the notorious treatise, *De tribus impostoribus*, a legendary black book that treated of the charlatanry of Moses, Jesus and Muhammad.[5]

The notion of double truth functioned at several levels. Siger of Brabant, one of the most famous or notorious of the Averroists, argued not that Averroës was necessarily right about the unity of intellect, but that Averroës's reading of Aristotle on this point was correct. Averroism tended to be popular among the Ghibellines (those who supported the Emperor against the Pope). It may be for this reason that Dante, who was an ardent Ghibelline, in his *Divine Comedy* put Averroës in Limbo with the virtuous pagans, while he put Siger in paradise.[6] Dante's *De Monarchia* was burnt as an Averroist text after his death. However, as we shall see, there is a problem with this interpretation of what Siger stood for.

This so far is the simple story of Averroism in the West, but things are never so simple. Our picture of the rise of Aristotelianism and Averroism in medieval Christendom is one that was first conjured up for us by Ernest Renan (1832–92), a figure whom Edward Said mistakenly believed to be the leading nineteenth-century Orientalist (though Said's knowledge of what Renan actually wrote was rather skimpy). Renan had studied for the priesthood, pursuing Hebrew and Arabic in the furtherance of Biblical studies. His Hebrew seems to have been pretty good, as was his Latin, but his Arabic was extremely poor as he himself admitted. In the course of his studies at the seminary of St Sulpice in Paris, he lost his faith and he went on to become France's most famous atheist. He wrote the novelistic *Vie de Jesus*, a biography of Jesus the man (and this was also translated into Arabic by Antun). He was an extremely prolific writer on an almost limitless range of subjects. He had an elegantly expressed opinion on everything.[7] Albert Hourani has written of 'that extraordinary style, limpid, moving and not quite serious'.[8] He was the apostle of Comteanism, preaching that Europe was inevitably in the process of moving from an Age of Religion to the Age of Science. The way Renan thought about other cultures was shaped by his thorough grounding in the Germanic science of philology. As he saw it, the Semites were limited by their linguistic structures. Semites, including most obviously Jews and Arabs, were good at generating monotheisms, but were more or less incapable of the more elaborate reasoning necessary for philosophy, science and mysticism. Those were fields in which Aryans excelled. So it was that Persians and Berbers did most of medieval Islam's philosophical and scientific thinking, while Sufism was an import into Islam from other cultures. 'What is Arabic in this so-called Arab science?' asked Renan, 'The language, nothing but the language ... Is it at least Muhammedan? Has Muhammedanism been in any way a support for those rational studies?' Renan answered himself: in no way. Here there was certainly a message for nineteenth-century Muslims. They would achieve science and a civil society only by freeing themselves from the shackles of their language and religion. The Muslim world was prevented from contributing to the advance of science by 'a circle of iron'. But Renan's real target was the Catholic Church, and the subtext was that Europe also had to advance further by casting off the old Semitic thrall.[9]

All this by way of a background to the general drift of Renan's thought. At the beginning of his academic career, at a time when he was thinking hard about the destiny of the human soul in an atheist's universe, he researched the thesis that he successfully defended in 1852 and later published as *Averroès et l'averroïsm*, in two fat, footnote-laden volumes.[10] This superficially impressive treatise sought to trace the impact of the great Arab philosopher on medieval scholasticism and to show how his writings created in the West a school of Averroists who were free thinkers and sometimes crypto-atheists. These men denied the possibility of the supernatural and sought to undermine the authority of the Church. This school eventually acquired an informal centre at the University of Padua, which Renan stylishly described as the *quartier latin* of the Venetian Republic. There were still representatives of the Averroist tradition to be found in Padua in the seventeenth century. As long as Averroism's opponent was blinkered pietism, it flourished. What doomed it was the rise of science, as scientific thinking offered a better alternative than Averroism to the old monkish ideas. As for the Islamic world, Arab philosophy was just Greek philosophy in disguise. Neither philosophy nor science was fully part of an Arab culture that, in essence, consisted of the monotheistic religion and the language in which that religion was expounded. Averroës's death marked the end of the progress of Muslim culture. The rise of the West was concurrent with the stagnation of Islam. Six centuries of questing uncertainty were to be followed by six centuries of bigoted certainty in the Muslim lands.

All this has the coherence of a good story. There are, however, several problems with it. Since his Arabic was poor, Renan's thesis relied excessively on Latin and Hebrew sources. So rather than quote Averroës directly from the Arabic, he relied on bad medieval Latin translations and these he translated into rather elegant French. The leading Orientalist Ignaz Goldziher (who was ignored by Said) was swift to point out that Renan had failed to use the Arabic texts of both al-Ghazali's pietistic attack on the philosophy of Averroës and Averroës's response to al-Ghazali.[11] Renan's main source on Averroës as one can see from the footnotes was a Latin translation of the *Tahafut al-Tahafut*, even though, as Renan himself noted, that translation was very bad and actually misrepresented the philosopher. Renan knew almost nothing about the main works of the Arab philosopher and neglected the overwhelming importance of the *Sharia*, or Islamic religious law, in the thought of Averroës. Averroës's allegedly cynical notion about the interchangeability of faiths was Renan's fantasy – just the sort of thing he would have wished to find in his sources. Renan had envisaged Averroës as an early version of Renan – a polymath who popularised the research of others and who was incapable of doing new things: 'He was one of those latecomers who compensate for their lack of originality by the encyclopaedic character of their work, commenting because it is too late to create ...'[12] It was important to deny both the originality and the Islamic spirituality of Averroës, and it was easy to do so by ignoring most of what he had written. As Raymond Schwab has suggested in *La Renaissance Orientale*, in the nineteenth century Orientalism became a refuge for clergymen who had lost their faith.[13]

Another misleading feature of Renan's version of the history of Islamic philosophy is that it is not true that history came to an end with Averroës, nor is it true that Ghazali and a bigoted crew of Islamists had decisively triumphed over speculative thought. It is true that Averroës was the last major thinker in the western Islamic lands, but other kinds of philosophy were to flourish in the eastern Islamic lands, particularly in Iran, during the fifteenth, sixteenth and seventeenth centuries: the names Nasir Tusi, Mir Damad and Mulla Sadra come to mind. Avicenna, though not Averroës, had plenty of intellectual heirs.[14]

The idea that there was a school of Latin freethinkers and atheists also seems doubtful. There is no evidence in Europe of an Averroist school of thought as such. Renan had combed Jewish and Latin sources to produce a composite portrait of medieval rationalism. The evidence for Siger having been an Averroist rather than Aristotelian is slim indeed.[15] Renan believed that the Averroist medical school, centred in Padua, despite its various faults, was the intellectual ancestor of modern science. He was one of the earliest scholars to study medieval science and philosophy and created the legend that the West's knowledge of Aristotle came via translations from Arabic. In fact, most of it came directly from the Greek.[16] His book is not so much a serious study of Islamic philosophy as a fable about the rise of rationalism in the West. Arabists who later worked on Averroës found Renan's view that the Muslim philosopher was a secret atheist to be unfounded. Moreover, Padua did not become Venice's intellectual quarter until the fifteenth century. For a large part of the medieval period, it was estranged from Venice or actually at war with it. And Bologna, not Padua, was the centre of Averroism.[17]

So where does Petrarch fit into all this? Petrarch was not an Arabist or a philosopher. And that perhaps is the point. Francesco Petrarch is a leading figure in both Italian and Latin literature.[18] He was born in 1304 in Arezzo and died in 1374 in Arqua, a village outside Padua. He became famous for his *Canzoniere*, love poems in Italian addressed to Laura, but also for his Latin epistles and such polemics as *Contra medicum quondam* and *De suis ipsius et multorum ignorantia*. He had a limited interest in the Middle East. He had written in Latin a short guide for pilgrims going to the Holy Land, though had not been there himself. However, he ransacked the Bible and his favourite Latin texts in order to draw attention to sites that would be of interest to humanist antiquarians en route to Jerusalem.[19] The Arabs do not feature in this work of classical piety. It also seems that he owned a manuscript vocabulary of Latin, Persian and Cuman (studied by Klaproth), which he had presumably purchased from a Genoese merchant who had been trading in the Black Sea.[20]

Petrarch's Latin polemics are key documents in the history of Renaissance humanism and it is due to some of their contents that Renan made him a key witness for the prosecution. Petrarch did not like what he had heard of Averroës and expressed his dislike quite vigorously, referring to Averroës as '*illem canem rabidum*'.[21] For Renan, Petrarch was the first modern man and by the same token the first person in the Middle Ages to feel real empathy with Antiquity. What on earth had Petrarch got against Averroës? What had Averroës done to him that he should feel so strongly? According to Renan, Petrarch reacted against the writings of Averroës because 'they represented the Arab spirit – that is to say fatalism and incredulity'.[22] So one can see, I think, that when it suited his overall vision of history, Renan presented Averroës as the spokesman of free thought, but when Renan's mind was running on other matters, Averroës became the spokesman of benighted fatalism.

The sources of Petrarch's hostility were many and various. First, Averroës was a Muslim, whereas Petrarch was an extremely pious Christian who sought to model himself on the pattern of St Augustine of Hippo. Secondly, Petrarch hated doctors and medicine. It seems to me that in medieval times this was such a reasonable prejudice as not to be a prejudice at all, since medieval doctors mostly did more harm than good. Academic medicine in medieval Europe, as opposed to folk medicine, was based above all on Avicenna's great medical encyclopaedia, the *Qanun*.[23] The main thing to note about this learned work is that it is mostly nonsense from start to finish, based on false ideas about how the human body and nature more generally work. Avicenna's medical treatise would admittedly be very useful to anyone wishing to diagnose and treat lycanthropy. Werewolfism most commonly occurs around February. Werewolves tend to have a yellow complexion, sores on their legs, a dry tongue and lurk around cemeteries. The condition is treated by bleeding, moisturising baths and meals of whey, followed by laxatives. If all this does not work, then the werewolf's head should be cauterised.[24] Averroës's medical concepts did not differ significantly from those of Avicenna, as Averroës was not an original thinker in that field. The learned tradition of medicine in the West was slavishly dependent on the Arab writings, but Petrarch was not having any of it. Quite apart from the physicians' dependence on the infidel Arab material, their practice of inspecting urine samples was disgusting and Petrarch reproached the physicians, saying, 'Your own wasted pallor comes from the chamber-pots you study every day.'[25]

Thirdly, Arab medicine was closely linked with astrology, and Averroism accepted astrology. Petrarch, following St Augustine, regarded astrology as an abominable superstition that denied human free will and perhaps even put limits on God's absolute power.[26] Fourthly, Petrarch was a fastidious stylist. Unlike many of the succeeding generations of humanist scholars, he knew no Greek. Yet he was confident that Aristotle could not have written as badly as his translators and commentators had made it seem. More generally, he hated the barbarous Latin used by contemporaries working in philosophy and medicine and their occasional use of transliterated Arabic in their Latin texts. Petrarch was not alone in condemning the ghastly Latin of the Arabists. Roger Bacon wrote of certain translators of Arabic into Latin who 'understand neither the subject matter, nor the languages – not even Latin'.[27] Fifthly, Averroës was a commentator on Aristotle. Petrarch, who followed Augustine, did not regard Aristotle as God. He mocked the superstitious and erroneous snippets of natural history that he thought he had found in Aristotle, though the errors were really those of Pliny's *Natural History* rather than of Aristotle.[28]

Petrarch attacked Averroës and the Averroists in several places. In a letter to Boccaccio, Petrarch gave an account of how he had been visited by an Averroist who had described St Paul as a 'word-sower' and a 'madman'. The visitor proclaimed that his only master was Averroës.[29] One might wonder if this visit ever really occurred. Petrarch's letters were of course not chatty notes keeping in touch with friends, but works of studied prose destined for publishing in so far as literature could be published in the age before printing. In *Contra medicum*, a letter to a certain Dondi, Petrarch railed against doctors and Arab science more generally. Averroës was the particular target: and 'this one dog who barks not at the moon, but, as the phrase has it, who barks with the foaming mouth at the very sun of justice ... You physicians worship Averroës; you love him; and you follow him simply because you oppose and hate Christ who is the living truth.'[30] The theme of the rabidity of the Arab philosopher recurs in a letter that Petrarch addressed to Fra Luigi Marsigli of the Order of St Augustine: 'I beg you ... write one book against that mad dog Averroës, who moved by unspeakable madness, barks at his Lord, Christ, and the Catholic Faith. Collect his blasphemies from all over.'[31] Petrarch claimed to have made a start on this project but was hampered by lack of time and knowledge.

However, the main attack on Averroism came in *De Sui Ipsius et Multorum Ignorantia* (c.1368–70). This polemic was provoked by hearing that four acquaintances of his in Venice had been discussing Petrarch and described him as 'a good man, but uncultured'. In his lengthy reply, he professed his own ignorance (St Augustine was a model for castigating his own failures), but he also denounced the intellectual darkness of Averroism in the context of a broader attack on the emphasis on the sciences, an attack that curiously anticipated by several centuries F. R. Leavis's famous literary polemic against the scientifically-minded novelist, C. P. Snow. More generally, Petrarch attacked the excessive reverence paid to classical authorities. Aristotle and Cicero must necessarily have had a limited perspective on life since they had not been vouchsafed the Christian revelation. They were invincibly ignorant.[32]

By the way, Renan claimed that the four individuals whom Petrarch was responding to were members of the Averroist school and thus evidence of a continuing tradition of Averroism in Padua that began in the fourteenth century and lasted till at least the sixteenth century. However, those four individuals – who have been identified – had no particular connection with Padua, unlike Petrarch who lived just outside.[33]

But I would like to turn now to an earlier letter, one written to Giovanni da Padova, a well-known physician, with reference to Arab medical authorities. In it Petrarch returns to his familiar Arab-bashing: 'But be an enemy of Averroës, the enemy of Christ ...' Although the letter was mostly concerned with medical and theological issues, he also has something to say about Arab poetry: 'I hate the entire race ... I know what kinds of poets there are. There is nothing more charming, softer, in a word, more base ... I shall scarcely be persuaded that anything good comes from Arabia.'[34] If Petrarch had read the Arab poets, this is amazing. He is the only European poet anywhere at any time in the Middle Ages to have made that boast. Not until the seventeenth century do a few scholars make a serious start at translating the great Arab poets, such as al-Tughrai. If Petrarch was familiar with Arab poetry, that would be exciting.

It is quite possible that Petrarch was simply lying about his knowledge of the style of Arab poets. As Enrico Cerulli has shown, the softness of the Arabs was a classical stereotype – found in Catullus, Virgil Manilius and others.[35] Those who have seen the film *Lawrence of Arabia* or who have read Wilfred Thesiger on the Bedouin of the Empty Quarter, might find the *topos* of the softness of the Arab rather curious. But what Roman authors like Juvenal were thinking of when they wrote of soft Arabs were city-dwelling Arabs, mostly Syrians, many of whom had settled in Rome – significant numbers even settled in Britain – and many of whom worked in the entertainment industry or were masseurs or prostitutes.[36] The softness of the Arab was kept alive in medieval Christian polemic about the sensuality of the Muslim paradise. The Arab nature was to succumb to promises of the sensual allurements of the *houri*. So it may be that Petrarch, who had not read or heard any Arab poetry, was simply striking a rhetorical posture and drawing on well-known classical precedents to do so.

But maybe only: would Petrarch, who sought to model himself on St Paul and St Augustine, have come out with such a flagrant lie, especially one he could easily be challenged on? It is after all just possible that he did know something of Arab poetry. One's first thought is that if he did, then his characterisation of that poetry as 'soft' is curious. What stands out in the best Arab poetry, that of the Jahili period, is rather its bleakness, its confrontation with single combats, hard journeys, old age and death. One thinks here of Imr'ul-Qays, Shanfara and others. But, of course, this was probably not the poetry that Petrarch would have encountered. If he heard Arab poetry recited, and perhaps kindly translated and explained to him, it would have been poetry of the Ayyubid and Mamluk period, by which time Arab versifying had travelled a long way from the austerity of the earliest *qasidas*. Poetry by Ibn Sana al-Mulk, Baha al-Din Zuhayr and Ibn al-Farid is the sort of thing he might have encountered.[37]

Ibn Sana al-Mulk (d.1211) was an Egyptian who nevertheless specialised in the distinctive form of the *muwashshah*. I will come back to the *muwashshah* in a moment. Baha al-Din Zuhayr (d.1258) was also an Egyptian. He specialised in panegyrics, light satirical verse and love poetry. Ibn al-Farid (d.1235) was famous as the *sultan al-'ashiqin*, or king of lovers, and was the mystical poet *par excellence* who used the tropes of sensual earthly love and of the *khamriyyat*, or wine-poetry genre, to evoke mystical ecstasy. It so happens that in the nineteenth century Pietro Valerga, a Carmelite scholar who worked on manuscripts in Turin and Florence, came across Ibn al-Farid's poetry, some of which he translated and published as *Id divano di Omar ben-al-Fared tradotto e paragonato col canzoniere del Petrarca*.[38] The thing about the *paragonato* or comparison of Ibn al-Farid's mystical verse with the *Canzoniere* of Petrarch was that the similarities were so very striking that Valerga judged that Petrarch was literally a reincarnation of Ibn al-Farid. Ibn al-Farid wrote of the agonies of love – love that is like a terrible sickness:

> My heart is flaming
> like a torch,
> My eyes awash
> in endless torrents.
> This is the lover's law:
> Bound to a fawn
> Every limb
> Is racked with pain.
>
> Fool
> Blaming me for loving them,
> Enough!
> Could you love, you wouldn't blame.[39]

Ibn al-Farid and Petrarch are on common ground in evoking the sufferings of love, which is such a tearful business. This, for example, is

Petrarch:

> I thrive on pain and laugh with all my tears;
> I dislike death as much as I do life:
> Because of you, lady, I am this way.[40]

But the reincarnation theory is not now a fashionable tool of literary criticism. And though the poems employ similar imagery, Petrarch was writing about a young woman while Ibn al-Farid was writing about God – and that was something that Valerga failed to recognise. Petrarch himself may have regretted his failure to seek to reach the mystical level aimed for by Ibn al-Farid. Here is Petrarch again:

> I go my way regretting those past times
> I spent in loving something which was mortal
> Instead of soaring high, since I had wings
> That might have taken me to higher levels.[41]

The idea that Italian *literati* might be familiar with contemporary Arabic literature may seem on the face of it improbable. When Asin Palacios wrote *Escatalogia musulmana en la Divina Commedia* (1919), suggesting that Dante's *Divine Comedy* was based in part on Arabic literary versions of the Afterlife, many critics challenged him to suggest how Dante could possibly have had access to such material even at one or two removes.[42] But in 1944, the year of Palacios's death, Bonaventura of Siena's *Liber de Scala Machometi* (The Book of Muhammad's Ladder – or Ascension) was discovered and found to have quite a few images and incidents that anticipated those found in the Divine Comedy. Meanwhile, Dante's debt to Arabic literature continues to be contested.[43]

In recent decades Samuel Stern and others have made a special study of the *muwashshah*, a strophic form of verse in non-classical Arabic that was usually sung to a musical accompaniment and which first evolved in al-Andalus before being taken up in Egypt.[44] The odd thing about this type of verse is that it can be just in Arabic, but there have been examples of linguistically mixed *muwashshahat* – Arabic-Romance, Hebrew-Arabic and Hebrew-Romance. A significant number of scholars believe that both the form and the themes of the troubador lyric were crucially influenced by the *muwashshahat*, though again the matter remains controversial. Ibn al-Khatib, the fourteenth-century Granadan statesman, whom I believe to have been the real architect of the Court of the Lions in the Alhambra, also put together a great anthology of *muwashshahat*, the *Jaysh al-Tawshih*.⁴⁵ The *kharjas* or concluding exit lines of those *muwashshahat* that are in a romance language may be the oldest surviving fragments of romance poetry – but, as I say, the matter is extremely controversial.

We should also bear in mind that there was still a significant Muslim Arab population in Sicily and southern Italy in the thirteenth century. Back in the 1930s the great Orientalist Sir Hamilton Gibb noted that 'it is a significant fact that the metric of the early popular poetry of Italy, as represented by the canticles of Jacopone da Todi and the carnival songs, and with more elaboration in the *ballata*, is identical with that of the popular poetry of Andalusia'. And he continued, 'Even Petrarch's violent nationalist outburst against the Arabs proves at least, if it proves anything, that the more popular kind of Arabic poetry was still known in Italy in his day.'⁴⁶

Recently, a less dramatic explanation for Petrarch's vaunted knowledge of Arabic poetry has been advanced and that is that some small fragments of Arabic poetry had indeed been translated into Latin. What had happened was that when Averroës translated Aristotle's *Poetics*, he ditched the examples that Aristotle had provided from Greek poetry and substituted 68 fragments from well-known Arab poets. Then, when the euphoniously named Hermann the German translated the Averroës text into Latin (in 1256), Hermann translated those fragments of Arabic verse also. Some of Hermann's translations were painfully literal prose versions, but in a few cases he relaxed and went for a freer rendering of the poetry. Hermann had a rather dour Teutonic view of Arabic poetry which he suggested was often composed in order to stimulate sexual intercourse and evoke the gamut of human pleasures. Hermann's condemnation echoed in a distorted fashion Averroës's quotation of the tenth-century philosopher al-Farabi's condemnation of the *nasib*, the opening part of the *qasida*, or ode, in which the poet traditionally lamented his lost beloved. So Petrarch may well have got his ideas about Arabic poetry from the introduction without even bothering to read the extracts themselves.⁴⁷

Whatever the truth of the matter, the probability is that Petrarch did not know anything much about Arab poetry, just as he knew rather little about philosophy. He was an essayist rather than a deep thinker. Though he attacked various aspects of Averroism, it is striking that he seems to have been unaware of earlier attacks by weightier figures such as Albertus Magnus, Thomas Aquinas and Ramon Lull. Incidentally, Lull had an especially virulent hatred of Averroës. Richard Southern mentioned Lull in his famous book, *Western Views of Islam in the Middle Ages* (1962) but declined to discuss him, as he claimed that Lull possessed 'a streak of madness to which I cannot do justice'.[48] Petrarch was out of his depth and his critical friends in Venice had judged him correctly. Yet, for all his ignorance and prejudice, he was a herald of an important feature of late medieval western culture. That culture was turning its back on Arab learning. This happened in the course of the fourteenth and fifteenth centuries. Arabism became a pejorative term as Christian scholars wearied of mangled and inaccurate translations of Arabic versions of Greek philosophy into barbarous Latin. A few stylists devoted themselves to improving the Latin style of the translations of Avicenna and Averroës. Others preferred to get their Greek philosophy from Hebrew translations. Others again redoubled their attempts to find the Greek manuscripts of the relevant works.

But it was also the case that Latin *literati* such as Cicero, Catullus and Juvenal were supplanting Greek philosophers as role models for Renaissance men. The fifteenth-century Florentine Platonist Marsilio Ficino libelled Averroës by claiming that he did not understand Aristotle because he did not know any Greek. The Venetian humanist Ermolao Barbaro the younger, looking back on the scholastic philosophers, the Aristotelians and Averroists of Paris, Oxford and Bologna, described them as 'dull, rude, uncultured barbarians'.[49] It is true that Barbaro's disparagement of the scholastic tradition provoked a response. The Florentine humanist and cabalist, Count Giovanni Pico della Mirandola wrote a letter to Barbaro sarcastically apologising for having wasted the best years of his life in studying those dull folk and in the preface to his *Conclusiones*, Pico claimed to abjure eloquence in the classical stylishly Latinate manner, in favour of 'the manner and diction of the most celebrated Parisian disputants'. In 1486 he had studied Arabic with an Averroist Jew called Elias de Medigo, and also with Flavio Mithridates. In the 1490s Pico's library had seven Arabic manuscripts, though it is likely that some or all of them dealt with Christian matters. And only seven![50] In *The Oration on the Dignity of Man* (1486), he quoted 'Abdala the Saracen', to the effect that 'There is nothing to be seen more wonderful than man'. Perhaps the reference here is to Avicenna, or Ibn Sina who was Ibn Abdullah.[51]

But Pico was like the man in the notorious schoolboy essay who 'stands with one foot in the Middle Ages, while with the other he salutes the rising sun of the Renaissance'. Elsewhere, Pico wrote, 'Leave to us in Heaven's name Pythagoras, Plato and Aristotle and keep your Omar, your Alchabitius, your Abenzoar, your Abenragel'.[52] For Pico, as for Petrarch, it was perhaps more a matter of striking rhetorical postures than of maintaining a consistent position. There were other flickering sparks of interest in Arabic in Renaissance Italy. The famous humanist scholar Lorenzo Valla apparently owned five Arabic manuscripts – and this at a time when it was difficult to get hold of worthwhile manuscripts and even whole copies of the Qur'an were rarely encountered in Europe.[53] Francesco Colonna's strange architectural allegory of love, the *Hypnertomachia. Poliphili* (1499), featured cod Arabic inscriptions in its woodcuts.[54] But these are the final embers of what had once been a more extensive engagement with Arabic language and thought. As Richard Southern noted, fourteenth-century Christendom knew less about Islam than had the twelfth century.[55] Averroës was the last Arab philosopher to be translated into Latin until the seventeenth century (which is when Orientalism in its true sense starts).[56] For Renaissance European culture, it was childhood's end, as western thinkers let go of the hand of their Oriental guardian and began to voyage on strange seas of thought alone.

The Argentinian Jorge Luis Borges wrote a famous short story, 'Averroës's Search'. In that story, Averroës, ensconced in his study in twelfth-century Cordova, struggles to understand what Aristotle meant by tragedy and comedy. (You must remember that there was no significant theatrical tradition in medieval Islam.) At the last, a series of what seems to Averroës serendipitous incidents leads him to the conclusion that by tragedy Aristotle meant panegyric and by comedy he meant satire and anathemas.[57] Borges's story may serve as a final comment on what I have been talking about, for I have been tracing the course of a long series of misunderstandings. Averroës misunderstood the Greek philosophers and was himself misunderstood by both the scholastics and the critics of scholasticism; the story of their interaction with the Arabs was misunderstood by Renan, who was in turn misread by Edward Said. Borges commented on his own story as follows: 'I felt that Averroës, trying to imagine what a play is without ever having suspected what a theatre is, was no more absurd than I, trying to imagine Averroës, yet with no more material than a few snatches from Renan, Lane and Asín Palacios. I felt, on the last page, that my story was the symbol of the man I had been as I was writing it, and that in order to write that story I had to be that man, and in order to be that man I had to write that story, and so on, *ad infinitum*.'[58]

Notes

1. Ibrahim Fawal, *Youssef Chahine* (London: British Film Institute, 2001), pp. 169–86.
2. Albert Hourani, *Arabic Thought in the Liberal Age 1798–1939* (London: Oxford University Press, 1962), p. 148. See also Donald M. Reid, *The Odyssey of Farah Antun* (Minneapolis: Biblioteca Islamica, 1975).

3. On the life and writings of Averroës, see Oliver Leaman, *Averroës and His Philosophy* (1988; rpt. Richmond, Surrey: Curzon, 1998); Majid Fakhry, *Averroës (Ibn Rushd), His Life, Works and Influence* (Oxford: One World, 2001); Dominic Urvoy 'Ibn Rushd', in Seyyed Hossein Nasr and Oliver Leaman, eds., *History of Islamic Philosophy*, 2 vols. (London: Routledge, 1996): 1: 330–45.

4. On the fortunes of Averroism in Europe, see Pierre F. Mandonnet, *Siger de Brabant et l'averroïsme latin au XIIIe siècle ... Deuxième edition revue et augmentée*, 2 vols. (Louvain: Academia Lovaniensis, 1908, 1911); Fakhry, *Averroes*, pp. 129–64; John Marenbon, 'Medieval Christian and Jewish Europe', and Catherine Wilson, 'Modern Western Philosophy', in Nasr and Leaman, eds., *History of Islamic Philosophy*, 2: 1006–7, and 2: 1017–19.

5. Wilson, 'Modern Western Philosophy', p. 1018.

6. Dante, *Inferno*, canto 4, line 144; *Paradiso*, canto 9, line 136.

7. On the life and writings of Renan, see John M. Robertson, *Ernest Renan* (London: Watts, 1924); Jean Pommier, *La pensée religeuse de Renan* (Paris: [n.p.], 1925); David C. J. Lee, *Ernest Renan. In the Shadow of Faith* (London: Duckworth, 1996); Charles Chauvin, *Renan* (Paris: Desclée de Brouwer, 2000). On his early foray into Arabic, see Johann Fück, *Die arabischen Studien in Europa biis in den Anfang des 20. Jahrhunderts* (Leipzig: Otto Harrassowitz, 1955), pp. 201–2.

8. Hourani, *Arabic Thought*, p. 254.

9. On Renan's thoughts about Arabs and science and his clashes with Kurd Ali and Jamal-al-Din al-Afghani on the subject, see Hourani, *Arabic Thought*, pp. 110–12, 120–3, 135; Joseph Escovitz, 'Orientalists and Orientalism in the Writings of Muhammad Kurd "Ali" ', *International Journal of Middle Eastern Studies* 15 (1982): 98, 99–100; Edward Said, *The World, the Text and the Critic* (London: Faber, 1984), pp. 279–81; Zachary Lockman, *Contending Visions of the Middle East: The History and Politics of Orientalism* (Cambridge: Cambridge University Press, 2004), pp. 78–83.

10. Renan, *Averroès et l'averroïsm* (Paris: Michel, Lévy Frères, 1861). On this work, see Jean-Paul Charnay, 'Le dernier surgeon de l'averroïsme en Occident: Averroès et l'Averroïsme de Renan', in Jean Jolivet and Rachel Arié, eds., *Multiple Averroès* (Paris: Belles Lettres, 1978), pp. 333–48.

11. On Goldziher's hostility to Renan, see Lawrence I. Conrad, 'The Pilgrim from Pest: Goldziher's Study Tour to the Near East (1873–4)', in Ian Richard Netton, ed., *Golden Roads: Migration, Pilgrimage and Travel in Mediaeval and Modern Islam* (Richmond, Surrey: Curzon, 1993), pp. 143–5; and see Maurice Olender, *The Languages of Paradise: Race, Religion and Philology in the Nineteenth Century* (Cambridge, MA: Harvard University Press, 1992), p. 121.

12. Renan, *Averroès*, p. 2; and see Lee, *Ernest Renan*, p. 171.

13. Raymond Schwab, *The Oriental Renaissance: Europe's Rediscovery of India and the East 1680–1880*, trans. Gene Patterson Black and Victor Reinking (New York: Columbia University Press, 1984), p. 103.

14. On later Islamic philosophy, see Nasr and Leaman, eds., *History of Islamic Philosophy*, 1: 527–670.

15. Fernand van Steenberghen, *Aristotle in the West: The Origins of Latin Aristotelianism*, trans. Leonard Johnston (Louvain: Nauwelaerts, 1955), pp. 209–29, and the same author's *The Philosophical Movement in the Thirteenth Century* (Edinburgh: Nelson, 1955), pp. 75–93.

16. Charles Burnett, 'The Introduction of Arabic Learning into British Schools', in Charles Butterworth and Blake Andrée Kessel, eds., *Introduction of Arabic Philosophy into Europe* (Leiden: Brill, 1993), p. 49.

17. Paul Otto Kristeller, 'Petrarch's "Averroists": A Note on the History of Averroism in Venice, Padua and Bologna', *Bibliothèque d'Humanisme et Renaissance* 14 (1952): 59–65.

18. On the life and works of Petrarch, see Morris Bishop, *Petrarch and His World* (London: Chatto and Windus, 1964); Kenelm Foster, *Petrarch, Poet and Humanist* (Edinburgh: Edinburgh University Press, 1984); Ugo Dotti, *Vita di Petrarca* (Bari: Laterza, 1987).

19. Donald Howard, *Writers and Pilgrims, Medieval Pilgrimage Narratives and Their Posterity* (Berkeley, CA: University of California Press, 1980), pp. 32–3.

20. Julius von Klaproth, *Vocabulaire Latin, Perse et Coman d'après un manuscrit écrit en 1303 et provenant de la Bibliothèque du célèbre poète Francesco Petrarca* (Paris, 1828).

21. Petrarch, *Letters of Old Age. Rerum Senilium Libri*, trans. Aldo Bernardo, Saul Levin and Reta A. Bernardo, 2 vols. (Baltimore: Johns Hopkins University Press, 1992): 2: 580; and see Ernst Cassirer, Paul Otto Kristeller and John Herman Randall, Jr., eds., *The Renaissance Philosophy of Man* (Chicago: Chicago University Press, 1948), p. 143.

22. Renan, *Averroës*, pp. 328–38.

23. Haskell D. Isaacs, 'Arabic Medical Literature', in M. L. J. Young, J. D. Latham and R. B. Serjeant, eds., *The Cambridge History of Arabic Literature, Religion, Learning and Science in the 'Abbasid Period* (Cambridge: Cambridge University Press, 1990), pp. 356–8.

24. Michael Dols, *Majnun: The Madman in Medieval Islamic Society* (Oxford: Clarendon, 1992), pp. 84, 87, 89, 485.

25. Petrarch, *Invectives*, David Marsh, ed. and trans. (Cambridge, MA: Harvard University Press, 2003), pp. 78–9.

26. Petrarch, *Invectives*, pp. 128–9.

27. Burnett, 'The Second Revelation', p. 186.

28. Paul Renucci, 'Pétrarque et l'Averroïsme de son temps', in *Mélanges de philologie romane et de littérature médiéval offerts à Ernest Hoepffner* (Paris: Publications de la Faculté des Lettres de l'Université de Strasbourg, 1949), p. 340n.

29. Cassirer, et al., *Renaissance Philosophy*, pp. 140–1.

30. Petrarch, *Invectives*, pp. 68–9.

31. Cassirer, et al., *Renaissance Philosophy*, p. 143.

32. Petrarch, *Invectives*, pp. 222–63.

33. See Kristeller, 'Petrarch's "Averroists" '.

34. Petrarch, *Letters of Old Age*, 2: 472.

35. Enrico Cerulli, 'Petrarca e gli arabi', *Rivista di cultura classica e medioevale* 7 (1965): 331–6.

36. On Roman attitudes to the Arabs and Persians and on Arabs settled within the Roman Empire, see Irfan Shahid, *Rome and the Arabs: A Prolegomenon to the Study of Byzantium and the Arabs* (Washington, DC: Dumbarton Oaks, 1984), and Kevin Butcher, *Roman Syria and the Near East* (London: British Museum, 2003).

37. On Mamluk poetry, see Muhammad Zaghul Sallam, *Al-Adab fi al-'Asr al-Mamluki*, 2 vols. (Cairo: Dar al-Ma'arif, 1971); Robert Irwin, 'Mamluk Literature', *Mamluk Studies Review* 7 (2003): 1–29.

38. Franceso Gabrieli, 'Il Petrarca e gli Arabi', *Rivista di cultura classica e medioevale* 7 (1965): 487–8
39. Thomas Emil Homerin, *From Arab Poet to Muslim Saint: Ibn al-Farid, His Verse and His Shrine* (Columbia, SC: University of South Carolina Press, 1994), p. 6.
40. Petrarch, *Selections from the Canzoniere and Other Works*, ed. and trans. Mark Musa (Oxford: Oxford University Press, 1985), p. 50.
41. Petrarch, *Selections*, p. 77.
42. The thesis of Miguel Asin Palacios's *Escatalogía Musulmana en la Divina Commedia* (Madrid: Estanislao Maestre, 1919), translated and abridged by Harold Sutherland as *Islam and the Divine Comedy* (London: Cass, 1926), is still controversial. See also, Richard Southern, *Western Views of Islam in the Middle Ages* (Cambridge, MA: Harvard University Press, 1962), pp. 55–6, and Southern, 'Dante and Islam', in Derek Baker, ed., *Relations between East and West in the Middle Ages* (Edinburgh: Edinburgh University Press, 1973), pp. 133–45; Philip F. Kennedy, 'Muslim Sources of Dante', in Dionysius A. Agius and Richard Hitchcock, eds., *The Arab Influence in Medieval Europe: Folia Scholastica Mediterranea* (Reading: Ithaca, 1994), pp. 63–82.
43. See Fück, *Arabischen Studien*, pp. 268–9, and James T. Monroe, *Islam and the Arabs in Spanish Scholarship (Sixteenth Century to the Present)* (Leiden: Brill, 1970), pp. 174–82.
44. Samuel Stern, *Hispano-Arabic Strophic Poetry* (Oxford: Clarendon, 1974).
45. On Ibn al-Khatib, see Emilio Molina López, *Ibn al-Jatib* (Granada: Comares, 2001), and Robert Irwin, *The Alhambra* (London: Profile, 2004), pp. 82–8.
46. H. A. R. Gibb, 'Literature', in Thomas Arnold and Alfred Guillaume, eds., *The Legacy of Islam*, first edition (Oxford: Oxford University Press, 1931), p. 192, and see Gabrieli, 'Petrarca', pp. 487–94.
47. C. H. L. Bodenham, 'Petrarch and the Poetry of the Arabs', *Romanische Forschungen* 94 (1982): 167–78; Charles Burnett, 'Petrarch and Averroës: An Episode in the History of Poetics', in Ian Macpherson and Ralph Penny, eds., *The Medieval Mind: Hispanic Studies in Honour of Alan Deyermond* (Woodbridge: Tamesis, 1997), pp. 49–56, and 'Learned Knowledge of Arabic Poetry, Rhymed Prose and Didactic Verse from Petrus Alfonsi to Petrarch', in John Marenbom, ed., *Poetry and Philosophy in the Middle Ages: A Festschrift for Peter Dronke* (Leiden: Brill, 2001), pp. 29–62.
48. Southern, *Western Views*, p. 72n.
49. Brian Vickers, *In Defence of Rhetoric* (Oxford: Clarendon, 1988), pp. 184–96.
50. On Pico della Mirandola, see Eugenio Garin, *Giovanni Pico della Mirandola: Vita e dottrina* (Florence: Università degli Studi di Firenze, 1937); Pearl Kibre, *The Library of Pico della Mirandola* (New York: Columbia University Press, 1936); Cassirer, et al., *Renaissance Philosophy*, pp. 215–54; Joseph L. Blau, *The Christian Interpretation of the Cabala in the Renaissance* (New York: Columbia University Press, 1944); François Secret, *Les Kabbalistes Chrétiens de la Renaissance* (Paris: Dunod-Sigma, 1964); K. H. Dannenfeldt, 'Renaissance Humanists and the Knowledge of Arabic', *Studies in the Renaissance* 2 (1955): 96–117, esp. p. 101.
51. Cassirer, et al., *Renaissance Philosophy*, p. 223.
52. Montgomery Watt, *The Influence of Islam on Medieval Europe* (Edinburgh: Edinburgh University Press, 1972), p. 80.
53. On Arabism in the Italian Renaissance, see Dannenfeldt, 'Renaissance Humanists', and Charles Burnett, 'The Second Revelation of Arabic

Philosophy and Science: 1492–1562', in Charles Burnett and Anna Contadini, eds., *Islam and the Italian Renaissance* (London: Warburg Institute, 1999), pp. 185–98.

54. Francesco Colonna, *Hypnerotomachia Poliphili* (Venice: Aldus Manutius, 1499); Jocelyn Godwin, trans., *Hypnerotomachia Poliphili: The Strife of Love in a Dream* (London: Thames and Hudson, 1999). On this curious text, see Angelo Michele Piemontese, 'Le iscrizioni arabe nella *Poliphili Hypnerotomachia*', in Burnett and Contadini, eds., *Islam*, pp. 119–220.

55. Southern, *Western Views*, pp. 72–5.

56. On the origins of Orientalist scholarship, see Robert Irwin, *For Lust of Knowing: The Orientalists and their Enemies* (London: Allen Lane, forthcoming 2006).

57. Jorge Luis Borges, 'Averroës' Search', in Andrew Kerrigan, ed., *A Personal Anthology* (London: Cape, 1968), pp. 84–91.

58. Borges, 'Averroës' Search', pp. 90–1.

7
Arab Views of Europeans, 1578–1727: The Western Mediterranean

Nabil Matar

> Then she said, 'I will teach you to read *ifranji* [French].' And I
> became her pupil, and she began honouring my companions.
> Love [*mahabba*] grew between us so much that I was distraught
> by it and I said, 'Before meeting her, I was at odds with the
> Christians, and engaged in the holy fight for religion. But now,
> I am at odds with myself and Satan.'[1]

Ahmad bin Qasim was an Andalusian Morisco who fled from Spain in
1599 and settled, like many of his compatriots, in Morocco. He was pro-
ficient in Spanish and, to the surprise of his wary co-religionists in
Morocco, Arabic too. Sometime in early 1611, he was sent with five other
Moroccans by the ruler, Mulay Zaidan (r.1603–27), to France and the
Netherlands on a mission to retrieve goods that had been looted from
Moroccan ships – or to demand compensation for them. During his
three-year stay in these two countries (one whole year was spent in
Bordeaux), he observed and reflected on the *nasara* among whom he was
staying, debated and argued with them, feasted and prayed, made friends
and enemies. He even fell in love, as the above quotation shows. Much
as he was inimical to infidel Europeans who, knowing little about Islam,
did not hesitate to denounce it, he still sought engagement with
Christian men and women, scholars and princes, and developed complex relations, even relationships, with them. After returning to
Morocco, and from there going on to Egypt, he wrote a memoir of his
escape from Spain to North Africa, and his subsequent journey to Europe.

With the exception of Alastair Hamilton and G. A. Weigers, scholars
have ignored the corpus of western Arabic writings in the early modern

period, specifically those writings that describe meetings and encounters with the Europeans. What did Arabic-speaking Muslims (as distinguished from Turkish-speaking Muslims) in the Maghrib know about Europeans, and how did they view the *nasara*? Did they see them as the adversarial Other, as religious enemies, or as partners in Mediterranean trade, diplomacy and acculturation? Given the growing body of European knowledge about Moors and Turks from Fez to Istanbul and from Jerusalem to Mocha, was that process of collection reciprocated by Muslims? Throughout this period of expanding markets, diplomatic alliances and military conflicts, European imaginations became deeply informed about Turks and Moors – the 'Mahometans'. What attitude did Muslims develop in their oral and written traditions towards the European *nasara*? And given the fantasy and the Orientalism that marked early modern and modern European perceptions of Arabs and Muslims, did an Occidentalism evolve in Arab-Islamic thought? Did the military polarisation that marked the two shores of the Mediterranean produce an Arab fantasy and invention similar to that characterising a large amount of European writings about Muslims?

Historians have shown that the Arabs of the medieval period were not as interested in Latin Christendom as they were in the Far East since there were no comprehensive surveys of medieval Christendom as there were of China or India. Aziz Al-Azmeh explained that medieval Arab travel and geographical sources viewed the Europeans as barbarians of little interest: because Europeans were Christian, and because Muslims knew Christianity through the Qur'an, Muslims did not bother to study European society since, in their view, that society was summed up in its theology, which was, according to the Qur'an, false and distorted.[2] Tarif Khalidi contested this position by showing the various geographical, historical and cultural views of Europe in the classical period of Islam.[3] Writing from the perspective of a cultural historian, Muhammad Nur al-Din Afaya focused on the medieval Arabic corpus of geography, trying to see how and if the paradigms of an 'imagined West' would be of value in the contemporary encounter with the West;[4] while Abdallah Ibrahim focused on Ibn Fadlan, Ibn Batutah and Ibn Khaldun, and analysed how the Other – *al-aakhar* – was seen in the Islamic imaginary of the medieval period.[5]

In the study of the modern period, Ibrahim Abu-Lughod noted that in the eighteenth century, the Arabs of the Levant (he did not examine the Maghrib) showed no interest in Europe, believing that the heritage of the Middle Ages had given them the edge over the Europeans.[6] In his *Iktishaf al-taqaddum al-urubbi* ('The [Muslim] Discovery of European Progress', 1981), Khalid Ziadeh completely ignored the Islamic West,[7] as did, to a large extent, Bernard Lewis in *The Muslim Discovery of Europe* (1982). Although Lewis touched on Arabic sources, he focused chiefly on the Ottoman experience, concluding that early modern Muslims had little 'curiosity' about Europeans.[8] Charles Issawi argued that in the nineteenth century, the Arab peoples felt hostile to Europeans and therefore wrote little about them,[9] but Susan Gilson Miller showed in her study of Muhammad bin Abdallah al-Saffar's journey to France (1845–6) that curiosity predominated over antipathy,[10] while Nazek Yarid argued for a mix of curiosity and hostility among nineteenth- and twentieth-century Arab Middle Eastern travellers to the West.[11] The survey of Moroccan ambassadors in Europe between 1610 and 1922 by Abd al-Majid Qadduri presented the 'official' court view about Europe: empirical and sometimes anxious.[12] With the rise of postcolonial theory, historians and cultural critics argued that the imposition of European political and cultural hegemony on the colonies led to the suppression of native views and expressions. The Arabs, like other subalterns, did not 'speak'.[13]

But the Arabs did speak, as can be seen in the varied writings of Moroccans, Tunisians and Algerians – with the chief emphasis falling on Moroccans, who remained the only Mediterranean Islamic people outside the hegemony of Ottoman political power and the Turkish language. It has been the misfortune of Morocco that in studies of the early modern Islamic world, it was subsumed under the Ottoman Empire – as happened in Fernand Braudel's *The Mediterranean and the Mediterranean World in the Age of Philip II* (1949; trans. 1972). But Morocco's separation from the Ottoman Empire ensured that the Arab legacy continued to flourish in a Turkish-dominated Mediterranean basin. Along with writings produced in Morocco, there were also writings from Tunisia and Algeria – regencies that gradually acquired some autonomy from the Sublime Porte in diplomatic relations, economic policies and cultural identity. In light of the pre-eminence of Morocco, however, the period that will be studied in this essay will extend from 1578, the date of the decisive battle of Wadi al-Makhazen/Alcazar (*al-ghazwa al-udhma*, or the 'Great Raid' as Moroccan historians remembered it) and the accession of Mulay Ahmad al-Mansur to the throne, to the death of the Moroccan ruler, Mulay Ismail, in 1727 – a century and a half which saw Europeans and Magharibi engaging in diplomacy, war, alliance, trade and sometimes falling in love.

Terminology

Magharibi is a term that is used in modern political and geographical historiography to describe the peoples of the Maghrib and Libya.

The terms that were used in early modern Arabic writings to designate travellers from those regions were Tunisian (*tunisi*), Algerian (*jazairi*) and Moroccan (*maghribi* from *al-Maghrib al-Aqsa*): evidently some consciousness of national identity was slowly emerging in the early modern period. More often, however, the term *muslim* was used in the context of the encounter with Euro-Christians.[14] As a result of confrontation and hostility, ethnicity and religion became the dominant dividers. Writers who found themselves in military, social or theological polarisation with the Europeans saw themselves as Muslims confronting Christians.

The first Europeans whom the Magharibi encountered were Catholics – which explains why they used the term *salibiyyun*, or 'cross-bearers', to refer to them. On many occasions writers also referred to them as *ahl u-saleeb*, 'people of the cross', or *abadat al-saleeb*, 'worshippers of the cross'. Although these were terms that had been widely used in medieval Arabic writings, they became even more appropriate in describing the peoples of Spain, Italy and France, especially during the Counter-Reformation when church symbolism and iconography became pre-eminent in worship, government and military institution. Other terms confirmed the religious character of the adversary, but were harsh and antithetical: *mushrikeen* and *kuffar*, polytheists and infidels; and *ahl u-shirk* and *ahzab al-kufr*, 'the people who associate [other deities] with God' and 'the parties of unbelief'. The Christians were those who came from the land of human and divine natures – '*dawlat al-uqnum wal nasut*' – wrote Ahmad al-Mansur after his son's victory over the Spanish-backed invasion of Morocco in 1595.[15] Such allusions appear frequently in inter-Magharibi communication about the dangerous enemies who were invading and pillaging the region under the banner of the cross.

At the end of the sixteenth century, the Marrakesh-based historian and Sa'adian court scribe, Abd al-Aziz al-Fishtali, used the terms *latarin* and *qalabin*, Lutherans and Calvinists, to describe the *nasara* who rejected Catholicism. Meanwhile, the Moriscos had come in contact with Protestants (Huguenots) as a result of which they learned about some of the differences between Catholicism and Protestantism: how Protestants detested the sacrifice of the mass; how they rejected papal authority; and how they were in agreement with the Jews in their rejection of religious ornamentation.[16] The word 'Protestant' does not appear in Arabic, although the Moroccan ambassador, al-Ghassani, did mention at the end of the seventeenth century that the English were known as *haratiqeen*, or 'heretics', to the worshippers of the cross.[17] His king, Mulay Ismail, like him, thought the term a proper noun: *antum ma'shar al-ricks* – 'you the *ricks* people' – he wrote to the exiled James II.[18] There is no indication that Magharibi writers knew the theological differences between Catholics and Protestants, except in noting that the latter did not obey the pope nor worship 'idols'.

With the growth of commercial and political relations between North Africa and western Europe, and with the drawing of Europe's denominational and national boundaries, the Magharibi started using more specific terms. Actually, they used national designations for the Europeans once the Europeans themselves began to identify more clearly with their national rather than religious affiliations: it was not possible for the Magharibi to apply national designations when the Europeans were still unsure of their allegiances, and when there was still really no idea of Europe.[19] Thus, from the late sixteenth century, a dramatic change occurred in Magharibi usage: Ahmad bin Qasim spoke about the *ajam*, or Spaniards (not Persians, probably translating back the word *aljamiada*); he also spoke about *isbaniya*, as did later writers, too. Terms such as *ifranj* (French), *alman* (Germans),[20] the *burtuqal* (the Portuguese), the *estad*, from the Spanish *estados*, for the States General in the Netherlands, and the *ingleez* (the English) were repeatedly used. On some occasions, the Magharibi alluded to *banu al-asfar* in connection with the inhabitants of the Iberian Peninsula (and more generally, the *ruum*), and towards the end of the seventeenth century, *iflamank* replaced *estad* for the Dutch when William of Orange became King of England.[21] In the eighteenth century, there was reference to *deen mark* after the Danish fleet bombarded Algiers, and to *al-moscow*.

The Magharibi were aware of the different nationalities not in terms of cultural peculiarities as much as religious orientation and political stance. They separated Protestants from Catholics because they saw all Catholics as followers of the pope, whose inquisitional practices had traumatised and transformed the demography of the western Mediterranean. Repeatedly, they sought to learn about political alliances in order to coordinate their commercial and trading agreements. In this respect, their knowledge was dominated by the empirical and utilitarian. The very nature of the interaction with the Europeans, and of the information they gathered about them, provided them not with specialised or scholarly but with kaleidoscopic views of the peoples, languages, political differences and tensions in the lands of the Christians.

Sources

The Moors, wrote an English visitor in 1669, 'are sensible that the acquaintance with foreign nations, is very necessary for their more convenient subsistence'.[22] Indeed, the Moroccans repeatedly sought engagement with Europeans because of their separation from, or desire for protection against, Ottoman imperial aspirations. Many communities around the Mediterranean basin found themselves restricted by the Ottoman Empire's ideological exclusion and overbearing superiority. Eager to separate themselves from the Empire, these communities turned to Europeans to explore venues for exchange and dialogue: thus the Druzes and the Maronites in the eastern Mediterranean (Lebanon and Syria), and the Moroccans and other Magharibi in North Africa. Only among those Arabic-speaking communities (in the case of the Maronites, also Syriac- and Latin-speaking) was there cultural, commercial and diplomatic familiarity with Europeans. It is not a coincidence, therefore, that the first 'Islamic' book about Christian Europe in the early modern period was written in Arabic by a Magharibi, Ahmad bin Qasim. Neither Native Americans, Persians,[23] sub-Saharan Africans, Ottomans nor any of the peoples of the Far East, who traded with Europeans, wrote as much about Europeans as did the Magharibi. The Magharibi were the first non-Christians to write about early modern Christian Europe.

In turning to the Magharibi sources about Europeans, it will be necessary to adopt a different methodological paradigm from that applied to the western sources about North Africa and the world of Islam in general. In the Magharibi context, there were no published tomes about Europeans, nor were there grand narratives of sweeping coverage. The European culture of print had produced a plethora of books about European travels in North Africa, or research into classical and contemporary history; it had also inspired epics and dramas that described (and imagined) the peoples and civilisations of Islam. The absence of print in North Africa and the rest of the Islamic world in the period under study was instrumental in militating against the creation of such grand texts. But it did not militate against the creation of other sources of information: after all, the absence of print did not translate into illiteracy. There was a large reading public in North Africa, trained in Qur'anic elementary schools and then in Sufi circles and mosque corners: pupils – predominantly boys but sometimes girls too – studied under learned jurists who, at the end of the education cycle, issued them with an *ijaza* or 'certificate of achievement'. Unlike in Russia, Wales and many parts of Christendom, the Moroccan elite was well educated, and written documents were widely read, as the reference to dense libraries and book collections among scholars and courtiers attests.

In such a context of widespread literacy without print and without the diffusion of mass-produced books, and in order to locate the

Magharibi view of Europeans, it will be helpful to adopt Carlo Ginzburg's method which appeared in his study of a sixteenth-century miller, *The Cheese and the Worms* (1982). For the information that is available about Europeans in the Magharibi corpus is similar to Ginzburg's material about Menocchio: allusions, anecdotes, recollections, images and news that appear at unexpected moments in texts that may have nothing to do with the Europeans, but that record a story which the narrator remembered or had heard, or a tribulation he had experienced. Information about Europeans exists, but it has to be sought in a method that is different from the search for information about Muslims in European books. It also has to take into account an important difference in representation: the Magharibi information valorised narratives about individual experiences over descriptions of institutions and landscape, personal intimacies over ethnography and geography. Because the interest in the European Other was often personal, the information appears in hagiography, jurisprudence, epistles and history, in verse as in prose. With the exception of the travel accounts, there is no continuous narrative about an encounter with Europeans or a description of a region of Europe, nor is there a compendium of consistent, verifiable and documented data. There were anecdotes, memories, prayers, exegetical reflections and short exempla about the Euro-Christians. The Arabic sources are rich with information about the *nasara* – but not in the kind of sequential presentations, titled chapters or imaginative fiction which characterise European literature. Actually, with the exception of ambassadorial travel accounts, the material about the *nasara* never exceeded a few pages. Still, such material shows how much exchange was taking place, and how information and ideas, diseases and cures, jokes and banter were crossing between the two civilisations of the Mediterranean and reaching sometimes even beyond.

There are two kinds of information about the Euro-Christians in the Magharibi Arabic sources that, employing categories proposed by Edward Muir, we might call popular and elite.[24]

Popular sources

A valuable source of information about the European world appears in the anecdotal exchange in Magharibi popular culture and memory. Visitors, travellers, captives, converts and re-converts, traders, sailors and petitioners participated in the inter-acculturation of the Mediterranean. Many Magharibi introduced to their home communities stories that they told and re-told about the European Christians. Abu Abdallah Muhammad bin Khalil al-Tarabulsi wrote about a trustworthy merchant who told him that when he visited Valencia and went to its *souk*:

> A vendor asked me, when he saw my Maghribi looks, 'From which part of the Maghrib do you come?' I told him about my country [Libya]. He asked me: 'Do you build your houses in Tripoli with gold and silver bricks [*labin al-dhahab wal-fidda*]? Or is your city like the rest of the world?' I thought he was mocking me until he swore to me by the one they worship.[25]

As a result of all the booty taken by Magharibi privateers, the Spaniards thought them so rich that they built their houses with gold. Just as Magharibi information about Europeans was sometimes inaccurate, so European information was exaggerated and misunderstood – and reported back to amused Muslim listeners.

What the above anecdote and others show is that Magharibi informa-tion networks reached from the urban centres to the countryside, and from royal courts to Sufi lodges. Merchants, traders dispersed in European cities and harbours and diplomats in royal courts took back news that was then disseminated by the mosque sermons (the television news of the day), gossip and individual narratives. In a 1599 *Catechismo* intended to convert the Moors, Juan de Ribera, Archbishop of Valencia, noted how Moors crossed over to Spain and the rest of Europe claiming they wanted to convert to Christianity. But they had other reasons for coming, he added, such as learning about those kingdoms inhabited by their people; or they came to grow rich, feigned conversion in order to be well treated and then returned to North Africa and reported what they had seen and heard.[26] Many such Magharibi returned to North Africa, carrying with them not only images and stories, but also European material culture – from firearms to neologisms, from clocks and mirrors to paintings and ships, and from food bowls to the Christian calendar. The book *Kitab ul-izz wal-rifa'* by Ahmad bin Ghanem and translated by Ahmad bin Qasim in the second quarter of the seventeenth century shows the transmission of European knowledge about cannon casting from Spain to Tunis, and from Spanish to Arabic: 'This is what the Spaniards do in their country', wrote bin Ghanem, 'and I am hoping that the same, or something similar, would be implemented in the Magharibi lands'.

Other Magharibi who were experienced in military affairs similarly transmitted information about European countries to their rulers. In 1701, a naval officer who had been involved in *jihad* for seven years returned to Algiers and met the Governor. Upon presenting himself, he told the British secretary of state in his letter, 'the ruler had started asking me about the lands and the seas [that I had seen]. I answered him fully on everything he asked. Then the discussion touched on your country, so he, may God make him victorious, asked me about your affairs [*ahwalikum*]. So I told him all that I knew.'[27]

Meanwhile, accounts in autobiographies and histories described advancements in medicine and other sciences among the Europeans and the interactions that ensued between the two sides of the Mediterranean. A Muslim surgeon from Tangier, as the seventeenth-century jurist al-Yusi recorded, told his fellow doctors how he had met some Christian (*ruum*) surgeons who had laughed at him for treating his patients with *couscous*. Later, the surgeon travelled across Bahr al-Ruum to visit one of those doctors where he found him giving wine to a patient with a high fever. Upon inquiring why he was doing that, the *ruumi* doctor answered that wine would not hurt the patient ' "because [he said] he has been drinking it since he suckled at his mother's breasts." So I exclaimed: "Glory be to God! So too have we suckled *couscous* at our mothers' breasts since we were children. Why should it hurt us?" He replied: "You are right," and he had nothing more to add.'[28]

Differences in cuisine, religious culture and medical treatment were underpinned by amicability and a desire to learn from each other. When Abd al-Karim bin Mu'min the renegade (*ilij*) travelled to see a Jewish doctor in France and inquire of him about a cure for syphilis (*al-habb al-ifranji*, or 'French pimples') he saw no transgression in his quest, since the science of medicine was *mushtarak* – common to all peoples.[29] In 1682, the Moroccan ambassador in France examined the potions and powders used by doctors and reminded his hosts that many of the ingredients came from his country: 'aussi-bien que la Science des Médecins, qui tiroit, de là son origine.'[30] After a severe bout of the plague (*al-humma*) in Tunis during the 1690s, Husayn Khujah wrote how he had travelled to the lands of the Franks (*ard al-faranj*) in a quest for cures for the deadly disease. He returned with quinine (*kina*) and described his interactions with the European doctors he had met, not only in France, but in Tunis too – where the number of 'Frankish doctors [had] increased'. He reported how he corresponded with French physicians whom he had known personally, sending and receiving numerous letters from them. The physicians sent him an epistle (*risala*) containing the views of a physician by the name of Insanu, but it was in 'their own language', and only after the *humma* reached Tunis did Khujah realise the need to translate it to Arabic. To do so, he turned for help in the medical terminology to the physician Harun Abi al-Uyun (possibly a Jewish physician in Tunis), and then presented the final document to his community.[31] When Abdallah bin Aisha visited France in 1699, he returned with a letter from the chief astronomer in Paris addressed to the 'Astronomes de Fez & de Maroc' in which the French wanted to exchange information: 'Nous en avons observé plusieurs de nos jours, & je croy que vous en avez observé aussi.'[32] Science and medicine were valuable means for communicating across the religious and military boundaries.

Shadow theatre was also instrumental in providing general information about Europeans. This theatre was popular in Egypt and other parts of the North African Mediterranean, especially after the arrival of the Moriscos, who re-enacted scenes from their Spanish experience before their new co-religionists.[33] It disseminated images and news about European affairs to the wider and illiterate public. A reconstructed text from a seventeenth-century shadow piece performed in Alexandria tells of a Moroccan (*Magharibi*) who arrives from Venice to announce an imminent attack by the *nasara*. He tells the Muslims about the military forces that were preparing to strike them and calls on them to 'break the army of the Christians, and destroy the walls' of their fortifications. Significantly, he alludes to European attacks that had been rebuffed and to territories that, by the early 1600s, had been seized from them by the Muslims: 'The lands of Cyprus and Algiers obey his [Muslim commander's] order; send a letter to Rhodes, and all the Christians around. The ships are ready to fight with two thousand soldiers.'[34] How the puppets – were puppets being used in the non-representational culture of Islam? – portrayed the Christians is not known. But they would have served to bring images of Euro-Christians to the centre of the Islamic community. Similarly, the 1607 'Tragicomédie Prophétique des Affaires des Bays Bas' introduced the pasha of Tripoli in Syria to the paradoxes, rivalries and slapstick of European affairs. In five acts, the actors burlesqued the relations between Spain and Holland, while alluding to the legendary Don Sebastian and to Britain's enmity with Spain. What the pasha made of this is not recorded, but like other Muslim potentates around the Mediterranean, he would have learned about the intriguing, confusing and perhaps amusing affairs of Europe.[35] Similar dramatic art of the European West found its way into the heart of Islamic society and power. Jerónimo de Alcalá showed in the second part of his *El Donado hablador* how a group of Spanish actors, seized and taken to Algiers, performed a play about the rebellion of the Moriscos of Granada – a performance that so angered the pasha that he had them all executed. Doubtless, their interpretation of the events, and possible denunciation of Islam, sealed their fate.[36] For the Algerians who were not familiar with theatre, it may not have been possible to separate fiction from reality.

At the same time, European diplomats, merchants and commercial factors passed on information to the North African leaders in the hope of winning support for their projects, commercial as well as diplomatic and military. European kings and ministers often instructed their representatives to inform – and misinform – the Muslim rulers about changes of alliances in Europe, so that the rulers would change their policies and re-evaluate their strategies. In 1599, Jasper Tomson, the English agent in Marrakech, was asked to give an account of the Ottoman invasion of Hungary in 1596, in which he had participated – which account was 'sett downe in Larbie tonge ... [by] the Kinges cheiffe interpretour for the Latine and Spanish tongues. Where we spent 6 howres together till the night approched.' And when he received letters from overseas about Ottoman affairs, Tomson 'advertised the Vicerey thereof'.[37] In a letter of 1608 to Philip III, Mulay Zaidan explained that he relied on European merchants for information: 'Merchants who travel in distant horizons and reach faraway lands are the tongues of time, and from them pencils [draw information] about lands and the news of mankind.'[38] Sometimes, however, the information which was passed on to the Magharibi was inaccurate. In 1680, the English factor in Tripoli, James Baker, reported that French agents and their Jewish employees were falsely informing the local population about 'the late conspiracie in England against his Majesties Royall Person'.[39] Indeed, throughout the second half of the seventeenth century and until the end of the War of the Spanish Succession, agents from both France and England repeatedly spread false rumours in order to undermine treaties signed by Morocco or Algeria with their rivals. When information about Europeans was inaccurate, it could well be that it had been inaccurately, and deliberately, relayed to the Magharibi.

Meanwhile, on the occasion of victory over the *nasara*, Magharibi writers composed poems that described the course of battles, the casualties, the tactics and finally the glorious ascendancy of the Muslim warrior or his martyrdom. Such oral recitations were memorised and repeated, and became the bases for the construction of national identity. They were in harmony with a culture that emphasised the orality of religious education where students listened to and repeated the words of their teachers.[40] Such emphasis on one-on-one orality required extensive abilities in memorisation – after which students were able to recite vast amounts of Qur'anic material and *hadith*, along with poems and doggerel describing battles against the infidels. Following the battle of Wadi al-Makhazin, many were the poems written to praise al-Mansur and to describe the battle: Ibn al-Qadi's poem recounted the history of the whole event. It mentioned the appeal of the exiled Moroccan princes to the *nasara*, the number of the enemy soldiers (100,000), the death of Sebastian and Muhammad, and the glory of al-Mansur, the descendant of the Prophet.[41] While there is no known contemporary Arabic prose account of the battle, Ibn al-Qadi's poem, along with numerous others which were memorised and later transcribed in al-Fishtali's chronicles, provided the immediate listeners as well as future generations with a Moroccan record of the battle. Similarly, poems by al-Fishtali and other court scribes which were recited before al-Mansur (and later transcribed) provide the only detailed description of the palace of al-Badee' which al-Mansur built during his lifetime; the accuracy of their description can be verified by reference to European published accounts that gave similar descriptions of the palace. After Mulay Ismail retook Tangier in 1684, poems describing the sieges and battles were composed, memorised and recited.[42] Such doggerel was very popular in Magharibi culture.[43] Following the victory over al-Araish in 1689, the jurist Abu al-Mahasin al-Shudri al-Tatwani composed a poem of 170 lines describing the negotiations before the battle, the Sunday of the day of the battle, the Christian captives who were later seized and the *qissees* who negotiated on their behalf.[44]

Every chronicle of the history of a Magharibi region, written from the eighteenth century onwards, contained orally transmitted poems which described the weapons used in battle, the ammunitions, the plans, where each famous leader was stationed and how they had been dressed – their swords, horses and flags. The poems narrated the course of events leading up to the battle: how the call for *jihad* had been sounded, how students (*talaba*) had flocked from all regions to join the battle, how and when the battle site had been seized by the infidels, its place in the history of Christian–Islamic confrontation, and then the day, and even the hour, on which the battle occurred wherein the infidels had been defeated. When ships were built that were to serve in the *jihad* against the invading infidels (*kafirin*) poems such as those recorded in *Al-Kitab al-Bashi* by Hammouda bin Abd al-Aziz (d.1788) were circulated in Tunis in anticipation of victory.[45] After the Danish attack on Algiers in 1770, a song described *qissat dha al-bonba – kaif jabouha a'dna* – the account of the bombardment, which our enemies brought upon us – a song that remained in recitation until it was recorded at the beginning of the twentieth century. Where print in Europe preserved information, the poetic and oral traditions preserved the historical and theological record in the Maghrib. After J. Morgan translated a Morisco treatise (which he had bought in Tunis on 27 September 1710, as he himself wrote on the manuscript),[46] he was stunned to hear some Tunisians 'of both Sexes, sing, in Concert, whole chapters out of this Work, to the Sound of Lutes and Guitars'.[47]

Many writers prefaced their material by confirming the trustworthiness of oral sources. Indeed, the tradition of *tawaatur* (repetition with the same content), which had been used in the establishment of Islam's religious canons, widely served in the authentication as well as the dissemination of early modern information.[48] '*Hadhihi al-akhbar tusaddiq an dhalika al-makan wa-l-khabar mutawaatir anhu*', wrote Ibn Abi Dinar about a specific place in Tunis: 'this information validates [the information] about that location, and the information is validated by repetition.'[49] Of course, orally transmitted information could prove inaccurate – just as much as written histories could be tainted by individual prejudices and biases. In *al-Hulal al-Sundusiyah fi al- Akhbar al-Tunisiyah* (written 1726–31), Muhammad bin Muhammad Wazir al-Sarraj describes how he queried descendants of individuals who had witnessed certain events in Tunisian history. On one occasion, his transmitters corrected an account recorded by the historian Ibn Abi Dinar (fl.1698). The latter had mentioned that at the beginning of the rule of Ahmad Khujah, Maltese ships had attacked the Tunisian harbour of Halq al-Wadi. After citing Abi Dinar, al-Sarraj added: 'But I was told by one whom I trusted that the attack was carried out by the English, who burned eleven ships, one of which belonged to Salee. And it was said that the English ships fired that day fifteen thousand shells which, because of the smoke of gunpowder, turned day to night.'[50] Al-Sarraj's informant was correct. A culture without print is not without accuracy and memory.

Oral communication served in the dissemination of news at the local, national and even international level. When the anti-Spanish warrior, Abu Abdallah al-Ayyashi, was killed in 1641, news of his death quickly reached Alexandria, where the Christians celebrated it. Even in Mecca a man dreamt about the death of the warrior, which was soon confirmed.[51] When the French delegation reached Mulay al-Rashid in the mid-1660s, they were amazed to find that he had 'caused to be spread abroad' a report of their visit which reached all the way to Fez.[52] Indeed, so successful were these reports around the country that 'all the high-wayes to the City thronged with ... vast multitudes'.[53] In Safar 1101 AH (November 1689), Abu al-Abbas al-Qadiri reached Egypt on his return from the pilgrimage to Mecca. A letter arrived from the Maghrib informing the caravan that in the month of Muharram, al-Araish had been reclaimed from the Spaniards by Mulay Ismail: the troops had laid siege to it for three months and then had blasted their way into it, and taken possession of all the booty there.[54] In less than one month, news had spread across all of North Africa. Even in the Far East, Magharibi travellers learned about events in their own countries as well as about events in Europe. Hammouda bin Abd al-Aziz reported meeting a traveller from Yemen who had met a merchant from India who had praised Ali Pasha, the ruler of Tunis. Upon being asked how he knew about the Tunisian, the Indian replied that the Franks who traded between the Maghrib and his country brought all kinds of information 'about the kingdoms they visited'.[55] The oral culture tied the world of the seventeenth century together – and continued to do so well into the eighteenth century and the modern period. Muhammad bin al-Tayib al-Qadiri (1712–73) confirmed in his *Kitab iltiqat al-durar* that some of his information came from eyewitnesses to the events he was describing.[56] Abu al-Qasim al-Zayani wrote that he had learned about England from sea-captains who had been sent there by the Moroccan ruler: the information had been communicated orally by Muslim merchants who were trustworthy and reliable.[57] Magharibi oral culture ensured the transmission of information from one region to another, and from one generation to another. A Moroccan writer could still describe the British violence against Tangier three-quarters of a century after it had occurred:

In the middle of Ramadan [1680–1], the Christians attacked from Tangier and fought the Muslims, of whom more than a hundred were killed. In Rabee' al-awal [1684], the siege on the *nasara* [Christians] was intensified, so they left Tangier after destroying its buildings and all that was within its walls, and they fled. So the Muslims entered Tangier, God be praised, and began to build its wall in Jamadi al-awal.[58]

In this context of popular oral transmission, material by and about Magharibi captives in Christendom constitutes the most extensive corpus of scattered anecdotes, recollections, biographical entries and letters. Cumulatively, this material provides a general portrait of the culture of captivity in the early modern Maghrib. This was a culture of the 'lower classes', to use Ginzburg's term, but it was also a culture that influenced the ruling and scholarly classes. This material does not belong to a distinct genre of writing with its distinct set of conventions, as in the European tradition, nor to a body of macro-historical documents and treatises: rather, it appears as subtexts in other texts, intrusions into larger polemics, hagiographies, or histories and religious expositions. But this 'meager, scattered, and obscure documentation can be put to good use'[59] – to provide a panoramic view of the Euro-Christians constituted from within the experience of the thousands of Magharibi men and women who were taken captive into Christendom.

Captives were sometimes the first conduits of reliable cultural, religious and military information about the Christians to their communities: they were the first commoners to see the European world from within, to experience the homes and gardens, galleys and slave markets of the *nasara*. Notwithstanding their bias, the captives' narratives still conveyed observations about the Christians, and evaluations about religious or social codes of behaviour. The captives were the first to (be forced to) learn European languages and to observe Christian rituals and social customs (in order to avoid punishment or retribution for breaking codes). In the same way that the published captivity corpus served to inform Europeans about the world of the Muslims,[60] so did the anecdotes, tales and memories of the captives serve to inform the Magharibi public about the world of the Christians. Accounts of captivity were stamped in the annals of Magharibi memory, providing, as they did in the European tradition, the most lasting image of the dangerous, predatory and different Other. The *corpus captivitis* records the voice of Muslims who have more often than not been heard: it brings this hitherto lost group into the historical evidence about the early modern Mediterranean, and provides an important corrective to the Eurocentric discourse about the Christian–Muslim encounter – and to all other discourses that resulted from European military and imperial hegemony.

Official sources

While popular information presents the views that prevailed in oral culture, ambassadorial accounts are of paramount importance for expounding, in writing, the official Magharibi view about Europeans. Travel accounts by Magharibi ambassadors or royal envoys provided a rich source – the richest in writing – of information about Christendom. The account by al-Tamjarouti of his journey to Istanbul in 1590–91, for instance, furnished al-Mansur with information about the Mediterranean coastline and its European pirates. There were also writings by Ahmad bin Abdallah (c.1609);[61] Ahmad bin Ghanem and Ahmad bin Qasim in the second quarter of the seventeenth century; Muhammad Temim's *Kitab al-Ajaib* (now lost) in 1682;[62] al-Ghassani's travelogue of 1691, and Abdallah bin Aisha's letters in 1700.[63] Qasim's memoir was the first Arabic account to provide a description of France and Holland by a Muslim in the early modern period. Along with other accounts by Arab writers of North Africa, including the *mashriqi* account about Fakhr-u-Din's journey to Italy by Ahmad al-Khalidi al-Safadi in the second decade of the seventeenth century,[64] Qasim's account provides the earliest, most extensive and varied description of Europeans by a non-Christian.[65]

There are records (and sometimes summaries) of about 80 or so ambassadorial delegations from North Africa into western Europe in the period under study. Although there are no written descriptions of most of the journeys, the ambassadors reported orally what they learned to rulers and courtiers and families (very much, for instance, as Sir Francis Drake reported in 1581 on his circumnavigation of the globe to Queen Elizabeth in a six-hour session). Monarchs and rulers were often more eager to listen than to read, and as Fatma Göçek has shown about Ottoman ambassadors in the eighteenth century,[66] ambassadors always gave extensive oral accounts of their trips to their rulers and members of the court.[67] In similar manner, in November 1616, 31 Muslim delegates were sent to Marseilles, and upon their return, 'raconté qu'ils avaient été comblés d'amabilités'.[68] Abdallah bin Aisha stated that after his return from European journeys, his ruler, Mulay Ismail, would quiz him for months about all aspects pertaining to the lands and peoples he had visited. So frequently did he tell his family about the ladies he had met in France and the friends he had made that the French community became a raging topic of conversation in Meknes. Ambassadorial communication informed the court and the family, the ruler and the tribe.

Magharibi ambassadors and envoys did not write as European visitors to the world of Islam did, not because they lacked curiosity about the European world, but because the traditional goal of travel was much more personal than it was for a European. The vast Arabic travel corpus of the early modern period shows the importance of human contact for the Muslims. Travellers did not travel to see 'things' but to meet scholars and jurists, and to acquire learning or fulfil pilgrimage rites. Because they travelled in a world with which they shared both religion and language, they engaged in personal relations as well as in intellectual pursuits: they wrote about men and sometimes women, books, Sufi circles, holy 'saints' libraries, shrines and only tangentially did they describe landscape and ruins and institutions. That is why a Moroccan visiting Jerusalem could not but describe a very different Jerusalem from what an English traveller saw – because of different empirical premises and religious assumptions and, most importantly, personal and emotional contacts.[69] Such contacts were clearly unavailable to them when they travelled in Christendom where they found themselves without any previous written models they could emulate or travelogues from which they could borrow – except Arabic material of the early Islamic conquests (and that only in the case of Spain). Where European travellers could rely on classical, biblical and pilgrimage sources – inaccurate and biased as they often were – for descriptions of North Africa and the Levant which would prepare them for their encounter, the Magharibi had no Arabic sources about Europe, and no learned and deeply cherished scholars in whose houses they could sleep and by whose wisdom they could grow.

Still, the ambassadors were inquisitive and had access to various levels of social, religious and political venues of information. The Moroccan ambassador to England in 1682 was observed by the English captive Thomas Phelps to try to improve 'his knowledge of English affairs'.[70] What enabled the ambassadors to come to terms (in part) with the new cultural environments was their educated backgrounds: the Moroccan ambassador to Spain in 1690, al-Ghassani, commented on Spain's decline through the historiographical perspective of Ibn Khaldun. Even when some envoys found themselves taken hostage by their hosts, they still tried to gather practical information for future negotiations and treaties.[71] The ambassadors recorded, or had scribes who recorded, all significant details; they were careful and precise, counting columns, registering the names of the villages through which they passed and distances between them, and describing meetings and conversations, encounters and amicable engagements. They wrote with 'le sérénité d'un observateur impartial', as Henri Pérès noted about the Moroccan ambassador to Spain in 1690, al-Ghassani.[72] The ambassadors knew that they served their rulers best by providing precise and useful information in their final reports – many of which have survived in numerous manuscript copies attesting to their wide circulation.

*   *   *

From before 1578 until 1727 and after, the Arabs of the western Mediterranean had a broad engagement with Europeans. In chronicles and biographies, religious polemic and theological rulings, royal epistles and ambassadorial memoirs, captives' accounts and commercial exchange, in verse and prose, rulers and commoners developed a view of the Europeans as partners and rivals, sailors and ambassadors, captors and captives, husbands and wives. On the Magharibi side, there was no structural aversion to Europeans: the Magharibi had fought with Europeans as well as converted to Christianity, just as some Europeans had converted to Islam. The two communities visited each other's lands as well as raided and looted them; they loved and hated, debated and traded, ate and drank with each other. The relationship was ambivalent and harsh, friendly and adversarial, short-lived and long-term, polarised and hybrid.

As Europeans borrowed from the Islamic East, so did the Islamic West borrow from Europeans. The Moriscos who arrived in North Africa brought with them aspects of the Renaissance which were integrated into Magharibi culture: *Don Quixote* was read in Tunis as well as in London,[73] and Christian architectural designs appeared in North African mosques just as Turkish carpets and Arabic calligraphy appeared in churches.[74]

A searching curiosity governed Magharibi travellers who sought out churches, European art and European perceptions and images of them. Although the Magharibi did not formulate a secular 'worldview' into which they fitted the Europeans – their view was always religious – in the manner that European scholars and antiquarians did about the world of Islam, their writings reveal an array of allusions to, and insights about, the *nasara*, both hostile and amicable, from the lands of the *ifranj* to those of the *ingleez*. Their descriptions of the Christians show how relations were not always oppositional – that while there were battles and kidnappings, captivity and humiliation, there was also diplomacy, amicability, cooperation and negotiation – that in the same manner there were different perspectives in European literature about early modern Islam and Muslims, so were there different views and emotions among the Magharibi about early modern Europeans.

Notes

1. From the autobiography of Ahmad bin Qasim, *Kitab nasir al-din ala al-qawm al-kafirin* in Nabil Matar, trans. and ed., *In the Lands of the Christians: Arabic Travel Writings in the Seventeenth Century* (New York: Routledge, 2003), p. 15. See the edition of the text by Muhammad Razzuq (al-Dar al-Bayda': Kulliyat al-Adab wal-Ulum al-Insaninyya, 1987) and the translation and edition by P. S. Van Koningsveld, Q. Al-Samarrai, and G. A. Wiegers (Madrid: Al-Majsli al-A'la lil-Abhath al-Ilmiyya, 1997). Unless otherwise indicated, all references

are to the Koningsveld text. For studies on Qasim, see Gerard Wiegers, 'A Life Between Europe and the Maghrib', in Geert Jan van Gelder and Ed de Moor, eds., *The Middle East and Europe: Encounters and Exchanges* (Amsterdam and Atlanta: Rodopi, 1992): 1: 87–115, and 'Learned Moriscos and Arabic Studies in the Netherlands, 1609–1624', in Jens Lüdtke, ed., *Romania Arabica* (Tübingen: Narr, 1996), pp. 405–17.

2. *Arabs and Barbarians* (London: Riad El-Rayyes, 1991), p. 228.
3. Tarif Khalidi, 'Islamic Views of the West in the Middle Ages', *Studies in Interreligious Dialogue* 5 (1995): 31–42.
4. Muhammad Nur al-Din Afayah, *Al-Gharb al-Mutakhayyal* (Beirut and Dar al-Baida': al-Markas al-Thaqafi al-Arabi, 2000).
5. Abdallah Ibrahim, *Al-Markaziyya al-Islamiyya* (Beirut and Dar al-Baida': al-Markas al-Thaqafi al-Arabi, 2001). See also the brief study by Thabit Abdullah, 'Arab Views of Northern Europeans in Medieval History and Geography', in *Cairo Papers in Social Science* 19 (1996): 73–81.
6. Ibrahim Abu Lughod, *The Arab Rediscovery of Europe* (Princeton, NJ: Princeton University Press, 1963), p. 6.
7. Khalid Ziadeh, *Iktishaf al-taqaddum al-urubbi* (Beirut: Dar al-Nashr, 1981).
8. Confirming that conclusion, Stuart B. Schwartz does not include any material on the Islamic perception of Europeans in his *Implicit Understandings: Observing, Reporting, and Reflecting on the Encounters between Europeans and Other Peoples in the Early Modern Era* (Cambridge: Cambridge University Press, 1994), nor did Anthony Pagden in his two-volume survey, *Facing Each Other: The World's Perception of Europe and Europe's Perception of the World* (Brookfield, VT: Ashgate, 2000). Alastair Hamilton surveys *Arab Culture and Ottoman Magnificence in Antwerp's Golden Age* (Oxford: Arcadian Library, 2001) in an attractive coffee-table book that does not, however, analyse the relations of cultures and their implications.
9. Charles Issawi, *Cross-Cultural Encounters and Conflicts* (Oxford and New York: Oxford University Press, 1998).
10. Susan Gilson Miller, trans. and ed., *Disorienting Encounters: Travels of a Moroccan Scholar in France in 1845–1846* (Berkeley, CA: University of California Press, 1992); and the edition of the Arabic text by Miller and Khalid Bin al-Saghir (Rabat: Muhammad al-Khamis University, 1995).
11. Nazik Saba Yarid, *Arab Travellers and Western Civilization* (London: Saqi Books, 1996). See also Mohamed El Mansour, 'Moroccan Perceptions of European Civilisation in the Nineteenth Century', in George Joffe, ed., *Morocco and Europe* (London: Centre of Near and Middle Eastern Studies, 1989), pp. 37–45; Said bin Said al-Alawi, *Urubba fi mir'at al-rihla* (Rabat: Muhammad al-Khamis University, 1995); Gilles Veinstein, *Le paradis des infidels* (Paris: Maspéro, 1981); Fatma Müge Göçek, *East Meets West: France and the Ottoman Empire in the Eighteenth Century* (New York: Oxford University Press, 1987); and Michael Harbsmeir, 'Early Travels to Europe: Some Remarks on the Magic of Writing', in Francis Barker, et al., eds., *Europe and its Others* (Colchester: University of Essex, 1985): 2: 72–89.
12. Abd al-Majid Qadduri, *Sufara' Magharibi fi Urubba, 1610–1922* (Rabat: Muhammad al-Khamis University, 1995). See also the earlier survey by Henri Pérès, *L'Espagne vue par les voyageurs Musulmans de 1610 à 1930* (Paris: Librairie d'Amérique et d'Orient, 1937).

13. See Gaytari Chakravorty Spivak, 'Can the Subaltern Speak?', in Cary Nelson and Lawrence Grossberg, eds., *Marxism and the Interpretation of Culture* (Urbana and Chicago: University of Illinois Press, 1988), pp. 271–313 on the silencing of 'subaltern' subjects in colonial situations.

14. At the end of the eighteenth century, Hammouda bin Abd al-Aziz used the term 'islamiyyeen' in reference to converted Jews; see Muhammad Madhur, ed., *al-Kitab al-Bashi* (Tunis: al-Dar al-Tunisiyya Lil-Nashr, 1970), p. 303.

15. Abd Allah Gannun, ed., *Rasail Sa'diyah* (Titwan: Ma'had Mulay al-Hasan, 1954), p. 174.

16. Louis Cardaillac, *Morisques et Chrétiens: un affrontment polemique, 1492–1640* (Paris: Klincksieck, 1977).

17. All references to al-Ghassani's travelogue are from my translation, *In the Lands of the Christians*, p. 165.

18. Comte Henry de Castries, *Moulay Ismail et Jaques II* (Paris: Ernest Leroux, 1903), p. 7.

19. See the note by Daniel Goffman, *The Ottoman Empire and Early Modern Europe* (Cambridge: Cambridge University Press, 2002), p. 4 n. 5.

20. There is mention in both Moroccan and Algerian records of the capture of German (*alman*) ships.

21. See the letter from Mulay Ismail to King William, Public Records Office, London, *State Papers*, 102/4/102.

22. *A Letter from a Gentleman of the Lord Ambassador Howard's Retinue* (1670), p. 2.

23. The Persian convert Don Juan wrote his account of his travels from Persia to Spain in 1604 after, however, he had converted to Christianity. His text is therefore neither by a Muslim nor written in his native language.

24. Edward Muir and Guido Ruggiero, eds., *Microhistory & the Lost Peoples of Europe*, trans. Eren Branch (Baltimore, MD: Johns Hopkins University Press, 1991), p. x.

25. Ibn Ghalbun, known as Al-Tarabulsi, *Tarikh Tarablus al-Gharb* (Cairo: al-Matba'a al-Salafiyya, 1930), p. 165.

26. Quoted in Abd al-Aziz Shahbar, 'Al-Liqa' al-Islami al-Masihi', *Academia* 15 (1989), p. 62.

27. Public Records Office, London, *State Papers*, 102/4/122.

28. Hasan al-Yusi, *Al-Muhadarat*, ed. Muhammad Hajji (Rabat: Dar al-Maghrib, 1976), p. 81.

29. H. P. J. Renaud and G. S. Colin, trans., *Documents Marocains pour servir à l'histoire du 'Mal Franc'* (Paris: Libraire Larosse, 1935), p. 3.

30. *Mercure Galant* (February 1682), pp. 311–12.

31. Hussayn Khujah, *Al-Asrar al-Kaminah*, ed. Al-Karray al-Qusantini (Tunis: Beit al-Hikma, 1993), pp. 32–3.

32. *Mercure Galant* (April 1699), p. 249.

33. Ahmad Hamruni, 'Tastur', in *Dairat al-Maarif al-Tunisiyya* (Tunis, 1993): 3: 62–73.

34. Paul Kahle, ed., *Der Leuchtturm Von Alexandria* (Stuttgart: Kohlhammer, 1930), p. 19.

35. E. K. Purnell and A. B. Hinds, eds., *Report on the Manuscripts of the Marquess of Downshire preserved at Easthampstead Park, Berks* (London: HMSO, 1936): 2: 79–84.

36. *El Donado hablador* (Valladolid, 1626).

37. Henri De Castries, *Les Sources Inédités de l'Histoire du Maroc: Archives et Bibliothèques D'Angleterre*, 2 vols. (Paris: Leroux, 1918–36): 1: 358; Pierre de Cenival and Philipe de Cosse Brissac, *Les Sources Inédités de l'Histoire du Maroc: Archives et Bibliothèques D'Angleterre* (Paris: Geuthner, 1936): 2: 143–4.
38. García-Arenal Mercedes et al., *Cartas Marruecas* (Madrid, 2002), p. 226.
39. Public Records Office, London, *State Papers*, 71/22/18r.
40. It is important to remember that the *ijazah* carried not the name of an institution but of a jurist.
41. *Durrat al-Suluk*, Rabat, National Library, Ms Dal 1428, 14.
42. 'In the beginning of the month of Rabi' al-Awwal / No sound was left of the *ruum* in Tangier; / In the year a thousand, add to it nine and five, / It now has passed; / The sultan ordered the reconstruction, With no delay or question', quoted in Muhammad Dawud, *Tarikh Titwan* (Titwan, 1959–), vol. 1, 2nd part, p. 270.
43. For the importance of the *urjooza* in Magharibi literary tradition, see the discussion in al-Arabi al-Hamadi, 'Al-ta'leef al-tareekhi fee al-ahd al-alawi: Abu al-Qasim al-Zayyani nomoothajan', in Muhammad Lamiri, ed., *Nadwat al-Harakah al-Ilmiyah fi 'Asr al-Dawla al-'Alawiyah ila Awakhir al-Qarn al-Tasi 'Ashar* (Oujda: Mohammad I University, 1995), pp. 236–7.
44. Quoted in full in Dawud, *Tarikh Titwan*, vol. 2, part 1, 13–16.
45. Hammouda bin Muhammad bin Abd al-Aziz, in Madhur, ed., *al-Kitab al-Bashi*, pp. 169 ff.
46. British Museum, London, Harl. Ms. 7501, inside cover.
47. Muhammad Rabadan, *Mahometism Fully Explained*, 2 vols. (London, 1723–25), 1: 'The Author's Preface', n.p.
48. As Johannes Pederson has noted, many Arabic manuscripts and books often opened by including 'a record of the chain of informants (*isnad*)' representing 'an unbroken oral tradition': *The Arabic Book*, trans. Geoffrey French (Princeton, NJ: Princeton University Press, 1984), p. 23.
49. Ibn Abi Dinar, *Al-Munis fi akhbar Ifriqiyah wa Tunis* (Tunis: Matba'at al-Nahda, 1931), p. 177.
50. Muhammad ibn Muhammad al-Andalusi Wazir al-Sarraj, *al-Hulal al-sundusiyah fi al-akhbar al-Tunisiyah* (Beirut: Dar al-Gharb al-Islami, 1985): 2: 397.
51. Abu al-Abbas al-Nasiri, *Kitab al-*Istiqsa (al-Dar al-Bayda: Dar al-Kitab, 1954–56): 6: 92.
52. Roland Frejus, *The Relation of a Voyage made into Mauritania* (1671), p. 55.
53. Frejus, *Relation*, p. 57.
54. *Nasmat al-Aas*, Rabat, National Library, Ms Kaf 1418, fols. 139r–141r.
55. Madhur, ed., *al-Kitab al-Bashi*, p. 370.
56. Muhammad bin al-Tayib al-Qadiri, *Kitab iltiqat al-durar*, ed. Hashim al-Alawi al-Qasimi (Beirut: Dar al-Afaq al-Jajdidah, 1981): 2: 322.
57. Al-Zayani, *Al-Tarjumanah al-kubra*, p. 302. For a discussion of al-Zayani, see R. Le Torneau, 'Al-Zayyani, Historien des Sa'diens', *Études d'orientalisme dédiées à la Mémorie de Lévi-Provençal* (Paris: Larose, 1962): 2: 631–7.
58. Norman Cigar, trans. and ed., *Nashr al-mathani* (London and New York: Oxford University Press, 1981), pp. 25, 30.
59. Carlo Ginzburg, *The Cheese and the Worms*, trans. John and Anne Tedeschi (Harmondsworth: Penguin, 1982), p. xvii.

60. See the discussion of this thesis in the context of England in my Introduction to Daniel J. Vitkus, ed., *Piracy, Slavery, and Redemption* (New York: Columbia University Press, 2001).

61. G. A. Wiegers, 'The Andalusi Heritage in the Maghrib: The Polemical Work of Muhammad Alguazir (fl. 1610)', in Otto Zwartjes et al., eds., *Poetry, Politics and Polemics: Cultural Transfer between the Iberian Peninsula and North Africa* (Amsterdam and Atlanta: Rodopi, 1996), pp. 107–32.

62. As reported in *Mercure Galant* (January 1682), p. 332.

63. There were also writings by al-Ghazzal and al-Miknasi in the eighteenth century.

64. Asad Rustum and Fuad Afram al-Bustani, *Lubnan fi ahd al-amir Fakhr al-Din al-Ma'ni al-Thani* (Beirut: Manshurat al-Jami'a al-Lubnaniyya, 1969).

65. Only the Ottomans developed a corpus of writing about Europe – but the first account by Katib Chelebi appeared in the second half of the seventeenth century and the first account about France in 1721, nearly a century after Qasim's.

66. Göçek, *East Encounters West*.

67. The Persian convert Don Juan wrote how he started writing a diary as soon as he left Persia with the intent of recording his description of the journey and of the Christian world 'in order later to publish [it] in Persia', *Don Juan of Persia*, trans. G. Le Strange (New York and London: Harper, 1926), p. 294.

68. Eugene Plantet, ed., *Correspondence des Beys de Tunis* (Paris: Alcan, 1899): 1: 13.

69. See my 'Two Journeys to Seventeenth-Century Palestine', *Journal of Palestine Studies* 29 (2000): 66–79.

70. Vitkus, ed., *Piracy, Slavery and Redemption*, p. 205.

71. For captured ambassadors, see 'Une Ambassade en otage', in El Mokhtar Bey, *Le Fondateur Hussein Ben Ali (1705–1735/1740)* (Tunis: Serviced, 1993), pp. 557–84.

72. Pérès, *L'Espagne*, p. 12.

73. Jaime Oliver Asin, 'Le "Quchote" de 1604', in Miguel de Epalza and Ramon Petit, eds., *Receuil d'Etudes sur les Moriscos Andalous en Tunisie* (Madrid: Direction General de Relaciones Culturales, 1973), pp. 240–7; see also L. P. Harvey, 'A Morisco Reader of Jean Lemaire de Belges', *Al-Andalus* 28 (1963): 231–6.

74. J. D. Latham, 'Towns and Cities of Barbary: The Andalusian Influence', in *From Muslim Spain to Barbary* (London: Variorum, 1986), pp. 188–205.

8

'The Treacherous Cleverness of Hindsight':[1] Myths of Ottoman Decay

Caroline Finkel

'Anyone who wants an outline grasp of history, the core of all subjects, can grasp it here.' Thus wrote *The Economist* in 1993 of a short history of the world by an eminent Oxford historian. The index of the volume in question promises comprehensive coverage: all time from before *Homo erectus* to the fall of the USSR, and all geographic space including, literally, space. It comes as something of a disappointment, then, to find that when it comes to the Ottoman Empire – a state, a civilisation indeed, that occupied extensive territory on three continents for more than six centuries – the history is not only short, but also very short, brutish, and displaying worryingly little grasp of the subject in hand. I quote:

> The explanation of Ottoman decline lies partly in internal weakness. For all its huge extent on the map, Ottoman power varied very much from place to place ...
>
> There was no centralized administration worth the name; the Ottoman empire was in most places a matter of arrangements between the 'pasha'... and local bigwigs about the way in which taxes could be raised. This gave the pashas much power and some of them came to resemble dynastic princes as time went by ...
>
> The Ottoman 'state' had been put together more or less haphazardly in order to fight the infidels. Such organisation as it had was basically military; it was meant to provide recruits and taxes to pay soldiers and did this by arrangements not unlike the 'feudal' tenures of western Europe. This structure had already become corrupt by the seventeenth century ... The sultan himself was the centre of intrigue; favourites, the women of the harem, generals and religious leaders all

sought to influence him ... The most professional regiments which the Turks possessed were the Janissaries, but they were sadly decayed by 1700 ...

Finally, throughout the Muslim community at large, real power was exercised by the religious leaders ...

Of modernization there was little. Almost all that was successfully achieved was the conversion of the navy in the 1690s from the old oared galleyships to sailing ships of the European kind ... (one sign of Ottoman decline at this period is the increasing employment of Europeans in the navy and army).[2]

I think that I have not done injustice to this text by omitting the few additional details it contains. I quote it because it provides a not untypical analysis of the Ottoman state and its political culture, and indicates the Sisyphean struggle Ottoman historians face when they emerge from the company of their likeminded colleagues to engage in dialogue with historians of other times and places. Eleven years is a long time in historiography, but even allowing for the limited number of works on Ottoman history that were then available in contrast with the case today, such a mode of exposition fails to help readers understand anything about the subject in hand – neither how the Empire functioned internally nor its complex web of relations with contemporary states to west and east.[3]

When we examine the passages quoted above, we find that if the author had not announced that he was describing the Ottoman Empire, much of what he writes could as well be applied to other contemporary states – the uneven distribution of the application of power; provincial administration as a matter of local negotiation; power accumulated by local notables who became dynastic princes; raising men and taxes for the pursuit of war; the monarch jostled by competing factions; real power exercised by religious leaders. Yet put alongside what are intended to be peculiarly Ottoman or Muslim characteristics, these universal features are turned on their head and become pejorative judgements: features that are common to all states are here represented as being somehow peculiar to the Ottoman context. Still more negative are the following notions: 'the Ottoman "state" had been put together more or less haphazardly in order to fight the infidels'; 'such organisation as it had was basically military'; the land-for-military service structure 'had become corrupt by the seventeenth century'; 'its military forces were 'sadly decayed'; 'of modernisation there was little'.

Here we have a cogent expression of how the Ottoman Empire appears to many of today's non-specialists. Driven by the crusading military spirit (*jihadist*, in today's parlance), their institutions corrupted, their armies decayed and held in the grip of religious authority, the Ottomans become – in Eric R. Wolf's memorable phrase – a 'people without history'.[4] What never fails to surprise Ottoman historians is that European historians may be quite excellent analysts of the time and place of their immediate interest, but when they look beyond, their critical faculties seem to shut down – though it is true that Ottoman historians have been regrettably slow in making available the fruits of their labours to non-specialist readers. The example I cite here is only one: many historians of Europe seem to believe that none of the criteria according to which they analyse their own history applies to the history of other societies. For them the pursuit of war and the grip of an unquestionable religion are the salient features of the Ottoman state – as if warfare and religion had no place in the history of Europe – and as though that was all there was to Ottoman history.

The Ottoman Empire, it is widely accepted by non-specialists, rose, declined and fell within the span of some 600 years – and that is about all anyone needs to know about it. The Ottomans had no Renaissance, no Reformation, no Enlightenment – and once the state could not expand territorially, it turned in on itself and its history came to an end until military reform along European lines rescued it for a while from its inevitable demise. Moreover, we are told by leading authorities that the Ottomans were quite uninterested in what was happening elsewhere in the world because they had an innate sense of superiority; that they conducted trade with Europe through the Sultan's Christian and Jewish subjects because Muslims knew no foreign languages – and in any case, no self-respecting Muslim would dirty his hands with commercial transactions. The Ottomans, it is said, had no curiosity and failed to discover new worlds. 'What', it has recently and hubristically been asked by one best-selling author, 'went wrong?' Why, indeed, could they not be like us?[5]

This Eurocentric view of how things were offers a more sinister version of the mindset with which I began. Where the Oxford historian produced a pejorative statement of how things were supposed to have been that stemmed from ignorance, the 'what went wrong?' mode derives rather from deep knowledge of Ottoman culture and betrays an implicit mission: to compare the Muslim world with Europe and to find the Muslim world wanting. Why, one might better ask, should they be like us? As put by Walter Mignolo in discussing the 'darker side' of the

Renaissance in the Americas:

> It is unfair to ask members of a culture different from ours how
> they do something we do. It is not fair because it assumes that
> whatever we do has a universal value and, as such, every culture on
> earth has to do it, one way or another, if they pretend to be
> human.[6]

Holding up the standard of what evolved into western capitalism to
analyse Muslim societies like that of the Ottomans, and then asking the
'what went wrong?' question, closes our minds to the possibility and
value of other ways of being than our own, and shuts off many more
avenues of historical enquiry than it opens up.

Another mode of writing about the Ottoman Empire – I will refer to it
as the 'fantasticatory' mode – similarly obstructs our ability to understand Ottoman history on its own terms. Unlike the foregoing, however,
this mode is implicitly sympathetic to the Ottomans and their world.
Fantasticators seek to entertain their readers – a laudable aim – but they
are able to do so only by turning Ottoman history into a theatre of the
absurd. Their efforts might be described as 'more caricature than charac-
terization'.[7] Thus, in a recent popular volume, we find such mellifluous
sentences as the following:

> The Ottomans were born to move, and this fact had made them war-
> riors: for upon the frontiers of the empire, movement inevitably
> means war ...
> The Ottoman urge to motion craved satisfaction. The *kul* [servant
> of the Sultan] could leave nothing to his sons, and their status
> required continual display. Power, like the grandeur of the palace,
> could not be still; it could not be stored, as it was in the palaces of the
> West or the bloodlines of European aristocracy ...
> By the eighteenth century the calcifying empire appeared
> encrusted with peculiar polities that had grown up in the vacuum of
> initiative, waiting in vain to be reorganised and digested by the cen-
> tral authority. They achieved a sort of ramshackle permanence
> instead, like eccentric lodgers in a rambling country house.[8]

I am not sure what any of this means, but in works of fantastication,
entertainment is valued over content, whose quality as history is unim-
portant as long as the narrative zips along at a spanking pace. The
problem, however, is that neither wondering what went wrong nor

fantasticating centuries of experienced history can help in the urgent task of portraying a past that can have given rise to the present.

* * *

Happily, the picture is not entirely gloomy. The coinage I have borrowed for my title comes from the pen of another Oxford historian who sees matters differently. Writing of the later centuries of the Ottoman Empire, he reminds us that it was not ever thus, that hindsight – and, one might add, teleology – compound the distortions already implicit in the historian's efforts to recover an understanding of the past. This is particularly the case for the period we know as the Renaissance, a nineteenth-century concept that is still widely accepted as the overarching framework for explaining why the 'West' is as it is – modern, civilised, free and democratic – and why the 'East' is not. However, as the present volume demonstrates, the scholarly output of historians who eschew such old narratives in favour of new ways of thinking is gradually reaching a wider audience. And for the specialist historian writing of the Ottoman Empire, recent years have seen wide interest among non-specialists in 'bringing the Ottomans back in', to adapt the title of another seminal work.[9] More European historians than ever before are now alive to the ways in which they constrict the telling of their own story if they fail to acknowledge that the lines of separation on the modern map conceal a shared and complex past.

Ottoman history is a relatively new field of enquiry and the visible successes in war of the Empire in the fifteenth and sixteenth centuries, and the warrior-sultans who ruled then were, inevitably, among the first topics to draw scholarly attention. It cannot be denied, therefore, that Ottoman historians must share the blame for the state of our field today. The reigns of Mehmed II 'the Conqueror' (1444–6, 1451–81), Bayezid II 'the Saint' (1481–1512), Selim I 'the Grim' (1512–20), Süleyman I 'the Magnificent' (1520–66) – the sultans who ruled when the Renaissance was in full swing – were viewed by a nostalgic and influential group of Ottoman intellectuals as a golden age, the high point against which all Ottoman history must be measured – *après eux le déluge*. The 'decline' thus set in – though there is no unanimity about timing – with the reign of Selim II 'the Sot' (1566–74). There were of course dissident voices, both then and today, but these were not allowed to cloud the myth, and like believers in the literal truth of the Bible, today's historians have been led astray by the writings of contemporary Ottoman commentators who had their own ideas of how they wanted to portray society and their place in it. Just as Renaissance scholars confront their own ghosts – those of Michelet, Burckhardt and the rest – Ottoman scholars have a mythical legacy of their own to contend with. Ottoman historians have long spoken of a 'Classical Age' extending between Mehmed II's succession in 1451 and Süleyman's death in 1566; though sometimes it has been allowed to reach as far as 1600. Perhaps it is not by chance that it corresponds with the Renaissance in European history.

The other era of Ottoman history that has attracted an abundance of scholarly attention is the nineteenth century, the time of reform under the European tutelage that supposedly saved the Empire from imminent demise and allowed it to limp along for another century and more. The two centuries between the Renaissance and the beginnings of 'westernisation' in the Empire – roughly from 1600 to 1800 – were until very recently very poorly known.[10]

This very selective interest in the span of Ottoman history until recent years was reflected in Lord Kinross's classic *The Ottoman Centuries*, which appeared in 1977.[11] Kinross allots some 200 pages to the little more than a century between Mehmed II's succession in 1451 and Süleyman's death in 1566, and another 200 to the 250 years from Süleyman's death to 1800. The imbalance in favour of 'the Conqueror' and 'the Magnificent' is still more pronounced, since the reigns of Bayezid II and Selim I are covered in a mere ten of these 200 pages. The form of Kinross's book, too, reflects perceptions of the Empire at the time when he wrote. The imperial *topoi* beloved of generations of historians are all there: dawn of empire, new Byzantium, zenith of empire, seeds of decline, age of reform. My intention is not to denigrate Kinross's study – which may be deemed of greater value than several of the works referred to so far – but mention him here to illustrate how far his understanding of Ottoman history reflected the sources available to him at the time, both in the relative amount of space he devoted to each century of Ottoman history and in the rise and decline framework within which he told the story of the Empire. This framework was widely accepted at the time he was writing; Ottoman historians themselves have only slowly begun to free themselves from its embrace and to consider the Empire in new ways.

The idea that the Ottoman history was part and parcel of European history is a quite unremarkable notion to an Ottoman historian. The British have perhaps the best excuse for thinking this a little far-fetched since geography set them at great distance from the Empire. Yet, as Gerald MacLean observes in the Introduction to this volume, imported eastern goods affected economic and social life in England in unanticipated and far-reaching ways. For the contemporary states of Europe, whether friend or foe in the long or short term, the Ottoman Empire was a physical presence that loomed large in the thinking of people at all levels of society. Travelling east across Europe, and having passed through the modern successor states of territories that once bordered the Empire – the Habsburg Empire, Venice and the Commonwealth of Poland-Lithuania, where war with the Ottomans was an ever-present possibility – the traveller reaches states that were once part of the Empire and where Ottoman history, whether in its political, economic or cultural form, *was* everyday life, and the history of the Empire *local* history. This was certainly the case in the buffer vassal states of Transylvania, Wallachia and Moldavia, and the several fully incorporated small states of the Balkans, and throughout Hungary. In such places the Ottoman presence could not be ignored.

The perception that there has always been a clash of civilisations between the Ottoman Empire – between the Muslim world at large – and Christian Europe has lost little of its appeal. Part of the reason for its resilience is that respected authorities and popular writers alike refuse to let it die. Why, we must ask, do they prefer to emphasise the divisive forces of war and religion, allowing these to obscure the uniting bonds of art, science, trade, diplomacy and other forms of exchange for mutual benefit? A colourful expression of the preference for the markers of difference over those held in common is the image devised by Perry Anderson some 30 years ago, that the Ottomans 'camped' in Europe and that the state was 'an Islamic intrusion into Christendom'.[12] Such snappy sound-bites are dangerous. Emphasising contrast where close similarities exist makes for a better story, but renders it harder to construct an alternative view of the past.[13]

The other face of the coin of difference is decline. It cannot be coincidental that the decline of the Ottoman Empire is deemed to have begun when territorial conquest slowed: emphasis on the martial characteristics of a state rather than the pacific inevitably leads to such a conclusion. However, stable borders or territorial contractions are *per se* erroneous measures of the health of any state. From around 1600 warfare everywhere in Europe, as on the eastern frontiers of the Ottoman Empire, became more static, more destructive and less glamorous, once it came to be dominated by infantry sieges of fortified positions. Yet the Ottomans were able to hold their own, showing themselves for almost another century to be as successful in playing the waiting game as they were on the battlefield. Their navy, too, had singular success in the sixteenth and seventeenth centuries with the capture from Venice of Cyprus and Crete – though the latter took many years. Diplomacy was another weapon in their arsenal: some ten years before the conquest of Cyprus the Ottomans had reached an understanding with Portugal, their naval rival in the East, over their respective commercial spheres in the Persian Gulf, and did so in the West with Spain by the treaty of 1580.

Nevertheless, the martial continues to occupy the foreground and obscure everything else. A reviewer of Kenneth Setton's otherwise useful volume *Venice, Austria and the Turks* notes the gap in coverage of the seven decades between the Ottoman–Venetian treaty of 1574 and the start of the Cretan war in 1645 during which there was peace between the Empire and the Republic and, more than that, pursuit of commercial and diplomatic interests the two states had in common, for instance against Spanish Milan and Naples.[14] Like the Ottomans of the Classical Age, the European states of the Renaissance employed both diplomacy and military might, and it is not solely the latter that is considered a measure of their health; this depended, rather, on the 'navigators, explorers and settlers' of the time, and on developments in intellectual life and the visual arts – though there are those who believe the latter to have been exaggerated, and much of what supposedly made the Renaissance, a myth.[15]

As the possibility of Turkish membership of the European Union looms – and, at time of writing, tantalisingly recedes – Turkish scholars are revisiting the notion of the Renaissance in relation to the Ottoman Empire. Can this interest have arisen at this time, one might ask, because the Renaissance was the only time in the long existence of the Empire when the Ottomans were thought of favourably by contemporary Europeans? The preferred approach of Turkish scholars writing on the Renaissance is the 'we too' approach, whereby they set out to demonstrate that the Ottomans matched the accomplishments of Europeans, but that their side of the story has been expunged from the record: after all, it is the winners not the losers who write history. Showing that the Ottomans did what the Europeans did is one way of investigating the topic, for it reveals that whatever went on in Europe in the fifteenth and sixteenth centuries was not confined to Europe and could not, therefore, alone account for what followed. Emphasising that the Ottoman Empire did not share in Europe's semblance of coherence and common purpose – a strategy that enables many, despite evidence to the contrary, to continue to talk about a continent-wide Renaissance[16] – but that it 'decayed' throws into relief the notion of the inevitability of the 'rise of the West', the embarkation of Europe on its path to the modern world, and consigns those beyond its borders to backwardness and ignominy. We should not forget, however, that all is not well within Renaissance studies, where there is lively debate about when and where the Renaissance was, and in what it consisted – even whether the term has objective meaning. Showing that the Ottomans in many important respects shared in the cultural and other developments taking place in Europe at this time surely suggests that an explanation for the subsequent divergence in their fates must be sought elsewhere.

An alternative tack, and a harder one to sustain since the voices of those from the periphery who challenge received wisdom invariably fail to be heard, is to eschew the concept that was created with the benefit of hindsight to account for a particular historical moment in a particular location – Europe, or some part of it, in the fifteenth to sixteenth or seventeenth centuries. The task for the Ottoman historian thus becomes one of showing that the specifics of the European case cannot usefully be applied to other societies whose *raison d'être* and rhythms differed from those of Europe. Furthermore, the political contexts in which East and West operated were very different. In what follows I will address elements of the two approaches to the Renaissance outlined here – the 'we too' approach, and the alternative that doubts the usefulness of the concept of the Renaissance as applied to Ottoman history. To illustrate the first approach I will consider, from among the many symptoms of the Renaissance, the following: display of kingship, acquisition of exotic goods, everyday commercial activity and the Ottoman model of the 'Renaissance man'. Discussion of why the Ottoman Empire did not match European exploits in the Americas with its own 'Age of Discovery' in the Indian Ocean will serve to illustrate the futility of such a comparison. Even cultural equivalence should not be pursued too far. All too often, when viewed from the western perspective, comparison of the Ottoman Empire with Europe inevitably results in unwarranted disdain of the former for not matching up to a standard that many fondly imagine to be universal.

Sultan Mehmed II was the contemporary of illustrious monarchs such as Matthias Corvinus of Hungary, and of Ferdinand and Isabella. Süleyman's reign coincided with those of the Holy Roman Emperors Charles V of Habsburg, his brother Ferdinand I, and Charles's son Philip II of Spain; the French Valois kings François I and his son Henri II; the English Tudors, Henry VIII and his children, Edward VI, Mary I and Elizabeth I; and Ivan IV 'the Terrible', Tsar of Muscovy. The Safavid Shah Ismail still ruled in Iran when Süleyman came to the throne and the Mughal emperor Akbar governed in India. Ottoman sultans were as familiar as other rulers of the time with the language of kingship – the game of one-upmanship whereby monarchs tried to outdo one another in magnificence and claims to legitimacy. The Ottomans could take on allcomers. In the early centuries they had told stories about themselves to prove they had greater right to rule than their Muslim rivals, the other emirates of Anatolia. During Mehmed's reign they responded to the threat posed by the White Sheep Turcomans under Uzun Hasan and, beginning in the reign of Bayezid II – Mehmed's son and Süleyman's grandfather – reacted to the alternative to their rule offered by what they saw as the heretical creed of Shiism espoused by Shah Ismail. When they needed to, the Ottomans could also compete with European monarchs in the fashioning of their image. Mehmed II commissioned medals with his likeness on them and was the most active patron of Italian medalists in the Quattrocento. Moreover, he was depicted by a greater number of medalists than any other patron, and the breadth of his patronage is demonstrated by the fact that he was never depicted more than once by any artist.

Süleyman took on Charles V. In 1530, the year after the failed Ottoman siege of Vienna, Charles had been crowned Holy Roman Emperor amid great pomp and circumstance, with his claims to universal kingship made plain. Süleyman took this as an affront, and addressed him in his correspondence simply as 'King of Spain' rather than in the grandiloquent fashion that was usually accorded fellow rulers. His grand vezir, Ibrahim Pasha, saw a more visible way to respond, and in 1532 arranged for a crown resembling Charles's to be commissioned in Venice for the Sultan. This fantastic and expensive object, in fact a helmet-crown, was intended to be worn on Süleyman's march to besiege Vienna or on a campaign to conquer Rome that he was planning. Süleyman did indeed take the helmet-crown with him, and it was prominently displayed at the triumphal parades along the way and when he received the Habsburg envoys who were suing for peace. Many contemporary European sources refer to the helmet-crown, indicating that observers were well aware of the challenge to Charles it boldly embodied.[17]

Such competition over the symbols of kingship was only one aspect of monarchical magnificence espoused by rulers in both East and West. Some Ottoman sultans saw themselves as partaking in a common civilisation encompassing their realm and the West – at the time of the conquest of Constantinople in 1453 the Venetian Niccolò Sagundino reported that Mehmed II was fascinated by the Spartans, the Athenians, the Romans and the Carthaginians, but that he identified above all with Alexander of Macedon and Julius Caesar.[18] In the preface to his eulogistic biography of the Sultan, the Byzantine Kritovoulos of Imbros wrote that Mehmed's exploits equalled those of Alexander. Mehmed fostered this identification of himself with great warriors of the past. On his way to win Lesbos from the Venetians in 1462 he visited Troy, where he viewed the ruins, noted the advantageous location of the site, enquired about the tombs of the heroes of the siege – Achilles and Ajax and others – and reportedly remarked that they had been fortunate indeed to have been extolled by a poet such as Homer.[19] Soon after, he had both the *Iliad* and the standard life of Alexander – Arrian's *Anabasis of Alexander the Great* and the *Indica* – copied for his library.[20] Like Mehmed, Süleyman I wanted to take Rome and reunite East and West.[21] Between 1529 and 1532 there was great fear throughout southern Italy that he considered the time was ripe and that an attack on the kingdom of Naples was imminent.[22]

Mehmed II patronised Gentile Bellini and Constanzo da Ferrara – to name only two of the artists and scholars he supported – in Istanbul, and had his new palace of Topkapı, his mosque complex and his fortress of Yedikule, 'Seven Towers', on the Istanbul land walls all constructed according to Italian forms.[23] His son and successor, Bayezid II, invited Leonardo da Vinci to build a bridge across the Golden Horn and another across the Bosphorus. Michaelangelo was also invited to construct a bridge over the Golden Horn, and in 1519 was encouraged by an Italian merchant to come to Selim I's court at Edirne since the Sultan had recently bought a statue of a reclining nude with her head resting on her arms and might be open, the merchant thought, to further artistic patronage.[24] If the merchant's letter is genuine its contents come as a surprise, because Selim I, the conqueror of the Mamluk state and the Sultan who brought the Muslim Holy Places of Mecca and Medina within the Ottoman Empire, is generally considered to have been stern and puritanical in outlook and therefore unlikely to have appreciated such figural representation.

At the same time that the silver of the Americas was working itself eastwards, the Ottoman elite was enjoying the riches amassed on many campaigns of conquest and the revenues of an efficiently functioning system of tax. There was wealth enough to spend ostentatiously, as well as on goods for private contemplation, and diplomatic goods, luxury goods and everyday trade goods travelled from East to West and West to East in abundance. An idea of the goods entering the Ottoman palace – possibly, on this occasion, for subsequent dispersal in connection with the inauguration of the mosque of Bayezid II – is given in an inventory of 1505 examined by Michael Rogers.[25] Rogers observes that the contents of the inventory attest to the similar tastes of the highborn in East and West. Many of the goods listed – luxury garments, textiles, hangings and furnishings – could as easily have been part of a contemporary European inventory, or indeed treasury. Like the Mediterranean *lingua franca* in matters marine and culinary, so the description and terminology of the textiles in this inventory were, with minor exceptions, such as would have been employed in an Italian inventory. In addition to goods from India and Iran, the inventory contained silver vessels from Venice, South German clocks and astronomical instruments, and Murano glass, as well as items such as pictures, paintings, silver cups, an illustrated book, playing or tarot cards – these last were designated *gebr* or 'Christian', and Rogers suggests they incurred disapproval because they were decorated with figures.

That the same types of luxury goods were appreciated by those who could afford them in both East and West should not surprise us, Rogers reminds us, since at this time the Ottoman elite was largely composed of individuals of Balkan or other European origin who might have ended up anywhere on the continent but who, thanks to the accident of being taken captive or selected for the youth-levy, converted to Islam and made a career serving the Sultan. Notable Balkan aristocrats who became high-ranking Ottomans included Mahmud Pasha Angelović, Mehmed II's grand vezir for many years, whose family was of the Byzanto-Serbian nobility, and Sokullu Mehmed Pasha, grand vezir between 1565 and 1579, who came of Serbian rural nobility. Of Italian origin were Cigalazade Sinan Pasha, born c.1545 as Scipione Cicala, son of the Genoese Visconte Cicala, a vezir who briefly rose to the post of grand vezir, and Gazanfer Agha, who was born a Venetian, son of Giacomo Michiel, chancellor of the *podestà*, and served for the last three decades of the sixteenth century as the chief white eunuch, or chamberlain of the palace pages.[26]

Rogers has written extensively on cultural exchange between the Ottomans and the West in Süleyman's reign in particular – as Julian Raby has on the reign of Mehmed II – and also on Süleyman's patronage of domestic artists; we therefore have quite a good sense of Ottoman court taste in the Classical Age. Writing of the booty Süleyman brought back from his campaigns, Rogers notes that he removed classical manuscripts to Istanbul from the library of Matthias Corvinus in Buda in 1526, and also a Florentine sculptural group with classical figures which was set up outside the palace of Ibrahim Pasha in the hippodrome in Istanbul – where it survived only until Ibrahim's execution ten years later when it was destroyed. From the conquest of Belgrade five years earlier he had brought back an icon of the Virgin. Booty apart, the Ottomans imported silver- and goldsmiths' work from south Germany,

Transylvania, Venice and Dubrovnik, and fine woollens and velvets, brocades and other silk textiles from the Italian city-states. Amber, furs and slaves and much else besides came from Poland and Muscovy, and also luxuries and precious commodities from the East – silk from Iran, and jewels and spices via the entrepôt of Egypt. Like many other sultans, Süleyman was a poet of skill and discernment, with a copious output in Persian and Ottoman. Rogers' account of the age, to which no summary can begin to do justice, demonstrates parallels with contemporary Europe in the arts of the book, carpet-weaving, pottery and tiles, architecture, floriculture, technology and science.[27]

In 1541, the year in which Hungary was effectively partitioned between the Habsburgs and the Ottomans, Ferdinand of Austria sent Süleyman a magnificent silver planetarium made for his grandfather, Maximilian I. Two years later the French king François I presented the Ottoman grand admiral Hayreddin Pasha (Barbarossa) with a clock-cum-terrestial globe, and in 1547 Süleyman was the recipient of a table fountain-cum-clock made at Lyons. European goods also reached the Ottoman court as tribute from other rulers, both great and small. Clocks were stipulated as part of the tribute the Habsburgs paid to the Ottomans on account of the complicated power-sharing arrangements in Hungary from Süleyman's reign.[28] In 1569 Selim II received clocks with hunting animals and birds as part of the tribute, and in 1573 his grand vezir Sokullu Mehmed Pasha also received a timepiece, as did another vezir, Semiz Ahmed Pasha, who made sure he would get exactly what he wanted by giving the Habsburg ambassador sketches. (The order was, it seems, delayed, as no one in Augsburg could understand the accompanying instructions written in Ottoman Turkish.) Both Sokullu Mehmed Pasha and Semiz Ahmed Pasha specified that they wanted vegetal ornament decorating their clocks, and specifically excluded human images. In 1582 Murad III, on the other hand, demanded of the Habsburgs human and animal figures moved by clockwork – as table decorations, it is thought.[29] Towards 1600 the Venetian ambassador obtained goods for the ladies of the *harem* – fabric dolls 'as those made by Venetian nuns', small dogs, gyrfalcons, cushions, cloths, chairs, rock crystal, clocks, French sugar, cheese, glass vases, glass for windows, lamps, mirrors, spectacles and 'feathers' made of Murano glass.[30] Ottoman sultans, their vezirs and their households patronised the arts and collected the curiosities of the other, exotic, western world. There is evidence that the curiosity for European luxury goods and trifles extended deeper down into Ottoman society but we so far have little information on this.

Venice to date provides the best-researched example of the Ottoman desire to acquire novelties from far and wide, and also of the trade in essentials. The Ottomans received reciprocal trading rights in the Republic by a treaty concluded in 1419. Their merchants first traded through Ancona, but from 1546 also regularly through Venice. From around 1570 Venice displaced Ancona as the main hub for Ottoman commerce.[31] Venice was unable to feed itself and relied to a great extent on the Ottomans to provide the staple of wheat, as well as cloth and spices in particular. The presence of numerous Muslims in Venice could cause problems. Süleyman's grand vezir Rüstem Pasha was embarrassed by the volume of complaints about them addressed to the Venetian authorities, and in 1567 the papal nuncio observed that the 'multitude of Turks' in Venice might prove attractive to proselytising Jesuits.[32] But the greatest threat to commerce was war, which disrupted the smooth flow of goods as merchants were arrested and their merchandise seized. When hostilities broke out between the Ottomans and Venice over Cyprus in 1570, 75 Muslim and 97 Jewish Ottoman merchants were arrested by the Venetian authorities. The next year the situation was back to normal – but only briefly, for soon news of the Sacra Liga victory at Lepanto caused them to flee. Following the conclusion of peace in 1573, however, there was a boom in Ottoman activity in Venice, just at the time, Cemal Kafadar has observed, that Ottoman 'decline' was supposed to be setting in.[33] From soon after the 1570–3 war the Venetian authorities became aware that the Muslim merchants scattered throughout the city needed to be housed in their own building; this was in part justified by the desire to keep them from behaviour considered antisocial by the Venetians, such as mixing with Christian women. Despite continuing opposition from the authorities, by 1579 a building had been allotted to the Bosnians and Albanian Muslims, though it proved too small to accommodate the Anatolians as well.[34] By 1621 the building known as the Fondaco dei Turchi was allotted to the Muslims, and most were housed here. Until the outbreak of war over Crete in 1645, the Ottoman-Muslim export trade flourished, despite the myriad troubles the Empire was suffering at the time from provincial revolt and currency debasement. Particularly striking is the participation in this trade of Anatolian Muslims,[35] who were not there at the order of the state, but clearly saw commerce with the West to be a profitable way of making a living.

Contrary, then, to what for many years was accepted as the conventional wisdom – that Ottoman Muslims avoided direct contact with foreign merchants for fear of contamination – the evidence of a range of Venetian documents utilised in recent research confirms beyond doubt that Ottoman-Muslim merchants did indeed conduct trade inside Europe both in person and face-to-face. Links with Venice were strong: Ibrahim Pasha's commissioning of the helmet-crown was not the only occasion on which a grand vezir sought to please his master by presenting him with an ostentatious western product. Shortly before his murder in 1579 Sokullu Mehmed Pasha – who only a few years before had not wanted human images decorating the clock he ordered from Augsburg – commissioned a set of portraits of the sultans from the school of Paolo Veronese, which influenced Ottoman miniature painting during the succeeding years. In 1543, the winter that the Ottoman fleet wintered in the port of Toulon, the grand admiral, Barbarossa, presented to Virginio Orsini dell'Anguillara, a commander in the French navy, a set of eleven miniature paintings of the Ottoman sultans by a sea-captain who was also a talented painter. Writing of this painterly exchange Julian Raby notes that it worked both ways: these portraits influenced western representations of the sultans thereafter, first through the agency of the physician, bishop and historian Paolo Giovio, who was also a collector of Ottoman portraits and artefacts, and whose own collection was enhanced by a gift of a portrait of Süleyman given to him by the Sultan himself.[36] Further discussion of the transit of luxury and mundane goods from the Ottoman Empire westwards during the Renaissance is better left to Renaissance than to Ottoman historians – MacLean's Introduction gives more than a hint of their volume and impact.

Ottoman monarchs of the Renaissance period could match their European counterparts in splendour and in the kinds of goods they enjoyed, and could probably surpass most of them in the quality of the poetry they wrote. But where else than to the rulers themselves might we look for the Ottoman 'Renaissance man', and what characteristics might he possess? Who was the Ottoman Cosimo de Medici or Leonardo? Allowing that our models of Renaissance virtue come from Europe, who were the towering figures of the Ottoman Classical Age, to be compared with their European fellows? One candidate might be Mehmed II's grand vezir, the Serbian noble Mahmud Pasha Angelović, who held the office for some 17 years. A warrior and a diplomat, he was also a poet; he patronised some of the most notable poets of his time, supported men of learning and students alike, and assembled a library of which most of the 300 volumes known were theology and legal sciences (75 per cent) and language (17 per cent). He established charitable foundations to provide food for the needy, religious colleges, fountains to bring water to parts of the newly conquered capital where it had not reached under the Byzantines, public baths, inns and bazaars for merchants and traders – as well as mosques and palaces.[37]

Credit for the Ottoman conquest of Thrace must in large measure be attributed not to the Ottoman dynasty *per se*, but to the various marcher-lords who pushed the frontier forward. Members of the Turahanoğulları family were the architects of the conquest of Thessaly where the patriarch, Turahan Bey founded the town of Larisa. He, his son Ömer Bey, and his grandson Hasan Bey, left a rich legacy of charitable foundations throughout Thessaly, amounting to some 60 buildings, including 19 mosques, twelve dervish lodges, eight bathhouses and three public kitchens.[38]

Might our Renaissance man be Süleyman's boon companion, Ibrahim Pasha? He was from Parga, on the mainland opposite Corfu, and had very close contact with Venice through the Istanbul-based merchant Alvise Gritti, with whose help he acquired the helmet-crown. The *bailo* of the time reported that Ibrahim Pasha avidly read the stories of Hannibal and Alexander the Great, and also gathered information about the monarchs of his own era.[39] Like Mahmud Pasha and the Turahanoğulları, Ibrahim Pasha was renowned for his philanthropy. He established foundations in Istanbul, Thessalonica, Razgrad, Kavala and Mecca. Süleyman's eager collecting and patronage would not have been possible without Ibrahim, his grand vezir from 1523 until his execution in 1536, after which a more sober aspect has been detected in the Sultan's life as he foreswore extravagant display. In the later part of his reign he exchanged his 'magnificent' persona, for that of 'lawgiver', the soubriquet by which he is known in Ottoman sources.

Süleyman's Bosnian son-in-law, Rüstem Pasha, was a controversial figure who may also qualify as an Ottoman 'Renaissance man'. He served as grand vezir for nearly 15 years, and was the chief interlocutor of Ogier Ghiselin de Busbecq, Habsburg ambassador to the Sultan's court who had been charged with negotiating peace with the Ottomans. Accused by contemporaries of venality, he was described by Busbecq as 'a man of keen and far-seeing mind' – though Rüstem's subsequent 'customary rudeness' may have been the ambassador's abiding memory of him.[40] Built above an arcade of shops in the old commercial quarter of Istanbul, Rüstem Pasha's mosque is generally reckoned to have the finest tile decoration of any Ottoman monument, and the complex of which it is part is only one of the many charitable foundations he established across the Empire to promote trade and learning.

Sokullu Mehmed Pasha was another Bosnian, and also a sultan's son-in-law, the sultan in question being Selim II. Having served as grand admiral early in his career, he was later grand vezir uninterruptedly between 1565 and 1579, under three sultans. Like Leonardo, Sokullu Mehmed had grandiose plans, and like Leonardo's they too sometimes remained unrealised. One such was his project to cut a canal between the Red Sea and the Mediterranean at Suez, and another his scheme to link the Don and Volga rivers. He was by inclination a peacemaker, seeking to avoid conflict with traditional enemies and strengthening alliances with allies such as France and Poland. He built palaces in Istanbul and mosques across the Empire, as well as bridges and caravanserais to encourage commerce. Like other notable Ottomans he maintained links with his family and his homeland. In addition to the series of sultans' portraits Sokullu Mehmed commissioned for Murad III, he was apparently delighted to learn that his own portrait had been painted by a Venetian artist residing with the embassy in Istanbul.[41]

Men of letters, consummate politicians and administrators, lovers of splendour, patrons of the arts, dreamers of the impossible: Ottoman Renaissance men were all these things, but above all they were philanthropists. As well as advertising the power of the ruling dynasty and of themselves as servants of that dynasty, charitable works demonstrated the concern of both for the Sultan's subjects – philanthropy was where true virtue was to be found. Women of the royal house played their allotted role in furthering the interests of the Ottoman dynasty, particularly through the power they came to exercise as mother of the reigning sultan, and they too could garner goodwill by showing their concern for the public weal. The complex built in Üsküdar was the last major project of the court architect Sinan for Nurbanu, concubine of Selim II and mother of Murad III. It comprised eleven separate elements – a mosque, a religious college, a dervish lodge, a Qur'an school for young boys, a college for teaching the traditions of the Prophet, a college for readers of the Qur'an, a caravanserai, a hospice, a hospital, a kitchen and a bath-house.

Perhaps Sinan himself should be considered the archetypal Ottoman Renaissance man. He and his workshop were responsible for hundreds of structures in all corners of the Empire. Contrary to western perceptions that these were of a monotonous sameness – if not that many were identical – and could in no way compete on grounds of inventiveness and variety with the exuberant architectural forms of the Italian Renaissance, it has recently been argued that experiment and innovation, together with a remarkable ability to accommodate the demands of individual patrons, were the hallmarks of his style.[42] Should we consider the claims of the sheikhulislam Ebüssuud Efendi, who codified the laws of the Empire for Süleyman, or those of any of a multitude of other figures who are more or less well known to us – female (as MacLean has alerted us) as well as male – who made the Ottoman Empire of the Classical Age the 'cultural lite' equal of the Renaissance states of Europe? And if the Ottomans were in no way inferior to their European contemporaries according to measures as these men and women exhibited, why is the state that they built viewed with disdain? We must clearly look elsewhere to try to discover how they failed to match up to the West.

One of the most critical markers of the Renaissance was undoubtedly the 'discovery' of the Americas, and Ottoman 'failure' to match this feat is typically ascribed to a lack of curiosity and enterprise, as well as to the handicap of old-fashioned galleys that could not cross the ocean – as though there was an imperative that the Ottomans should seek to subjugate distant lands after the manner of their Portuguese and Spanish counterparts across the Atlantic. Yet, as Fernández-Armesto reminds us: 'In terms of territory added to their sovereigns' sway, the achievements of Columbus and Cortes were eclipsed by their Turkish contemporaries.'⁴³ Looked at without distorting spectacles, the story of Ottoman contact with distant lands across the ocean points up the differences between the two societies and shows what a futile exercise it is to compare them simplistically – always, it must be said, to the disadvantage of the Ottomans – when the historical circumstances and cultural norms of each society were so different.

In 1488 Bartolomeu Diaz rounded the Cape of Good Hope, and in 1492 Christopher Columbus came upon the Americas while sailing to India. Vasco da Gama reached India in 1498, and soon the Portuguese were in the Indian Ocean trying to monopolise the spice trade, which had hitherto been in the hands of Arab and other traders and had flowed west through Egypt to Venice. Portugal's appearance in the East worried the Venetians not a little. They looked to the Mamluks to resist Portuguese diversion of the spice trade, and following the end of the Ottoman–Venetian war of 1499–1502 Venice sent an embassy warning the Mamluks of the inevitable dire consequences if nothing was done to resist these interlopers. Venice was aware that the Mamluks were unable single-handedly to take on the challenge of protecting the trade routes on which the Republic depended for much of its prosperity. By 1509 Ottoman subjects were serving the Mamluks and local Muslim rulers on the coasts of the Indian Ocean as mercenaries, and from 1510 the Ottoman state provided direct assistance to the Mamluks. Following the overthrow of the Mamluks by the Ottomans in 1516–17, the latter were able to improve on the faltering start they had made together in protecting their vital interests on the Red Sea coasts from the Portuguese. The Ottomans now controlled the Holy Places of Mecca and Medina in the Hijaz to which thousands of pilgrims journeyed each year, and the obligation to provide for their security was added to the necessity to protect the spice trade.[44]

A former Mamluk sea-captain, Selman Reis, who had for some time been engaged in efforts to repulse the Portuguese advance, set out against them again in 1525 with a fleet of 18 ships and 299 cannon. The fleet's arrival caused the Portuguese to retreat, and Selman Reis reported upon his strategic goals in the region to his superior, Sultan Süleyman's grand vezir, Ibrahim Pasha, who had been sent to Egypt to restore order in the recently conquered province. The principal concern expressed in Selman's report was to safeguard the customs revenues from the spice trade, which the Portuguese were diverting to their own coffers. To this end he proposed bringing the ports of the southern Red Sea under Ottoman control, and insisted upon the need to control Yemen, Aden and Abyssinia – the latter as far inland as the Nile, with the important entrepôt of Atbara, and also ports south of the Bab al-Mandab. Selman died soon after this, but his plan to oust the Portuguese from the Indian Ocean lived on.

In 1531 an Ottoman fleet reached Diu in Gujarat and drove out the Portuguese, but when Bahadir Sultan, the ruler of Diu, called on Portuguese help in 1535 after being defeated by the Mughal emperor Humayun, and then thought better of it and appealed to the Ottomans, another was sent eastwards from Suez in 1538. This failed to capture Diu, in large measure because of the duplicity of the new ruler – Bahadir Sultan having been executed by the Portuguese in the interim – but as a result of the expedition Yemen and Aden were formed into a new province. This was just what Selman Reis had recommended. The port city of Basra at the head of the Persian Gulf, a conduit as important for westward trade as the Red Sea, had been taken by the Ottomans soon after their conquest of Baghdad in 1534, and by 1546 was constituted the centre of a province. The Portuguese continued to hold the island-trading centre of Hormuz at the entrance to the Gulf, however.

In pursuit of their aims in the Indian Ocean, the Ottomans created the provinces of Yemen (1539) and Habeç (1555) on the Red Sea, and Basra (1546) and al-Hasa or Lahsa (1552) on the southern shore of the Persian Gulf. In the late 1580s, in a final gasp that seemed to complete the real-isation of Selman Reis' plan, they briefly won the allegiance of local rulers on the east African coast and were thus able to hinder Portuguese use of the sea-lanes that led back to their Atlantic base.

Ottoman activity in the Indian Ocean contemporary with the European arrival in the Americas surely fails to match the high drama of the latter. So powerful is the motif of New World exploration in the telling of the Renaissance that it has been forgotten how the Portuguese and the Ottomans had rather similar *modus operandi* in the Indian Ocean, and that they eventually reached a compromise over control of the Gulf trade. The motives of both powers in the Indian Ocean were economic: they sought renewable resources, not plunder, as the Portuguese did in Brazil. Rather than seeking new riches the Ottomans wanted to hold on to and augment those they had, which they saw slipping away into the hands of a rival. Both were too thinly spread and too exposed to succeed by force, and worked to achieve their aims by alliance with friendly local rulers whom they used as proxies. They could usually rely on the co-operation of the rulers of the small but numerous indigenous Muslim states around the Indian Ocean whose interests were also adversely affected by the Portuguese presence, while the combination of the local knowledge and the vessels these states provided, together with the threat of Ottoman naval force, was sufficient to demonstrate to the Portuguese that they could not act with impunity. Colonies of Ottoman mercenaries were established at strategic coastal points from Gujarat to faraway Aceh, on the northwestern extremity of Sumatra, and these too played a part in foiling Portuguese attempts to establish full control of the spice trade. Ottoman vessels sailed regularly to Aceh and in the 1590s, for instance, considerably more pepper was arriving in the Red Sea from Aceh than the Portuguese were taking by sea to Lisbon.

The sultanate of Aceh, whose main export was pepper, was the most stalwart ally of the Ottomans in the region. Ottoman troops were in the service of the Sultan of Aceh from the 1530s, but the high tide of their co-operation was the 20 years from about 1560 when, sometimes in concert with Gujarat, they worked together to impede the Portuguese. The arrival of an Ottoman envoy in Aceh seems to have been decisive in cementing their relationship. Following his visit the Ottomans sent artillery experts to Aceh, and in 1564 the Sultan felt confident enough to refuse the Portuguese berth for the first time. When in 1565 news reached Istanbul from Aceh that the Sultan and fellow Muslim rulers in the region were reciting Süleyman's name in the Friday prayer, it was presented as a voluntary gesture aimed at winning Ottoman support in the struggle against the Portuguese. The Ottomans did not have to force the 'natives' to accept their authority in such matters – it was an arrangement of benefit to both parties. Ottoman documents of the 1560s and

1570s reveal also that gold coins were being paid to mosques in Calicut, Ceylon and Aceh for the support of imams who would say prayers in the Ottoman sultan's name. Such actions provoked the indignation of Jesuit missionaries who complained of the activities of itinerant Muslim clerics in the region. In 1567 the grand vezir Sokullu Mehmed Pasha prepared a fleet to sail to Aceh. Its departure was postponed because of a rebellion in Yemen, but 500 Ottoman mercenaries were instead sent to assist the Acehnese when they besieged the Portuguese outpost at Malacca in 1568.[45]

The Portuguese presence in the Indian Ocean consisted in strategically situated but widely scattered commercial bases. Establishing these outposts was slow at first, but by 1600 there were over 100. The Mughal emperors were not averse to the possibility of allying with the Portuguese against the Ottomans, as Emperor Akbar hoped to do in the 1580s – but his plans came to nothing.[46] In the end it was geopolitical shifts that drove the Portuguese from this Ottoman sphere of interest. From the late 1570s Ottoman attention was diverted to war against Iran, and soon thereafter against the Habsburgs in Hungary, while the Dutch and then the English entered the Indian Ocean and established a monopoly with which the Portuguese were unable to compete.

This brief sketch of Ottoman and Portuguese activity in the Indian Ocean should serve to illustrate how very different the situation there was from that of Portugal and Spain in the Atlantic, and how unlike the acquisitive European way of empire, as practised by the Spanish in Mexico at least, was the Ottoman. For a start, both the Ottomans and their Portuguese 'foes' were outsiders in the Indian Ocean; both had long experience of existing in the same European historical space. The Spanish encounter with the Aztecs, by contrast, saw a sophisticated empire of indigenous peoples overcome by an aggressive intruder that co-opted their local rivals and began within a few years to force its own, alien values upon these erstwhile allies with catastrophic consequences.[47] Measured against the mischief wrought by Spain and Portugal across the Atlantic, there was no 'darker side' to the Ottoman adventure in the Indian Ocean.

To see the sixteenth-century presence of the Ottomans in the Indian Ocean as but a pale imitation of the European voyages of discovery is to err profoundly, and we must look for another way of conceptualising these events. We might reconsider first the widely held view of the latter as driven by a spirit of inquiry unprecedented in human history. Fernandez-Armésto writes: ' "The great age of European expansion" was no outpouring of pent-up dynamism' but 'was launched from the insecure edges of a contracting civilization', and continues by describing the Iberian peninsula as 'an ill-favoured salient occupied by poor, marginal communities, coming from behind'. Echoing Linda Colley's characterisation of the British as 'a small people' who needed to find new lands,[48] Fernandez-Armésto considers Portugal and Castile in similar terms, as 'small countries, sparsely populated and scantily endowed with sources of natural wealth'.[49] Compared to the already extensive and richly endowed Ottoman Empire, which was then at the height of its power, these states were small indeed. We must also note that it was from the seaboard states, rather than from Venice, for instance, that the Atlantic voyages were made. Unlike Spain and Portugal, but like Venice, the Ottoman Empire was situated far from an ocean, and it was only once the Mamluk lands were conquered that they had clear access to the East. Unlike the Europeans, however, the Ottomans did not have the urge to impose their authority over distant territories. Very different ties bound different parts of the Empire to Istanbul, varying from direct administration in the heartland, to the lightest of touches further afield, as in the Maghrib.

Where the Ottomans did impose direct administration over regions far from Istanbul, it was applied from strategic nodes, while the hinterland of the provinces created at this time was largely ignored – either because it could not be controlled, as in the striking example of Yemen where resistance to the Ottomans was endemic, or because it was not needed. An example of this realistic exercise of power was the way the Black Sea became an 'Ottoman lake' by the late fifteenth century. As in the Indian Ocean, here too the Ottomans relied on proxies to do their work for them – the voivodes of their vassal states of Wallachia and Moldavia to the northwest, and the Tartar khans of the Crimea to the north. The Crimean Tartars were entrusted with the vital task of patrolling the great steppe lands to keep the trade routes open: the slaves, furs and other goods that reached Istanbul from the north were as important as spices to the Ottoman economy. What mattered to the sultans was that the treasury was full and that their heartland of Istanbul remained safe and its inhabitants provided for. Unlike the Spanish and Portuguese in the New World, the Ottoman Empire could also be a soft hegemonic empire of allegiance, not one of territorial conquest.

With an empire at the centre of the world – the notions of West and East must logically derive from a viewpoint between the two – and potential foes on many sides, imperial realism came to the Ottomans early on. The Ottoman vision of empire was one of consolidation rather than innovation, with the *pax ottomanicum* as the symbol of the integrity of the Sultan's realms. What counted was his ability to provide peace and prosperity for his subjects, and this conservatism was continually made explicit in the justification for measures taken because they were in conformity with the 'ways of old', the *kanun-i kadim*. This was very different from the Europeans of the Renaissance, with their plethora of small warring states of Europe, and there were further differences. Unlike the Spanish and Portuguese in the Americas, the Russians in their Far East and, later, the British, the Ottomans did not, with few exceptions, colonise native peoples whose indigenous modes of governance were very different from those of the imperial power. The heartlands of the Ottoman Empire had formerly been Byzantine, but even at the peripheries, those whose territories became incorporated into the Sultan's domains, whether fully or loosely, had similar expectations of government and spoke the same language of power as their new masters. Although part of Europe, the Ottoman Empire was not Europe, and Ottoman norms and ways of doing things were at many points driven by a logic greatly at variance with that of the West.

Views of the Ottoman Empire widely held today have been shaped less by knowledge of Ottoman history than by how Europeans wished to project themselves and their society in relation to the Empire. It is as if the individual prejudices of the travellers whose narratives are typically regarded as the embodiment of the Renaissance spirit of enquiry were writ large. When, in the nineteenth century, imperial, militaristic Europe reflected on how it had come to dominate the globe, the notion that it was uniquely qualified to set the civilisational standard to which others should aspire must have seemed self-evident. It was a short step from certain knowledge of European superiority to the imposition of tutelage, indeed quasi-colonialism, on the weakened Ottoman Empire whose own attempts to modernise were too faltering. Alongside economic measures went the disruption of the cultural integrity of Ottoman society through the decrying of its many features that were uncharacteristic of Europe. So resilient is this nineteenth-century legacy that few modern historians and commentators are able to look dispassionately at the Ottoman Empire. The result has been pervasive misunderstanding of an unfamiliar culture. Negative comparison with the West is usually implied, which is not the case in discussion of the more distant lands of China, Japan and India – and more often stridently asserted.[50]

Why did the Ottomans know no languages? Why did they not send permanent ambassadors abroad until the late eighteenth century? Why were they incurious about foreign lands? Why did they not travel and live abroad? Why did they not produce maps? Why was their society in the grip of religious obscurantism? Apart from the fact that ongoing research – such as that of Giancarlo Casale – is producing an unsuspected wealth of material that allows for a radical rewriting of the intertwined history of Europe and the Ottomans, and of Europe and the wider Muslim world – as exemplified by Nabil Matar in this volume and elsewhere – questions framed in this way, from a European perspective that ignores the Ottoman historical context, have little meaning. More than hindsight, even, it is perhaps western 'ownership' of the history of other societies that most effectively inhibits measured analysis of similarities and difference and, in the case of the Ottoman Empire, perpetuates the myth that for much of its history it had no history.

Acknowledgement

This essay is dedicated to Michael Rogers whose many books and articles are a source of inspiration to all those working on Ottoman–European cultural exchange.

Notes

1. Felipe Fernández-Armesto, *Millennium: A History of our Last Thousand Years* (1995; rpt. London: Black Swan, 1996), p. 223.
2. J. M. Roberts, *A Short History of the World* (1993; rpt. Oxford: Oxford University Press, 1997), pp. 319–20.
3. With so much now available in English, I mention only two recent 'crossover' books that provide a flavour of the contextualised and de-exoticised ways in which Ottoman historians are writing about the Empire today: Daniel Goffman, *The Ottoman Empire and Early Modern Europe* (Cambridge: Cambridge University Press, 2002) convincingly makes the case for considering the Empire as an integral part of Europe; Colin Imber, *The Ottoman Empire, 1300–1650. The Structure of Power* (London: Palgrave Macmillan 2002) concentrates on the internal workings of the Empire, focusing on its institutions and how they developed over the centuries.
4. Eric R. Wolf, *Europe and the People without History* (Berkeley, CA: University of California Press, 1982).
5. See Bernard Lewis, *The Muslim Discovery of Europe* (New York: Norton, 1982), and *What Went Wrong? Western Impact and Middle East Response* (2002; rpt. London: Phoenix, 2003).
6. Walter D. Mignolo, *The Darker Side of the Renaissance: Literacy, Territoriality, and Colonization* (1995; rpt. Ann Arbor: University of Michigan Press, 2003), p. 332.
7. Rhoads Murphey, review of Kenneth M. Setton, *Venice, Austria and the Turks in the Seventeenth Century* (Philadelphia: American Philosophical Society, 1991), in *Archivum Ottomanicum* 13 (1993–94): 371–83; this passage, p. 372.
8. Jason Goodwin, *Lords of the Horizons. A History of the Ottoman Empire* (London: Chatto, 1998), pp. 144, 145, 269.

9. Peter B. Evans, Dietrich Rueschemeyer and Theda Skocpol, eds., *Bringing the State Back In* (Cambridge: Cambridge University Press, 1985).
10. Although there is much new scholarship taking issue either explicitly or implicitly with the intellectual laziness that characterises these two centuries as a period of 'decay' or 'decline', they have still not been written about in ways that enable non-specialists to grasp the nonsensicality of these labels.
11. Lord Kinross, *The Ottoman Centuries. The Rise and Fall of the Turkish Empire* (London: Cape, 1977).
12. Perry Anderson, *Lineages of the Absolutist State* (London: Verso, 1974), p. 397.
13. In the rest of this essay I draw upon research conducted for my *Osman's Dream. The Story of the Ottoman Empire, 1300–1923* (London: John Murray, 2005).
14. See, for instance, the papers in *Toplumsal Tarih* 112 (August 2003): 66–95, on the 'Renaissance and the Ottoman World'.
15. Fernández-Armesto, *Millennium*, pp. 154–5.
16. Julian Raby, 'Picturing the Levant', in Jay A. Levenson, ed., *Circa 1492: Art in the Age of Exploration* (Washington, DC: National Gallery, 1991), pp. 78–81, passage cited, p. 79.
17. Gülru Necipoğlu, 'Süleyman the Magnificent and the Representation of Power in the Context of Ottoman–Habsburg–Papal Rivalry', in Halil İnalcık and Cemal Kafadar, eds., *Süleyman the Second and his Time* (Istanbul: Isis, 1993), pp. 163–94.
18. Niccolò Sagundino, 'Orazione al serenissimo principe e invitto re Alfonso', in Agostino Pertusi, ed., *La Caduta di Constantinopoli*, 2 vols ([n.p.], 1976), pp. 131–3.
19. Michael Critovoulos, *History of Mehmed the Conqueror*, trans. C. T. Riggs (Princeton, NJ: Princeton University Press, 1954), pp. 3, 181.
20. Julian Raby, 'Mehmed the Conqueror's Greek Scriptorium', *Dumbarton Oaks Papers* 37 (1983): 15–34, passages cited pp. 18, 21.
21. Necipoğlu, 'Süleyman', p. 190.
22. Jean Aubin, 'Une frontière face au péril ottoman: la Terre d'Otrante (1529–1532)', in Giles Veinstein, ed., *Soliman le magnifique et son temps* (Paris: Galeries Nationales du Grand Palais, 1992), pp. 465–84.
23. Gülru Necipoğlu, *Architecture, Ceremonial and Power: The Topkapı Palace in the Fifteenth and Sixteenth Centuries* (Cambridge, MA: MIT Press, 1991), p. 14.
24. These contacts are well known and have been written about in Turkish by Semavi Eyice, 'II.Beyazid devrinde davet edilen batılılar' [Westerners invited in the period of Bayezid 2], *Belgelerle Türk Tarihi Dergisi* 19 (April 1969): 23–30.
25. Michael Rogers, 'An Ottoman Palace Inventory of the Reign of Bayezid 2', in J.-L. Bacqué-Grammont and E. van Donzel, eds., *Proceedings of Comité international d'études pré-ottomane et ottomanes, VIth Symposium* (Istanbul: Isis, 1987): 39–53.
26. Maria Pia Pedani, 'Safiye's Household and Venetian Diplomacy', *Turcica* 31 (1999): 9–32, passages cited pp. 14–15. Nurbanu Sultan, consort of Murad III, was once thought to have been born a Venetian patrician, but it now seems probable that she came from a Greek family of elevated status from Venetian Corfu; see Benjamin Arbel, 'Nur Banu (c.1530–1583): a Venetian Sultana?', *Turcica* 24 (1992): 241–59.

27. Michael Rogers, 'The Arts under Süleyman the Magnificent', in İnalcık and Kafadar, eds., *Süleyman*, pp. 257–94.
28. Rogers, 'Arts', p. 289.
29. Suraiya Faroqhi, 'Moving Goods Around, and Ottomanists too: Surveying Research on the Transfer of Material Goods in the Ottoman Empire', *Turcica* 32 (2000): 435–46; passage cited p. 443.
30. Pedani, 'Safiye's Household', p. 12.
31. Cemal Kafadar, 'A Death in Venice (1575): Anatolian Muslim Merchants Trading in the Serenissima', *Journal of Turkish Studies* 10 (1986); 191–218; passages cited pp. 192, 195–9.
32. Eric Dursteler, 'Commerce and Co-existence: Veneto-Ottoman Trade in the Early Modern Era', *Turcica* 34 (2002): 105–33; passage cited p. 126.
33. Kafadar, 'Death in Venice', p. 201.
34. Lewis, *Muslim Discovery*, pp. 122–3.
35. Kafadar, 'Death in Venice', pp. 200–2.
36. Julian Raby, 'From Europe to Istanbul', in *The Sultan's Portrait: Picturing the House of Osman* (Istanbul: İşbank, 2000), pp. 136–63.
37. Theoharis Stavrides, *The Sultan of Vezirs. The Life and Times of the Ottoman Grand Vezir Mahmud Pasha Angelović (1453–1474)* (Leiden: Brill, 2001), pp. 187–326.
38. Machiel Kiel, 'Das türkische Thessalien: Etabliertes Geschichtsbild versus Osmanische Quellen', in R. Lauer and P. Schreiner, eds., *Die Kultur Griechenlands in Mittelalter und Neuzeit: Bericht über das Kolloquium der Südosteuropa-Kommission 28.-31. Oktober 1992* (Abhandlungen der Akademie der Wissenschaften in Goettingen. Philologisch-historische Klasse, Folge 3, Nr. 212) (Goettingen: Vandenhoeck & Ruprecht, 1996), pp. 109–96; passage cited pp. 150–1.
39. Necipoğlu, 'Süleyman', p. 168.
40. Edward Seymour Forster, trans., *The Turkish Letters of Ogier Ghiselin de Busbecq* (1927; rpt. Oxford: Clarendon Press, 1968), pp. 29, 91.
41. Raby, 'Europe to Istanbul', pp. 150–1.
42. Gülru Necipoğlu, *The Age of Sinan: Architectural Culture in the Ottoman Empire, 1539–1588* (London: Reaktion, 2005).
43. Fernández-Armesto, *Millennium*, p. 220.
44. This section on the Ottomans in the Indian Ocean is based on Halil İnalcık, 'The Ottoman State: Economy and Society, 1300–1600', in Halil İnalcık with Donald Quataert, *An Economic and Social History of the Ottoman Empire, 1300–1914* (Cambridge: Cambridge University Press, 1994), pp. 9–409, especially pp. 319–59.
45. Giancarlo L. Casale, lecture entitled 'A Previously Unknown Turkish Travel Narrative from the Sixteenth-Century Indian Ocean: its Discovery and Historical Significance' delivered at the Istanbul branch of the American Research Institute in Turkey on 18 October 2004. This lecture derives from Casale's unpublished doctoral thesis: 'The Ottoman Age of Exploration: Spices, Maps and Conquest in the Sixteenth-Century Indian Ocean' (Harvard University, 2004), which I have unfortunately not seen. We must assume that it supersedes İnalcık's narrative of sixteenth-century Ottoman expansion into the Indian Ocean.
46. Naimur Rahman Farooqi, *Mughal-Ottoman Relations (A Study of Political & Diplomatic Relations between Mughal India and the Ottoman Empire, 1556–1748)* (Delhi: Idarah-i Adabiyat-I Delli, 1989), pp. 20–2.

47. Ross Hassig, *Mexico and the Spanish Conquest* (London: Longmans, 1994), see pp. 144–58.
48. Linda Colley, *Captives: Britain, Empire and the World, 1600–1850* (2002; rpt. London: Pimlico, 2003), pp. 5–7.
49. Fernández-Armésto, *Millennium*, p. 155.
50. The labels 'East' and 'West' and, indeed, 'Europe' that I have used for lack of any more suitable alternatives throughout this essay as geographical markers are not without problems, for they imply the very lines of separation that I intend to challenge. Although, as I state here, the history of China, Japan and India may not be disdained as that of the Ottoman Empire has been, the lines of separation imposed in the historiography of these places is just as real as those made to divide the Ottomans from Europe. As recently put by Amartya Sen: 'The richness and variety of early intellectual relations between China and India have long been obscured. This neglect is now reinforced by the contemporary tendency to classify the world's population into distinct "civilizations" defined largely by religion (for example, Samuel Huntington's partitioning of the world into such categories as "Western civilization", "Islamic civilization" and "Hindu civilization"). There is, as a result, a widespread inclination to understand people mainly through their religious beliefs, even if this misses much that is important about them. The limitations of this perspective have already done significant harm to our understanding of other aspects of the global history of ideas'; 'Passage to China', *The New York Review of Books* 51:19 (2 December 2004): 61–5; this passage, p. 61.

Index